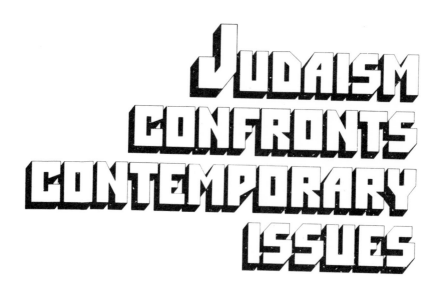

# JUDAISM CONFRONTS CONTEMPORARY ISSUES

## by Alex J. Goldman

SHENGOLD PUBLISHERS, INC.

NEW YORK

ISBN 0-88400-056-7

Library of Congress Catalog Card Number: 78-54570

Copyright © 1978 by Alex J Goldman

Published by Shengold Publishers, Inc.
45 W. 45th St., New York, N.Y. 10036

Printed in the United States of America

# PREFACE

Religions have a way of discussing their positions without providing precise views. Perhaps they would otherwise stagnate and be crippled by dogmatism. Some religions can offer official views; others cannot. Some can only give vague indications towards possible vantage points, while at the same time, reflecting a basic understanding of vital issues as they arise and impinge upon life.

New issues confront us today. Bioethics has become a major area of discussion. Religion is always asked where it stands. Man wants to know. Religion insists on its relevance to the issues of the hour and is called upon to prove it. What religion actually has got to say to the modern world, is rarely spelled out in detail. Although religion cannot always offer a precise, clear-cut statement of where it stands, it must attempt it.

Judaism has always been a vital, forceful, practical guide to living. It always derives its views from the massive, unbelievably comprehensive law and literature of the Bible, Talmud, Codes, Responsa and the viable interchanges of scholars and sages who, over the centuries, confronted the issues of daily life.

Some problems are already born, others are in the making. What does Judaism say about them? Does Judaism, in fact, have a position? Can it help, not only the Jew, but every man, clarify his thinking, direct him, clear the confusion?

To point up the relevancy of Judaism, this book seeks to suggest some answers. They will not be exact. They will, however, provide a broad frame of reference, so that an intelligent forum for discussion can be available.

This book will show that Judaism takes every issue of life seriously. Indeed, this volume is designed to be a source book for many of today's major issues.

Every statement is not an official one. Judaism speaks in many ways. There is no comprehensive line laid down by all groups. Orthodox, Conservative, Reform, and Reconstructionist groups have made statements; they are included here as are the views of rabbis who, while affiliated, reflect their own thinking. There are agreements and disagreements. All, however, represent the living struggle of a vital tradition. "These, too, are the words of the living God," the Talmud reminds us.

Orthodox Judaism, rooted in the Halakhah, does indeed confront issues. Many rabbinic journals, in Israel as in America, discuss new subjects. Cloning, sex-change, gene engineering, in vitro fertilization, have already begun to engage scholars. Rabbi Moshe Feinstein, the recognized authority of Orthodox Jewry, Rabbi J. David Bleich, Rabbi Immanuel Jakobovitz, Chief Rabbi of Great Britain, Rabbi Louis Jacobs, Rabbi Moses D. Tendler, Rabbi Abraham Scheinberg, Rabbi David Shohet, Dr. Fred Rosner, Rabbi Dr. Azriel Rosenfeld, Rabbi Norman Lamm, among others, have written extensively for *Tradition*, the excellent quarterly of the Rabbinical Council of America.

The Conservative movement boasts of a number of capable scholars who have challenged and confronted issues, often recommending varying attitudes, but always within the Halakhic spectrum and spirit. Rabbi Isaac Klein, Rabbi Robert Gordis, Rabbi Seymour Siegel, Rabbi David Feldman, Rabbi David Novak, Rabbi Ben Zion Bokser, Rabbi Daniel Goldberg, Rabbi Louis Epstein, among others. They have dug deep into the Halakhic world and have written for the Committe on Law and Standards of the Rabbinical Assembly as they have for their own publications. Many of their responsa have become the bases of Conservative Judaism's dynamic position.

Reform Judaism, to the largest degree, finds its position in the work of its Committee on Responsa and reports regularly to the Central Conference of American Rabbis. For decades, Rabbi Solomon Freehof, has stood out as its scholar. His responsa are published regularly and his erudition is reflected in the immense scope of questions raised by his colleagues and his prolific responses. From 1944, when he published *Reform Jewish Practice*, at least seven volumes on responsa have appeared. His predecessor in stature was Dr. Jacob Z. Lauterbach, who published *Studies in Jewish Law*, among other volumes.

A series of thirteen pressing subjects have been selected for consideration. Each is treated separately. The views of various groups, as of the recognized authorities, are included. Areas of differences are described and some official positions recorded. A general introduction designed to provide the perspective and thrust of the Jewish interpretation process precedes the chapter discussions.

I would like to acknowledge the following who granted permission to quote their works — the sources are fully noted in the Notes:

John V.R. Bull, Assistant to Managing Editor of the Philadelphia Inquirer, Rabbi Rudolph Adler, Dr. Fred Rosner, Dr. Robert Gordis, Rabbi J. David Bleich, Mr. Charles Bloch of Bloch Publishing Company, Rabbi Bernard Raskas, Rabbi Aaron Soloveichik, Dr. Fritz Bamberger, for the Hebrew Union College-Jewish Institute of Religion, Rabbi Marc D. Angel for *Tradition*, Mrs. Alan F. Guttmacher, Rabbi Moses D. Tendler, Rabbi Malcolm H. Stern for the Central Conference of American Rabbis, Rabbi Jules Harlow, for the Rabbinical Assembly, Dr. Solomon Freehof, Rabbi Isaac Trainin, for the Commission on Synagogue Relations, Federation of Jewish Philantropies, Mr. David Olivestone for Hebrew Publishing Company, Rabbi Eugene Borowitz for *Sh'ma* Magazine, and Rabbi Norman Lamm.

The monumental set, *Soncino Talmud*, published by Soncino Press, London, is an invaluable literary achievement which all serious students of Judaism must possess and study. Of equal brilliance is the new translation of the Bible by the Jewish Publication Society of America.

Gratitude must be recorded to those who made the publication of this book possible.

Mr. Moshe Sheinbaum, publisher of Shengold Publishers, whose excitement about the contents encouraged its completion.

Mrs. Bertha Klausner, International Literary Agency, is my literary agent, my dear friend and counselor for many years.

Dr. Freema Gottlieb, edited this book with extreme and devoted care. Dorothy Trompeter, Philip Morse, Lawrence Lowman, and Ralph and Helen Biernbaum had great confidence in this book.

Mr. Philip Diamant carefully read the galleys and typescript and offered valuable criticism and help.

My wife, Edith, who for almost thirty-eight years now, constantly inspired and encouraged me to write and to create. Her love and understanding made my life gratifying and fulfilling.

Alex J. Goldman

*Sarah Esther Goldman, my mother,*
*who loved her heritage and lived it*

Alex J. Goldman

*David Trompeter, inventor, creative genius,*
*who loved his heritage and sought to improve it*

Dorothy Trompeter

*Shimon Muszacki, Chana Muszacki,*
*Sheine Chaya Muszacki, Chaim Muszacki*
*who loved their heritage and died for it,*
*in the Holocaust*

Philip S. Morse

# CONTENTS

# INTRODUCTION

Understanding the pressing issues of contemporary life as they impinge upon Jews and Judaism requires a broad perspective to begin with. Simply to make a number of dogmatic assertions about Judaism without any understanding of the complexities involved is to make of Judaism an oversimplified, cut-and-dried religion, which it is far from being.

Judaism does not offer one limiting, precise answer to every issue. Nor does it maintain that an answer remains the same for all time. Much depends upon which of the denominational groups within Judaism one relies for direction. Thus, Orthodox Judaism may offer one view, Reform Judaism another, Conservative Judaism a third, and the Reconstructionists a fourth. Non-religiously oriented groups may hold yet other positions, or all groups may be unanimous on a specific issue.

This volume does not seek to dictate which view is correct; to do so would imply that there is no room for contradictions, and would deny the right of each Jew to his own individual approach, as if Judaism could mean exactly the same thing to everyone. Instead, this book will attempt to describe impartially the varying views, where they exist, towards the issues confronting Judaism today.

In fact, this notion of making allowance for differing points of view is the most characteristic feature of Judaism throughout history. Judaism has never been a static religion, but has developed organically with a wisdom as wide as the life-experience of its adherents.

# HALAKHAH

The purpose of this introduction is to offer an insight into the development of Jewish opinion through the principles of what is called *Halakhah*. This word means "walking," implying (a) how to walk in the way of religion, and (b) an on-going process. The tense is in the perfect. Judaism has adopted this word to signify the movement of Judaism throughout the ages — it suggests a constant activity, dynamic and creative in response to the changing forces of life. Thus, *Halakhah*, the process of development of Jewish law, is a key concept in our discussion. The principle underlying it comes into play as we confront every issue of contemporary life.

It must be understood from the outset that the English translation of the word *Halakhah* as "law" should not be taken literally, in the sense of a legal system that is rigid and unchangeable. On the contrary, the term must be understood in its widest sense to include not only religious principles, but experience and human relations of every conceivable type, both those between man and God, and those between people.

When we speak of the *Halakhah* in any given situation, we mean, not simply Jewish law in its narrower sense, but the whole vastness of Judaism with its large historic sweep as applied to that particular situation. Rarely is the simplest answer given without an analysis of all the intricate sources which interrelate with the issue at hand.

If we associate the term *Halakhah* with the recognized denominations within Judaism today we might say that Orthodox and Conservative Judaism are *Halakhah*-oriented. Reform and Reconstructionism are not; these groups do not consider themselves bound by traditional *Halakhah* or Jewish law. Non-religiously-rooted groups have no tie whatsoever with *Halakhah*.

## THE ROOTS OF JUDAISM

What we in modern times have come to know as Orthodox Judaism is the foundation from which the other forms of Judaism developed. Throughout Jewish history, with the exception of a few sects apart from the mainstream, it represented the only Judaism.

Orthodox Judaism must be considered as basic. One cannot understand the essential structure of Judaism without first coming to terms with its source. An appreciation of the tenets of Orthodoxy is necessary, even for those who are critical of them.

## THE BIBLE, WRITTEN LAW

The source book of Judaism is, of course, the Bible, in Hebrew called the Torah. A literal translation of the word "Torah" is "instruction" or "teaching." The Bible, consisting of three divisions (Tenakh), is referred to as the Written Law or Written Torah (in Hebrew, *Torah Sheh-bik'tav*).

The Bible begins with the creation of the world by God, the corrosion of the creation by evil, and the formulation of basic laws of human (not specifically Jewish) conduct. The Seven Laws of Noah or Man are: (1) establishment of courts of justice; (2) prohibition of blasphemy; (3) prohibition of idolatry; (4) prohibition of incest; (5) prohibition of bloodshed; (6) prohibition of robbery; (7) prohibition of eating flesh cut from a living animal. These ethical rules of conduct constitute what is known as Natural Religion.

Ten generations later, Abraham arrives on the scene of history as God's chosen instrument. God makes a covenant with Abraham and this personal revelation lays the foundation for Israel as God's chosen people, the external sign of which is circumcision. Abraham is succeeded by his son and grandson, Isaac and Jacob. The twelve sons of Jacob become the twelve tribes. They are slaves in Egypt for centuries and are then liberated and forged into a nation by Moses, under God's instructions.

Redemption leads direct to Sinai where God reveals Himself to Moses and the people. Moses is given the Ten Commandments and innumerable other laws. This revelation of God to the whole people, referred to in Hebrew as *Ma-amad Har Sinai*, or the Theophany on Mount Sinai (literally, the standing on Mount Sinai), is the high point of Jewish spiritual history. The Torah that Moses received on Mount Sinai was God-given and is referred to as *Torah min ha-shah-mah-yim*, or "Torah from Heaven."

The laws given to Moses on Mount Sinai are eternally binding, especially in view of the fact that they were wholeheartedly accepted with the response "*na-aseh v'nishma* — we shall do and we shall obey." The taking on of this responsibility was not an agreement limited to that particular time; it is eternally binding. This is the basis of *Halakhah*, which deals not only with civil, criminal and ritual law, but which includes, as we have mentioned, ethical and moral law affecting the most fundamental principles of human life. The principles of Halakhah underscore man's dignity as a free human being; indeed, they are the most humanizing principles ever found in any source.

There are 365 negative and 248 positive commands in the Bible, making a total of 613 regulations, mnemonically abbreviated to spell out the word TaRYaG, 613. Though many of these laws cover sacrificial arrangements which no longer exist, so that the laws themselves are therefore in abeyance, they are still studied.

The laws of the Bible are not all understandable on a rational basis. The rabbis admitted that there are different kinds of laws. Some are defensible on rational grounds; had they not been included in the Revelation on Sinai, they might have occurred to us by natural means. These laws are given the name *Mishpatim*, from the root of the Hebrew word "to judge." A second set of laws are called *Hukkim*, or "statutes," for which no explanations are given and which cannot be understood by human reason but are accepted on faith because of their origin. Both categories are subsumed under the Hebrew word *Mitzvot* (singular, *Mitzvah*), meaning duties or commandments.

These laws appear only in the *Pentatauch*, the first of the three divisions of the Bible, which begins with the account of the creation of the world, and comes to an end as Moses hands over the leadership to Joshua, who prepares to cross the Jordan into Palestine.

The second division of the Bible, called *Neviim* (Prophets), is further divided into historical and literary prophets. Living very close together in time, a group of prophets arose who served as oracles of God. They received Divine revelations, though of a lesser intensity than those experienced by Moses. These men and women were the political advisors of kings and, expanding upon the laws and principles laid down at Sinai, they placed an emphasis on the inspiration underlying those laws and the necessity for the incorporation of this spirit into the lives of the Jewish people.

They stressed principles of ethical conduct, social justice, the brotherhood of man and the fatherhood of God. Thus, while serving as links to the *Pentateuch*, the prophets amplified the principles enunciated by God to Moses, and by Moses to the Jewish people.

During this period the Torah, which had been recorded by Moses at the end of the events contained in the *Pentateuch*, reposed in the Holy Ark until the era of the kings; the Ark often travelled from place to place, although it also remained in one place for an extended period of time. Finally, the Ark came to rest in the Temple in Jerusalem.

The Torah was occasionally neglected and forgotten, and major historical events, such as the findings of the Scroll by King Josiah in 622 B.C.E., and the Torah readings instituted by Ezra the Scribe in 444 B.C.E., made the people commit themselves afresh to the laws of the Torah; its authority as the arbiter in Jewish life was reaffirmed.

## THE BIBLE, ORAL LAW, TALMUD

It is apparent that, as time went on, the Written Law required elucidation and interpretation. Scholars followed up the Written, with what became known as the Oral Law (in Hebrew, Torah *Sheh be'al peh*, Torah "by word of mouth"), which was at first transmitted orally from one generation to another. The Talmud is a synonym for Oral Law. The combination of both Torahs, Written and Oral, or better, the merger of the one into the other, that is, the superimposition of the Talmud's explanation and interpretation of the Torah upon the Written Law, forging both into one inextricable unit, became the basic source and inspiration of Jewish life.

A recent writer has put it this way: "The text given at Sinai was the seed which bore the fruit of rabbinic interpretation, thus investing the Oral Law with the binding authority of divine revelation and prompting our Sages to assert that 'even that which an advanced disciple would instruct in the presence of his master was already spoken to Moses at Sinai.'" Thus, every aspect of Jewish living, ethical and legal, is traceable to this central revelation. That was, and still is, the sum and substance of *Halakhah*: everything must go back to it. This does not mean, however, that only those laws deriving directly from Sinai are binding and authoritative. Laws based upon interpretative principles which the rabbis later evolved have equal force and are held to have been revealed at Sinai. From this we can see the reason for the dynamic development of tradition within Judaism.

## THE SANHEDRIN

The scholars and scribes came to their decisions only after serious thought and study. Imbued with a deep belief in God and Divinity of His law given at Sinai, their debates and decisions were tentative and governed by conservative principles. They were very hesitant to come out with definite decisions on their own authority

and relied heavily on group discussions on the basis of which a ruling might emerge. When no decision was possible they were honest
enough to say so, declaring that "Elijah in the days to come would
answer this question." (An acrostic, or abbreviated form of this, was
known as *Teku*, signifying the lack of final decision.)

One of the great institutions of Jewish history was the
Sanhedrin, a council of seventy-two sages. In courtly and precise
fashion issues were posed, evaluated, and decisions rendered, usually requiring a majority vote. New situations and problems affecting
the lives and destinies of Jewish people were openly considered and
resolved, never losing sight of reference to origins in the Written
Torah. The decision-making body was certainly not a monolithic
group, and decisions were arrived at only after long debate.

These councils, in turn, sought direction from smaller groups
of scholars in academies of higher learning. Erudite sages
magnetically drew hundreds of students. In both Palestine and
Babylon, schools sprang up, many continuing for generations.
Many of these schools, which flourished at the same time, developed
different perspectives in terms of interpretation, some being
stricter,and others more liberal. The best known were those of Hillel
and Shammai, the former being famed for its more liberal approach.

## STRUCTURE OF THE TALMUD

The Talmud developed out of these Rabbinic rulings and
debates. This massive compendium which contain innumerable discussions in the most minute of detail, of every conceivable phase of
living, arose out of interpretations of Biblical laws and principles
which had been handed down orally, with authority, each adding his
own analysis, while deferring to the teacher who had preceded him.

Gradually, the practical need arose to put down in writing all
these situations, teachings, laws and decisions, so that, while the title
"Oral Law" was retained, they were, in fact, all recorded. This com-
pilation also took successive forms. First came a code called the
Mishnah, from the word "to study." This contained the principles
and decisions which came into being up to about 250 C.E., and it
was edited by Rabbi Judah HaNasi (the Prince). Based on the pattern
laid down by the brilliant Akiba, the Mishnah had its own structure
and was divided into Six Major Categories or Orders, as follows:

*Ze'rah-im*, Seeds, dealing with laws bearing on agriculture.

16

*Mo'ed*, Seasons, dealing with the Sabbath, festivals, feasts and the fasts of the Jewish calendar.

*Nashim*, Women, dealing with marriage, divorce and family life.

*Ne'zikin*, Damages (torts), dealing with civil and criminal law.

*Kedoshim*, "Holy Things," — dealing with the Temple and sacrifices.

*T'horoth*, Questions of ritual purity.

Each of these Orders is further divided into volumes, called tractates, *Massekhot*, in Hebrew. In the Talmud there are sixty-three tractates which are further subdivided into smaller groupings containing chapters and paragraphs.

This codification did not mean that the law had been finalized. Discussions continued as life presented the rabbis with new experiences and new problems. The *Mishnah* became the basic text studied and was the source of debate for hundreds of years, until the oral discussion once again became too voluminous and had to be put into writing. In 500 C.E., the *Gemara* (learning) came into being. Based on the structure of the Six Orders of the Mishnah, the Gemara was edited by a number of sages, especially Rabina and Rabbi Ashi. The combination of both the *Mishnah* and the *Gemara* is the Talmud. The sages of the Mishnah were called the *Ta-na-im* (Teachers), and the sages of the Gemara, *Amo-ra-im* (Sayers). Both the Talmud and the Bible are the source of the *Halakhah*.

## PRINCIPLES OF INTERPRETATION

Since law must be consistent, the Talmudic masters had to develop a system by which law could be interpreted as it confronted ever new situations. Hence, principles of interpretation came into being, some more distinctive than others.

There was, for example, what is called the *Ge-zay-rah* (decree), a restrictive principle imposed by the rabbis to protect and safeguard the Scriptural law. Some principles were developed after study and analysis of given situations; others were issued for the purpose of "making a fence about the Torah," thus protecting the original law which might otherwise be infringed. There was also the *Takkanah*, a new regulation issued by the authorities confronting an entirely new situation, or to improve compliance with existing laws. The rabbis did not issue *Takkanoth* arbitrarily. Careful study preceded the decree. Another principle of interpretation was called *Minhag* (Custom). This had developed as a highly regarded tradition and was staunchly adhered to. Local customs were in time recognized as having the force of law.

By means of these principles, even after the closing of the Tamudic era, the two Torahs, Written and Unwritten, continued as one. After 500 C.E., in different periods, different groups of rabbinic leaders dealt with new situations. Academies were opened, leaders of which were called *Hakhamim* (originally, Wise-men), sages, or rabbis who were sought out for decisions as questions arose. Their responsa, after a great deal of contemplative analysis, always consulting the earlier sources, was accepted as binding.

An era of some 500 years, from the closing of the Talmud until about 1038, was called the Gaonic period. Gaon means "illustrious" and was the title accorded to the scholars who lived during the time. By a combination of their erudition and awareness of the new pressures of life, they were able to keep the people united within the *halakhic* framework. The law was constantly being developed and expanded. The underlying procedure by which these vital decisions were arrived at is called *She'ayloth u-teshuvot*, (Questions and Answers), and *Responsa*. The literature thus created became known as Queries and were forwarded to the Gaon, who would investigate the sources for precedent, seek to interrelate a present day issue legally, halakhically, with earlier events or experiences and, after added consultation, render a decision which became part of the process of *Halakhah*. The large accumulations of these questions were later also committed to writing, and were incorporated into digests of laws.

## THE RISHONIM AND CODIFIERS

There continued to be successive eras of commentators. Schools were established in various parts of the world to which historic and political forces drove the Jewish people. Jews residing in Southern Europe, North Africa, and Palestine became known as the Sephardic Jews, from the Hebrew word, *Sepharad*, Spain. They gradually grew into a separate body following the rite of the earlier Babylonian community.

The Northern European Jews, especially those in Poland and Russia, were known as Ashkenazim from the Hebrew word, *Ashkenaz*, Germany. They follow the school of study that originated in Palestine, and developed a different rite and outlook.

Both groups adhered completely to the Written and Unwritten traditions. The differences lay in emphases and living environments, but the authority of the Torah was unquestioned.

From the Gaonic period, a group of scholars, now called the *Rishonim*, or the First Expositors, in contrast to a group in later centuries called *Aharonim*, the Later Expositors, were the religious and intellectual authorities from about the year 1000 C.E. to the middle of the 15th Century. They and their schools developed commentaries on the Talmud which were accepted as authoritative and with each generation the compendia grew, the material becoming incorporated into the process of *Halakhah*.

Among the most respected was Moses Maimonides (1140-1205), known by the acrostic of his name, RaMBaM, Rabbi Moses ben Maimon. His code of Jewish law, Mishneh Torah, stands out as perhaps the most impressive in the whole history of the Halakhah. He wrote not only a simplified digest of the Talmud, but incisive commentaries and explanations as well. His code still serves as the best reference guide for deep study of Talmud.

Another of the greatest scholars of the period was Rabbi Shlomo Yitzhaki, known by the acrostic of his name RaSHI, the commentator par excellence. Without his brilliant, strikingly simple explanatory comments, the Talmudic text (as indeed the Bible) would have been a closed book.

While the authority of these commentators was limited to their immediate locale, their scholarship carried their reputation to many lands. They were succeeded by codifiers who were continuously organizing the massive literature that developed.

The first was Rabbi Jacob ben Asher who divided the traditional Six Orders of the Talmud into Four Pillars, or *Turim:*

> *Orakh Hayyim*, Way of Life, laws concerning prayer and the observance of the Sabbath and Festivals.
> *Yoreh De'ah*, Teacher of Knowledge, dealing with the dietary laws, certain prohibited matters, and the laws of mourning.
> *Even Ha-Ezer*, Rock of Help, laws of marriage and divorce.
> *Hoshen Mishpat*, Breastplate of Judgment, dealing with laws concerning the processes of judgment and matters of property.

19

The most extensive codification was the *Shulhan Arukh*, the Code of Jewish Law, literally, "Prepared Table." Completed in 1554 by Rabbi Joseph Karo, this became the most authoritative source of Jewish law since the Talmud. His work differed from the earlier Four Pillars in that he did not show the conflicting opinions, but followed the example of Maimonides, setting down the decisions finally arrived at in succinct, concise statements and noting the opinions of great masters. Since Karo was born in Spain and was a product of that environment, his work was authoritative for the Spanish-Portugese Jewish Community.

Another authority, Rabbi Moses Isserlis, the RaMAH, a Polish scholar, completed the Shulhan Arukh, including decisions which represented the results reached by codifiers in France and Germany. Isserlis originally planned to compose a work similar to Karo's but put off doing so, satisfying himself with his notes, which were incorporated into the Shulhan Arukh. His work is called Mapat Hashulhan, or the Table Cloth, since it puts the finishing touches to Karo's ready-laid table. In the completed volume containing the two texts, Karo's work appears in larger, and that of Isserlis in recognizably smaller typeset.

## THE REVOLT AGAINST THE HALAKHAH

The modern era has witnessed opposition to the Codes, some attacking their basic thesis and others their approach. The Hasidic revolt, for example, rebelled not against what we call Orthodoxy, or *Halakhah*, but rather against its legalistic approach to Judaism. Their philosophy of life emphasized joyous expression, comradeship, and delight in the Torah expressed through song and dance, rather than what they consider a more rigid and legalistic approach to Jewish living. In addition, they provided the people, who were not completely acquainted with the intricacies of law, with an opportunity of sharing in Jewish expression.

A revolt against the *Halakhah* itself was precipitated during the era of Enlightenment, propelled by a group known as the Maskilim, or Enlightened Ones. In the early 19th Century they severely criticized the rigidity of the *Halakhah* and its alleged emphasis on conformity to ritual. They rejected the authority of the rabbis of the Talmud and paved the way for the rise of the Reform movement in Europe which stressed the ethical ideals of the Hebrew prophets as against the legal authority of the Bible and Talmud.

In spite of the inroads made by the Maskilim and the attacks leveled against Orthodoxy, the Halakhah continued to flourish and to remain the authoritative guide to Jewish life, and digests of the Shulhan Arukh continued to appear.

## THE ORTHODOX POSITION

In 1815, a concise summary of the Shulhan Arukh, called the Hayye Adam, Life of Man, was edited by Rabbi Abraham Danzig of Vilna. In the latter part of the century, Rabbi Shlomo Ganzfried composed a digest, also of the Shulhan Arukh, for the layman, titling it the Kitzur Shulhan Arukh, or the Condensed Code, which became popular among the masses although it contained no materials other than dry legal decisions and stereotyped patterns of conduct.

Other digests continued to flow from gifted scholars. The latest is the work of Rabbi Israel Meir HaCohen, known as the Hafetz Hayyim (Desire for Life), published a half century ago, and entitled the Mishnah Berurah, or Clear Teaching or Study. In addition, the process of Questions and Answers continues to function as the traditional method of applying the Halakhah.

So, the entire process, from Moses through the Biblical period, the Talmudic and Gaonic eras, the Rishonim (First Expositors), Codifiers, and Aharonim (Latter Expositors), is part of an unending chain, one interpretation building upon the other. This is the traditional method — an issue arising today is discussed, evaluated and interrelated with sources, and a decision called a judgment or sentence is reached.

## THE REFORM APPROACH

Had the process of the Halakhah proceeded as smoothly as reflected here, there would have been only one Judaism to which to apply for decisions and guidance on contemporary issues. But this is not the case. One of the first movements to deviate from the mainstream of Judaism was what is now called Reform Judaism.

The seeds of the new group germinated when the National Assembly of France, on September 27, 1791, declared Jews citizens of that country. This was a major event for Jews, who had never before been recognized as free citizens. The doors opened to welcome them to a new and freer society. From France the fever spread to Germany.

At first, the pressing forces of change struck at the external structure of the synagogue. Impressed with the decorous worship of their Christian neighbors, individuals, led in 1810 by Israel Jacobson and others, tried to add beauty and dignity to the services. They at first introduced only minor modifications without any basic change in philosophy, but they still managed to dislocate the pattern to which Jews had been accustomed. Once changes were introduced, the process was speeded up, penetrating to the core of Jewish practice and belief.

These modifications had to have rabbinic justification, and there was reliance on the historic process of change — that is, precedents were sought in the Talmudic tradition and codes. Gradually, however, the younger, more militant rabbis, exposed to secular university studies where they had imbibed a basic knowledge of history, archaeology and philosophy, could not accept the traditional procedures and challenged not only the process of adjustment but also the whole *Halakhic* approach and the teachings of Judaism, its beliefs and practices.

An almost open conflict resulted. On the one hand, the rabbis sought to minimize differences which prevented fuller participation in civil life. On the other hand, they noted that many had renounced affiliation with their faith. The impulse to cross the imaginary line (to them not imaginary at all) into what appeared to be a welcoming society, was compelling. Judaism would lose greatly, and its future was gravely threatened unless something was done quickly. Caught in this overpowering dilemma, the young rabbis felt impelled to take severe if not radical steps.

First, the services and then the internal structure were singled out for change. The attack was directed not only at the methodology of the codifications of the laws, the Responsa, and the Shulhan Arukh but also against the Talmud itself as Oral Law. A reverse trend from that which had originally systematized the oral tradition set in, erasing layer after layer of that same tradition until the Reform movement openly denied the divine inspiration of the Talmud so as to abrogate many of its tenets.

This change in belief was not a sudden one. Differing views stirred within the minds of the young reformers of the early 19th century. One position held by some was that only the Shulhan Arukh of Joseph Karo had become accepted as the final authority, and was binding, and that codes that developed later were not. A middle-of-the-road position maintained that there should be a selective approach to Talmudic laws to determine which should be considered binding. This non-extremist view did not go so far as to impinge on the authority of the Bible. Still another more radical opinion was that the new movement for change must deny, not only the binding force of the Unwritten Law, the Talmud, but that of the Bible itself was to be called into question. They recommended that the ethical and moral concepts of the Bible be regarded as eternal, but that the ceremonial laws, which to them held credibility only during Biblical times, were no longer binding.

While the less radical leaders held out for group decisions, insisting that the major ones had been historically decreed by discussions of rabbis in the past, it was nevertheless agreed that the modern emphasis would be on the religious spirit of Judaism, rather than on the performance of ritual law. The *spirit* of Judaism was eternal. *Performance* externalized by ceremony and ritual was transitory and mirrored only the particular period in which it was carried out.

The 19th century witnessed the drive for complete separation from traditional Judaism. Underlying the move was the final denial of the binding nature of the Oral Law. Some of the leaders tried to convene conferences in which the rabbis would agree to discuss these basic issues. Their attempts were abortive, however; guidelines could not be agreed upon.

The Orthodox rabbis did not accept the new movement without protest. There were even threats of excommunications — a very natural response, since the new movement not only represented a threat to the rabbinic authorities of the time, but to the whole concept of Judaism as it had developed over the centuries.

The final schism came with the Pittsburgh Conference, convened by Dr. Kaufmann Kohler in November, 1885; the position adopted by the Pittsburgh Platform became the official view of the Reform movement, (until it was replaced by the Columbus Conference in 1937). The authority of the Talmud was denied and the conference stated that:

> We recognize in the Mosaic legislation a system of training the Jewish people for its mission during its national life in Palestine, and today we accept as binding only its moral laws, and maintain only such ceremonies as elevate and sanctify our lives, but reject

all such as are not adapted to the views and habits of modern civilization.

We hold that all such Mosaic and rabbinical laws as regulate diet, priestly purity,and dress originated in ages and under the influence of ideas entirely foreign to our present mental and spiritual state. They fail to impress the modern Jew with a spirit of priestly holiness; their observance in our days is apt rather to obstruct than to further modern spiritual elevation.

We recognize, in the modern era of universal culture of heart and intellect, the approaching of the realization of Israel's great Messianic hope for the establishment of the kingdom of truth, justice, and peace among all men. We consider ourselves no longer a nation, but a religious community, and therefore expect neither a return to Palestine, nor a sacrificial worship under the sons of Aaron, nor the restoration of any of the laws concerning the Jewish state.

At a later meeting, July, 1895, which was very poorly attended, the position was clarified:

> ... from the standpoint of Reform Judaism, the whole post-biblical and patriotic literature, including the Talmud, casuists, responses, and commentaries, is, and can be considered as nothing more or less than "religious literature." As such, it is of inestimable value. It is the treasurehouse in which the successive ages deposited their contributions to the never-ending endeavour to elucidate the same. Consciously or unconsciously, every age has added a wing to this great treasurehouse, and the architecture and construction of each wing bear the indelible marks of the peculiar characteristics of the time in which it was erected. Our age is engaged in the same task. We, too, have to contribute to the enlargement of this treasurehouse; but we have to do it in our own way, as the spirit of our time directs, without any slavish imitation of the past.

Rejection of Talmudic authority as expressed in the Codes, especially in the Shulhan Arukh, required the conscious development of a completely different structure of values for a different Judaism. Reform Judaism proceeded to confront each problem, custom and rite, and for a long time found its raison d'etre merely in negating the structure of prayer and custom that had endured over the centuries. But, even while they were abrogating the laws, many of the leaders inquired into the Talmudic sources for guidance as to how to proceed. Isaac M. Wise, on the other hand, tended toward a more moderate position, asserting: "To be sure, I am a reformer as much as our age requires, because I am convinced that none can stop the stream of time; none can check the swift wheels of our age, but I always have the *Halakhah* for my basis; I never sanction a reform against the law."

The tendency toward more radical reform continued until the so-called "classical" reform of the 1885 vintage was replaced as we have mentioned earlier, by a new balance sheet of Reform Judaism in the Columbus Platform of 1937. New developments, including the rise of Zionism, disappointment in socialism and other liberation movements, and the rise of Nazism, coordinated to bring about a new perspective even for Reform Judaism. The new platform reveals a major change of heart especially in the use of the term "Torah" rather than Bible, and reflects a more sympathetic appreciation of traditions. What had earlier been considered anachronistic is now appreciatively returned to. Special recognition of the Torah, both Oral and Written, speaks of a reversal from the original repudiation of Talmudic literature and the Shulhan Arukh. Although these latter are still not declared to be the products of direct Divine revelation, much of the antagonism levelled against them at the Pittsburgh Platform has become tempered.

This continuing trend to resort to Talmudic authority is evident in Reform literature and conventions. Leaders caution, however, that this can be overdone and an acceptance of the divinity of the Unwritten Law seems to be implied. Dr. Solomon Freehof, analyzing the changing positions of Reform says:

"We began to be interested, not as hitherto only in Judaism, but in Jewishness." He advises people to be careful not to overvalue the status of the new rituals, which should remain, at best, *minhagim* (customs) and not *mitzvoth* (laws), that is, Divine mandates. Yet he does not hesitate to express his admiration and esteem for Talmudic literature:

> These ceremonial experiments . . . . may well beautify and rein-
> spire our religious life. It may have also another benefit; it may
> bring us back to an intellectual interest in the vast learning which
> the old ceremonial observances created in older Judaism. We have
> been too scornful of that. If the great legal literature was not the

product of genius and inspiration as the Bible was, it is at least the product of immense talent and devotion. We do not accept even the Bible verbally, but search in it for that which can inspire. So we will search the great rabbinic literature and add greatly to the foundations upon which the creative Judaism of the future will be built.

Some Reform rabbis have asked for guidelines for Jewish observance, and individual rabbis have developed such manuals, basing them on modern interpretations of Talmudic law. One has suggested: "*Halakhah* represents the totality of the demands of God, as defined by Judaism and realized in Jewish experience. There is no Judaism without *Halakhah*." Present day majority thinking is associated with the views of Dr. Solomon Freehof who stresses the importance of retaining an element of *Halakhah* in Reform Judaism maintaining that the movement was always involved in post-Biblical Judaism, that is, Talmudic Judaism, as regards manner of worship, the structure of prayer in the synagogue, and those customs which have been retained within Reform Judaism. He argues that the Central Conference of American Rabbis has always had a Responsa Committee reporting to the annual conventions on issues presented to it for adjudication. While he cannot accept the Orthodox position, he does say in his Preface to Reform Responsa:

> ... whatever authority the *Halakhah* has for us is certainly only a selective authority ... we cannot believe that rabbinic law is God's mandate ... The law to us is a human project. That does not mean that God does not somehow reveal Himself in the "language of the children of men." Perhaps He does, but if He does, His self-revelation is not so perfect nor so clear nor so final as to make the whole law His sure commandment. To us the law is human ... developed by devoted minds who dedicated their best efforts to answering the question "What doth the Lord require of thee?" The law is authoritative enough to influence us, but not so completely as to control us. The rabbinic law is our guidance but not our governance ....

## THE CONSERVATIVE APPROACH

The extreme to which Reform was galloping generated intense reaction from still another perspective which sought to interrelate the ends of "maintaining the integrity of Judaism simultaneously with progress," as Zacharias Frankel noted. This thinking led to the emergence of the Conservative movement, often incorrectly called the middle way between Orthodoxy and Reform. The Historical School or Historical Judaism is another name ascribed to this vital current.

While in the third quarter of the 19th century, some Reform leaders hoped to bring all modern thinkers into one umbrella organization, the extremist forces prevailed, creating the schism that separated the two groups. In reaction to Reform, and with a real esteem for the vibrancy of traditional Judaism, the new group went forward with a thesis of its own.

On the whole, the Conservative Movement accepted as a fact of life the principle that definite change had entered into Judaism, as it had into every facet of existence, and that change was inevitable. No living organism is static. The new era had to permit and encourge freedom of thought, allow for serious questioning and criticism of every aspect of life, law or custom. It was good, rather than bad, for people to gain a full exposure to the new science. Recognition of scientific principles was not harmful, but helpful to a better understanding of Judaism and the observance of the faith, and should, indeed, even be assimilated into Judaism. Such an attitude would prove the dynamic vitality of *Halakhah* as an on-going process. The developing principles included (1) a positive attitude toward the law, *Halakhah*, as an inextricable part of Judaism and its religion; (2) the necessity of the observance of the laws and traditions of Judaism; and (3) a loyalty to the reality of Jewish nationhood.

Observance of the laws was to be viewed as the avenue by which the truths of Judaism were revealed and preserved, strengthening the continuity and transmission of the tradition to succeeding generations. Belief in the nationhood of Israel was not to be construed chauvinistically; rather it would stress the fact that the Jews were a distinct historic people, with a distinctive religion and laws. Also, both the religion and the nationhood of Israel were inseparable. It was the fact that the whole complex structure of law provided a central unifying force for the Jewish people that ultimately served as its justification.

The leading exponent of the budding Conservative movement was Zacharias Frankel, who vigorously opposed Reform Judaism. While he was part of the earlier drive toward Reform, participating in conferences, hoping to steer toward a clearer, historic, road, he withdrew when he saw the extreme toward which Reform was veering. Admitting that certain aspects of Judaism could not withstand the pressures of modern life, he was of the opinion that attempts had to be made to stabilize Judaism and prepare it for confrontations from within as from without, and that this could be accomplished only by diligent, honest research into the sources. Simply to negate and abstract as Reform had done was only destructive. "Religion has to be practical and tangible and any attempt to divest the Torah of its institution endangers the existence of the Jews. Only by diligent study and research will we be able to discover what is essential and what is non-essential . . . what are the accretions which could be disposed of and what are the religious forms which should be retained at all costs."[1]

The thesis with which the new movement started out was that "Judaism was a changing and developing entity which through the ages had recognized the temper of the times and changing conditions and had adjusted to them without sacrificing its own integrity."[2]

Again: "Judaism historically was both mobile and static . . . it must in measure adjust toward the spirit of the time and in measure resist it, and . . . a conclusive factor in all judgments must be a sensitivity to the history, needs, and unity of the people."[3]

Unlike Reform Judaism, which rejected the concept of Torah as a force for growth by denying the validity of Talmudic law and the codes and responsa developing from it, and unlike Orthodox Judaism which, by its rigidity, did not take fully into account the needs and social context of the Jewish people, Conservative Judaism has tried to intertwine the three parts of the formula, God, Torah, and the Jewish people; it considers each of equal validity. Whereas God and Torah are accepted basics of Judaism, the sentiment of the people, and their particular problems and situations, are equally vital in this formula. Each of the three principles contained in this triangle, with each attaching to the other, so as to project the totality of Israel, provides the most succinct formulation of what Conservative Judaism, and Judaism itself is all about.[4]

"There is no other Jewish religion but that taught by the Torah and confirmed by history and tradition, and sunk into the conscience of Catholic Israel."[5]

The second larger principle, Positive Historical Judaism, gives credence to those who would like to call Conservative Judaism, Historical Judaism. The appellation reflects the position of the

28

movement in terms of continuity of the past and a need to maintain that continuity, not blindly but in terms of a direction. The concept holds that Judaism retains a marked reverence for the system of Jewish life which developed in time, its religious-legal system, drawn from the Written and Oral Laws, and that while Judaism has changed because life has changed, the structure must be conserved. Hence, the name "Conservative Judaism," meaning to conserve the dynamic development of Judaism, and its religio-legalistic-cultural framework. In addition, the school holds that change should come through an evolutionary process and that these changes can come from within Judaism itself. Talmudic guidelines and mechanics for change within the bounds of the law have always been operative. Conservative Judaism holds that pressing issues of the day can be confronted within the framework of Talmudic law. Reform Judaism, while saying that it accepts the principle of interpretation, has in reality rejected the authority of the legal tradition. A few leading Reform rabbis often call for some minimal acceptance of the legal tradition, but their voices are thin and they evaporate in the face of overwhelming odds. Orthodoxy, while maintaining the principle of interpretation, grinds slowly as issues are addressed to individual rabbis. Their hold on the past is tenacious, thereby slowing the process of change to a trickle.

In addition, the Jewish people, as people, are completely intertwined in and determinant factors of the Halakhic process. This theme is reflected in the term Catholic Israel propounded by Solomon Schechter. In his words it is the "collective conscience . . . embodied in the Universal Synagogue . . .' with its long, continuous cry after God for more than twenty-three centuries,' with its unremittent activity in teaching and developing the word of God, with its uninterrupted succession of Prophets, Psalmists, Scribes, Assideans, Rabbis, Patriarchs, Interpreters, Elucidators, Eminences, and Teachers, with its glorious record of saints, martyrs, sages, philosophers, scholars, and mystics, . . . the only true witness to the past, and forming in all ages the sublimest expression of Israel's religious life."[6]

The term Catholic Israel "derives from the solid and meaningful phrase Klal Yisrael — the totality of Israel."[7]

"No other movement in Judaism has put as much emphasis on the Jewish people as the bearer of revelation as has the Conservative movement. Zecharias Frankel cited the following passage from the Talmud as his watchword:

*R. Yochanan said: Our Rabbis investigated the observance of the prohibition against the use of gentile oil, and they found that the observance of the prohibition had not spread amongst the majority of Israel, and our Rabbis relied on the word of R. Shimon b. Gamaliel and on the words of R. Eleazar b. Zadok, who were wont to say, 'We do not institute a prohibition on the community unless it is possible for the majority of the community to abide by it.*

"Solomon Schechter gave the idea of the centrality of the consciousness of the Jewish people in his celebrated statement about the locus of authority in Judaism: (that authority is in) 'some living body (which) by reason of its being in touch with the ideal aspirations and the religious needs of the age, is best able to determine the nature of the Secondary meaning (referring to the normative interpretation of Scripture). This living body, however, is not represented by any section of the nation, or any corporate priesthood or rabbinate, but by the collective conscience of Catholic Israel as embodied in the Universal Synagogue.'

"Rabbi Joshua b. Levi says: 'Whenever the Bet Din is in doubt as to the interpretation of a law, and you do not know how to comply with it, observe what the people do' (Yer. Peah 7:5, cf. Berachot 45a). Catholic Israel is the locus of authority, and Catholic Israel has adopted the Halakhah as its mode of religious expression — not its exclusive mode, but its most crucial mode.

"The idea of Catholic Israel has been widely criticized as being applicable only in times past, when the preponderant majority of Jews observed the Halakhah. Can it still be utilized in our own day?

"Robert Gordis attempted an interesting redefinition of the doctrine of Catholic Israel:

*"Catholic Israel is the body of men and women within the Jewish people who accept the authority of Jewish law and are concerned with Jewish observance as a genuine idea. The character of their observance may be rigorous and extend to minutiae, or it may include modifications in detail. Catholic Israel embraces all those, too, who observe Jewish law in general, though they may violate one or another segment, and who are sensitive to the problem of their non-observance because they wish to respect the authority of Jewish law.*

"Catholic Israel, theologically speaking, is the refractor of the voice of God in matters of Jewish law, because Israel is God's people. When the Jewish community speaks authentically out of its own integrity, it is the medium through which the divine intention for the people is expressed. The idea of Catholic Israel is basic to any understanding of the approach of Conservative Judaism to Jewish Law. It is the collective conscience which endows the Law with sanctity. It is the collective conscience which gives the ultimate judgment about how the law should be changed and modified."[8]

Conservative Judaism insists that to fulfill its aims (in Rabbi Siegal's words: "to validate and promote the observance of Jewish law, and to make modification and change possible"), it must assume the authority via "its rabbinical body acting as a whole to interpret and apply Jewish law." Some customs, procedures, traditions, have developed not by fiat or rabbinic decision but by daily living. They have become part of the recognizable substance of the the movement without examination and decree.

"The Rabbinical Assembly, the rabbinic arm of Conservative Judaism, operates through its Committee on Jewish Law and Standards. It consists of twenty-five rabbis who are appointed by the President of the Rabbincal Assembly, and is assigned the responsibility of interpreting Jewish law for the Conservative movement. Generally, the decisions made by the committee reflect a majority and a minority opinion. According to the regulations of the Assembly, individual rabbis have the privilege of following either of the opinions. The local rabbi, however, who is the *mara d'atra*, and who is most sensitive to the conditions and needs of his own congregation, has the authority to select the opinion he prefers and to act upon it. When, however, there is unanimous opinion rendered by the Committee, it is then considered to be a standard, and each and every rabbi of the Assembly is bound to comply with that unanimous decision."[9]

Rabbi Siegel points out that the methodology involved in a Halakhic rendering posits:

"1. Seek out the precedent. Unless there is good reason to do otherwise, we are bound to the precedent.
2. In seeking out the precedents, we do not necessarily limit ourselves to any specific code.
3. If the precedent is deficient in meeting the needs of the people, if it is clearly foreign to the group of law-observers in the community, if it is offensive to our ethical sensitivities,

or if we do not share its basic scientific, economic, and social assumptions, then the law can be modified either by outright abrogation, or by ignoring or modifying it. Thus, when we are faced with rendering a moral judgment about abortion, we are informed by the tradition, which expresses a bias for the life of the unborn fetus. We find in the tradition, however, that abortion to save the life of the mother is permitted. We find it possible to interpret the meaning of "saving the life of the mother," as involving economic, emotional and sociological components — thereby legitimating many abortions 'for cause.' "[10]

Another technique for legal action is represented in the establishment of a Joint Law Conference which includes members of the Rabbinical Assembly and faculty members of the Jewish Theological Seminary of America on issues dealing with marriage, divorce and the family. This group assumes the Jewish legal principle of issuing *takkanot* (injunctions or enactments) in areas concerning marriage and the family.

## RECONSTRUCTIONISTISM

The Reconstructionist movement, "dedicated to the advancement of Judaism as a religious civilization, to the upbuilding of Eretz Yisrael as a spiritual center of the Jewish people, and to the furtherance of universal freedom, justice and peace," was organized in 1934 by Professor Mordecai M. Kaplan. Most of the affiliated rabbis are members of the Conservative Rabbinical Assembly, their perspective left of center. Yet, the movement has its own fellowship, Seminary, and press, calling for the reconstruction of Judaism.

Of the principles significant for this book, the following are important:

> Judaism, or that which has united the successive generations of Jews into one People, is not only a religion; it is a dynamic religious civilization.
>
> The revitalization of Jewish religion can be best achieved through the study of it in the spirit of free inquiry . . .
>
> The continuity of a religion through different stages, and its identity amid diversity of belief and practice, are sustained by its *sancta*; these are the heroes, events, texts, places and seasons that the religion signalizes as furthering the fulfillment of human destiny . . .

The position of Reconstructionism on *Halakhah* is found in the following excerpt from Rabbi Jack J. Cohen appearing in the Reconstructionist Magazine:

> Life has irretrievably destroyed the *halakhah* as law . . . We have graduated from revealed monocracy to the age of civil democracy and religious voluntarism . . . For all of us, however, living without the positive values of *halakhah* and the knowledge of what it has meant to Jewish life would be impossible . . . we have absorbed the *halakhah* as part of our apperception of Judaism. The content of ritual *halakhah* is the starting point of our ritual observance; the ethical spirit and intent of civil *halakhah* has become part of our own ethical standpoint. Much of the subject matter of our study of Judaism is the *Halakhah* itself, both in content and method; and our commitment to our people and to the advancement of its tradition is a counterpart, in our lives, of the devotion of our ancestors to the halakhic way of life.
>
> What does it mean to live *with* the *halakhah* but not *by* it? It means precisely what is implied in living with the Bible but not by it. To be Jewish is to have one's whole soul suffused by the Bible, so that it becomes an element in the very structure of one's mind . . . And yet living with all this, we dare not live our lives within the constitutional limits of the Bible itself.
>
> In the same way, there is no Judaism for us without the Mishnah and the Talmud, the Codes and the Responsa. The magnificence of an ethic embodied in legislation, of a society founded on the study of law and the exploration of its spiritual significance, and of a tradition dedicated to holiness rather than power, is our life and the length of our days. And yet if we are honest with ourselves, we cannot live by Rabbinic texts. Instead we have to learn how to build our Judaism in our own style on what the *halakhah* has bequeathed to us.

The issues on which the Reconstructionist point of view has addressed itself are included in this book.

### REFERENCES

1. Meyer Waxman, A History of Jewish Literature, Vol. III, Bloch Publishing Company, New York, 1936, p. 381.

2. Mordecai Waxman, Editor, Tradition and Change, The Burning Bush Press, New York, 1958, p. 7.

3. ibid.

4. See Mordecai Waxman, ibid, p. 14.

5. Solomon Schechter, The Charter of The Seminary (1902), quoted by Mordecai Waxman, ibid, p. 103.

6. Quoted by Henrietta Szold in Mordecai Waxman, ibid, p. 111.

7. ibid, Mordecai Waxman, p. 14.

8. Seymour Siegel, Conservative Judaism and Jewish Law, The Rabbinical Assembly, New York, 1977, XVII-XVIII. See also Seymour Siegel's article in Conservative Judaism, Halakhah and Ethics, Rabbincial Assembly, Vol. 25, No. 3, Spring 1971, p. 33. See also article by Robert Gordis in same issue, p. 49.

9. ibid, Seymour Siegel, p. XIII. Rabbi Siegel's words have been paraphrased.

10. ibid, Seymour Siegel, p. XXIV.

# ABORTION

The pressing contemporary issue of abortion has, in fact, been discussed and evaluated in Jewish sources since biblical days. A number of different attitudes have evolved, which even now serve as guidelines when particular cases are presented for adjudication.

The basic premise to an understanding of the subject at hand is the unanimously held position that human life is sacred and cannot be tampered with at whim. Convenience is not a ground for abortion, nor does the mere desire not to have a child give one automatically the right to get rid of the living fetus. Abortion is not deemed a mere surgical procedure.

> The decision on whether and under what circumstances it is right to destroy a germinating human life depends on the assessment and weighing of values, on determining the title to life in any given case. Such value judgments are entirely outside the province of medical science . . . Such judgments pose essentially a moral, not a medical, problem. Hence, they call for the judgment of moral, not medical specialists . . . The decision on whether a human life, once conceived, is to be or not to be, therefore, properly belongs to moral experts, or to legislatures guided by such experts.[1]

Every group in Judaism agrees unequivocally that when the life of the mother is at stake, or even threatened, the fetus not only *can* but *must* be aborted.[2a] The life of the mother has undisputed priority in Jewish thought. Danger to life includes psychological, as well as physical hazard, provided it is genuine. Both physical and mental health stand on the same level of concern.

When an abortion is performed in such a case it is therapeutic, and therefore absolutely permissible; no censure, and certainly no guilt, is then in order.

Every group agrees also that where the fetus is in its more highly-developed stage, and ready to begin the birth process, the case for abortion becomes increasingly more difficult. Generally, the life of the fetus cannot then be destroyed, unless there is a hazard to the life of the mother. Both mother and fetus are then living entities, each entitled to the full measure of life. One life cannot, in Jewish law, be sacrificed for another, for that would invite the indictment of murder.

It is *almost* conceded, even from the Orthodox position, and the word *almost* is stressed, that the risk to mental, as well as to physical, health is included under this general heading of "hazard to life." In this case, a real threat to the mental life of the mother would, today, be sufficient ground for authorizing therapeutic abortion.

On the other hand, none of the official denominations would allow indiscriminate abortion, without justifiable cause. Recently some have recommended that the mother be given the final say without involvement of state or religion. Hawaii in February of 1970, became the first state allowing any woman who had resided there for at last ninety days to have an abortion simply on the grounds that she did not want to have a child. The new Maryland law requires only that the physician be licensed.

The differences in perspective lie in that vast but difficult middle ground which attempts to distinguish between the precise boundaries of law and legal interpretation. Orthodox Judaism, on the one hand, does not generally permit abortion for any reason except concern (physical and mental) for the life of the mother.

Abortions in cases of rape, incest, and German measles or rubella, are, therefore, not considered therapeutic since danger to the mother's life is not in question. While the fetus is not technically deemed a living being (*nefesh* is the Hebrew word) for which abortion would be classified technically as murder, it is nonetheless regarded as a crime because the fetus itself has the basic right of continuing to full term.

Real differences of decisions among the religious denominations, in sanction or in law, stem from the bases upon which the presentation is made and the authorities who are recognized and accepted. Thus, Orthodox Judaism,[2b] following the stricter position, has a set of perfectly clear-cut and logical premises. Reform, on the other hand, while seeking sources for precedents without necessarily being bound by them, accepts the more liberal sources. So long as there exists at least the suggestion of lenient opinion on the part of some great authority, Reform Judaism will rely on that, and allow for abortion on therapeutic grounds. The Conservative group, rooted more deeply in a respect for and acceptance of *Halakhah*, allows abortions in cases where there is a real hazard to life and also permits therapeutic abortion in certain cases. Under this head, Conservative rabbis in various parts of the country, have issued statements urging state legislatures to legalize abortion in cases of rape, incest, or rubella and the threat of malformed babies.

The differences in decisions of the various groups can also be understood from their manner of approach as to which is the more crucial in the decision-making process, the law as it has evolved out of the tradition, or the individual involved? Does the problem of the individual become a central concern when the decision is being made? Is the suffering of the mother or of the potential child the determining factor? Here, as we have seen, Orthodox, Conservative and Reform agree in regarding the life of the mother as having priority and the law is determined by this fact.

It should be noted that the Reconstructionist position, while it has not been made from any platform, also seems to take its stand with the liberal Conservative and Reform positions.[3]

It ought also be mentioned that, in the Orthodox view, abortion is not to be deemed a medical problem. Medicine alone cannot determine whether abortion ought or ought not to be effected. Some psychiatrists agree to this. Dr. Thomas S. Szasa, in *The Humanist*, writing on the subject, "The Ethics of Abortion," says:

> Abortion is a moral, not a medical problem. To be sure, the procedure is surgical; but this makes abortion no more a medical problem than the use of the electric chair makes capital punishment a problem of electrical engineering. The question is, What is abortion — murder of the fetus or the removal of a piece of tissue from the woman's body?[4]

Interestingly enough, as we shall see later, the latter phrase entered into Rabbinic Talmudic discussions of particular cases.

There are views, however, which hold that abortion must also be considered medical, which would draw in the issue of the fetus and its potential, as well as the effect on the mother from a medical point of view. Even in cases of rubella, the fetus is entitled to survive. The Reform and other liberal views, also take the child's right to live into serious account. For example, if the child, according to expert opinion, is certain to be deformed, the Orthodox, ignoring the medical prognosis, and basing themselves on an ethical and religious point of view, insist that even such a contingency does not permit life to be destroyed any more than it would be right to do away with the crippled or the insane.

> . . . any abortion of a human fruit for fear that it may be born deformed, must be condemned as tantamount to murder. This prohibition would stand even if it were certain that the child would be born deformed, just as it is forbidden to kill a crippled person.[5]

Thus, the Orthodox view seems to be closer to the official Roman Catholic stand, with the one crucial exception, that the child not only can, but must be sacrificed and the pregnancy terminated where the life of the mother is at stake. In official Roman Catholicism, this cannot be done because of the principle that "better two deaths than one murder," a position which has been official since 1869.[6]

## BIBLICAL BASIS

Only one source in the entire Bible relates to abortion. Under the general category of Civil Legislation and the division of the Rights of Persons, the Bible records:

> When men fight, and one of them pushes a pregnant woman and a miscarriage results, but no other damage ensues, the one responsible shall be fined according as the woman's husband may exact from him, the payment to be based on reckoning. But if other damage ensues, the penalty shall be life for life . . .[7]

Literally and by interpretation, this passage poses the basic legal principle that the destruction of the fetus is not to be considered punishable murder. Death of the unborn child is punishable by fine only,and capital punishment does not apply. Only if the mother is harmed, i.e., killed, does the law of capital punishment take effect.

Dr. Immanuel Jakobovits, Chief Rabbi of the United Kingdom,

and leading Orthodox exponent of the issue, finds in the biblical reference the very basis of the widely divergent views of Jewish Law and official Catholic doctrine. He emphasizes that capital punishment is not applicable if a miscarriage occurs and the woman remains alive. However, if she dies, then the full penalty of the law is rendered.[8] He establishes this premise by pointing out that a rabbinic commentary on a Biblical passage defining murder, recorded in the same chapter, elicits the principle that murder would indeed apply if a man, or human being, were killed. "He who fatally strikes a man, shall be put to death,"[9] says this passage. The rabbis deduce that this statement means that when a *man* is killed, the murderer is to be put to death and that this applies to a *man* and not a *fetus*. The unborn child is in an entirely different category from that of a human being, at least for the purpose of imposing capital punishment. While causing a miscarriage is indeed a crime, it is not a crime punishable by death.

The great commentator, Rabbi Shlomo Yitzhaki, known better as RaSHI, a contraction of the three first letters of his name, explains:

> . . . Then on the other hand, so far as concerns the statement, 'He who fatally strikes a man,' it might be held that even premature births at a term of eight months (the Talmud holds that while a seven month's child is viable, one born at eight months cannot be reared) are included in the term 'a man' to intimate that one is not subject to the death penalty unless he kills a viable child — one which is fitted to become a man.[10]

The Midrash, on the same Biblical sentence, comments:

> Observe how many commandments God concentrated into every detail in the Torah. It says that when men fight and one of them pushes a pregnant woman, then, if she dies, you shall give life for life, but if she does not die, there is monetary punishment, though the child had not seen the light, being still in the mother's womb; but the Torah gives injunctions to Israel concerning everything. (Not having yet been born, they cannot be called 'a soul' in order to incur the death penalty but there is a monetary punishment.)[11]

Rabbi Jakobovits, contrasts with this the Christian position which he derives from the same passage, asserting that an original mistranslation of the one Hebrew word "harm" has been retained, the constant repetition of which has hardened the Catholic position.

In the Hebrew, the word "a-son" means harm or accident, that is, not a fatal injury. A mistranslation of this word in the Septuagint, the Greek translation of the Bible, took it to mean "imperfectly formed."[12] Thus there arose a difference between an unformed and a formed fetus. The translation would then appear as:

> And if two men strive together, and hurt a woman with child so that her fruit depart *imperfectly* formed, he shall surely be fined, according as the woman's husband shall lay upon him. But if *perfectly formed*, then thou shalt give life for life . . .

This would mean that a miscarriage of the latter kind, when the fetus was perfectly formed, would incur the same penalty as murder. This mistranslation was later adopted as canon law. In time, the distinction between "formed" and "unformed" evaporated, leading to the one conclusion, that the killing of any fruit, from the moment of conception, was punishable as a capital offense. This distinction between the Catholic Church and Orthodox Judaism has become clear-cut; according to the latter, whatever the conditions in which an abortion takes place, the crime, though severe, is not a capital offense.

## TALMUDIC BASIS

The Mishnah, composing the first part of the Talmud, which provides only one source for an understanding of the Jewish position on the issue of abortion, assumes that the full title to life arises only at birth.

> If a woman has great difficulty in giving birth (and her life cannot otherwise be saved), it is permitted to destroy the child (literally, cut up the child) within her womb and extract it limb by limb, because her life takes precedence. But if the greater part (or head) has come out, it must not be touched because one life must not be taken to save another.[13]

A related source, though not exactly part of the Talmud, offers a similar presentation, with only slight variation:

> For a woman that is having difficulty giving birth it is permitted to cut up the child in her womb even on the Sabbath and take out limb by limb because her life takes precedence. If its head came out, it may not be touched even on the second day (of a festival) because one life may not be taken to save another.[14]

40

Where there is danger to *life*, and the word *life* is stressed, of the mother, embryotomy may, indeed must, be performed, because the mother's life has priority. This is the primary Talmudic source dealing with abortion, and all inquiry into the subject derives from it.

A Mishnah is simply a text elaborating on the Written Law, while the Gemara is an interpretation elaborating upon the Mishnah. The Gemara has this to say on the subject on hand:

> On the text, "Once his head has come out, he may not be harmed because one life may not be taken to save another," the question is asked, "Why should not, even in this case, the fetus be destroyed? It is, after all, an aggressor or pursuer, that is, is not the fetus pursuing the life of the mother, and hence, in self-defense could be destroyed, even if the head has come forth?" The answer provided, notes, that there is a difference in this case, because the mother is pursued by heaven, (that is, it is an act of God.)[15]

The fetus as aggressor is in the same category as an aggressor who can be killed in self-defense.

Once again the commentator *RaSHI* explains the reason why the fetus is spared once the head has appeared. So long as the fetus, or the most important part of it, its head, has not come out into the world, it is not called a *nefesh*, a human soul, and therefore its life can be taken to save the mother. However, once the head has protruded, it cannot be harmed because it is then considered to have been born, and one life may not be taken to save another.

For our purposes, an unborn fetus is not to be considered a living being, and therefore the taking of its life cannot be termed murder.[16] It still always must be kept in mind, however, that this taking life, although not equivalent to murder, is permissible only when the mother's life is in danger.

This view of *RaSHI* provides the reasoning behind the permission granted for therapeutic abortion when most of the fetus has not emerged because it is not deemed a living being.

Maimonides in the twelfth century provides us with another basis for permitting therapeutic abortion but his line of thinking is more restrictive than *RaSHI*. He cites the text in the Mishnah where it says that the reason the fetus can be dismembered is because it is to be considered an "aggressor" or "pursuer" after the mother's life, and reasons that a pursuer may be cut down in self-defense. Whereas Maimonides provides only *specific*, *RaSHI* offers a more *general*, foundation for therapeutic abortion. Although Maimonides introduces another element, that of removal of the fetus by drugs or other oral means, the reason on which he bases his argument, that of "pursuer" or "aggressor," would tend to limit other motives. The entire issue then comes down to whether, in abortion cases, the fetus is considered a living being.

> RaSHI explains this passage as resulting from the fact that "As long as it did not come into the world, it is not called a living thing." Maimonides, on the other hand, reasons that the child may be aborted because "it is regarded as one pursuing her and trying to kill her." Thus, it would seem that RaSHI would not consider the fetus a living thing; while Maimonides would consider it a living thing.[17]

Jewish sources have considered this issue from a different vantage point. Although the question as to when life begins or when the soul enters the body affect decisions on therapeutic abortion, Jewish scholars, however, insist that theological issues have no bearing on the question of abortion. Thus one says:

> In Jewish law, the right to destroy a human fruit before birth is entirely unrelated to the theological considerations. Neither the question of the entry of the soul nor the claim to salvation after death have any practical bearing on the subject.[18]

Another writes:

> The conclusion is inescapable that these Aggadic or theological reflections — or the actual spiritual destinies of the fetus — have no bearing on the abortion question. The Responsa accordingly omit them from consideration. With the soul's immortality as much irrelevant as the time of its endowment, the earthly court must concern itself with the human problem of murder and deprivation of life in this world. For the earthly court, the law is defined: before birth, the embryo is not a person; from the moment of birth and on, it is; the disposition of the soul, being pure to begin with, is unaffected. The Jewish and Catholic doctrine have once again parted company.[19]

Thus, what is involved, is whether the life of the mother is in danger. The Mishnah records a dialogue between Rabbi Judah the Prince and the Roman Emperor Antoninus:

> Antoninus asked Rabbi Judah, "When is the soul given to man?

At the time the embryo is formed or at the time of conception?" Rabbi Judah answered, "At the time the embryo is already formed." The emperor was surprised, and asked, "Is it possible for meat to stay three days without salt and not putrefy?
It must therefore have occurred at conception." Rabbi Judah (later) stated: "This thing Antoninus taught me and scripture supports him, as it is said in Job, 'And your visitation has preserved my spirit.' "[20]

Different views were held in ancient times regarding the time the soul enters the body. Aristotle says that the rational soul enters on the 40th or the 80th day after conception for male and female respectively. Plato holds that the soul enters at the time of *conception*. The Stoics maintained that the soul entered at *birth*. Roman jurists and common law, following the latter opinion which implies that the soul is not in the fetus until birth, did not view abortion as murder.

Plato's view, however, reinforced into Catholic position, is that since the soul entered at the time of conception, any removal of the fetus is murder.[21]

While medical science considers a fetus a living organism from the moment of fertilization, there is certainly a difference between a living thing and a separate entity. The Talmud refers to a fetus as being part of the mother and where an abortion is therapeutic, the fetus, like any other part of the mother's body, must be sacrificed where life is at risk.[22] While its removal in cases of danger to the mother's life remains in the category of destruction of potential life, it is not murder.

## APPLICATION OF HALAKHAH TO CASES

While the general principles are clear, applying them is more difficult.

For example, take the case where there is reason to fear, in the final stages of parturition, that unless the fetus-child is aborted, both mother *and* child would die. Dr. Jakobovits has indicated that in this case the fetus should be sacrificed. While the case is probably hypothetical, since the real danger to the mother would have occurred before this stage is reached, yet the issue is related to the question of breech birth, where the child's head cannot be withdrawn and the rest of the body has been born. Technically, since there is equality of life at that moment, the fetus cannot be sacrificed.

However, there are a few other indications which suggest that the balance tilts in favor of the mother. First, the child will probably die anyway. Second, Judaism does not consider a child fully alive until it has passed the thirtieth day of its life. Thus, when the two lives are equated, the mother's life is certain while that of the child is in doubt. Some authorities have allowed abortion in those cases only where physicians are confident they can save the mother's life.

In modern times, pressure has been exerted to permit abortion in cases of rape, incest, adultery, and rubella, or the contraction of German measles during pregnancy which causes deformed babies.

Dr. Jakobovits has noted that in the case of a fetus developing as a result of rape, no specific decisions have been issued. It is clear, however, that his position would be in the negative, since the life of the mother is not at stake. The question is that of the fetus, not the mother.

> . . . Jewish law would consider a grave psychological hazard to the mother as no less weighty a reason for an abortion than a physical threat. On these grounds a seventeenth century responsum permitted an abortion in a case where it was feared the mother would otherwise suffer an attack of hysteria imperiling her life. If it is genuinely feared that a continued pregnancy and eventual birth under these conditions might have such debilitating effects on the mother as to present a danger to her own life or the life of another by suicidal or violent tendencies, however remote this danger may be, a therapeutic abortion may be indicated with the same justification as for other reasons. But this fear would have to be very real, attested to by the most competent psychiatric opinion, and based on previous experiences of mental imbalance . . .[23]

The Conservative Jewish view has indicated that "termination of the pregnancy resulting from rape" would be allowed. "This is based on the statement that 'the tendency in Jewish law is to permit abortion . . . in grave situations as well.' While one ruling forbids it when the pregnancy results from an adulterous union because 'to permit abortion would open the floodgates of immorality,' another ruling would clearly allow termination resulting from rape."[24]

Conception from an adulterous union has often been discussed in Responsa literature. Where a married woman committed adultery, became pregnant, had pangs of conscience, wanted to do penance and asked for permission to take drugs to eliminate the "evil fruit" in her womb, Rabbi Yair Hayyim Bachrach (1639), a recognized rabbinic authority, noted that there is no relationship between the issue of abortion and that of illegitimacy. What is involved is only the question whether abortion is considered the taking of life. He evaluates differences between the various states of development of the fetus, 40 days after conception, three months after conception, etc., and concludes that *theoretically* abortion may be permitted in the early stage of pregnancy. However, since there is strong feeling against immorality, he cannot grant permission in this case. Rabbi Bachrach could not tolerate such a practice, since sanctioning abortion "would open the floodgates to immorality and debauchery." According to Dr. Solomon Freehof, reflecting the Reform Jewish position, Rabbi Bachrach "at first says that it would seem that a fetus is not really a *nefesh* and it might be permitted to destroy it, except that this would encourage immorality."[25]

One century later, Rabbi Freehof points out, Rabbi Jacob Emden, another recognized authority, decided affirmatively in a similar case. The reason, however, for allowing therapeutic abortion was curiously different, that "if we were still under our Sanhedrin (our own ruling court) and could have the authority to impose capital punishment, such a woman would be condemned to death and her child would die with her anyway." As an aside, Dr. Freehof notes that "then he (Jacob Emden) adds boldly (though with some misgiving) that perhaps we may destroy a fetus even to save a mother *excessive physical pain.*" This would suggest that danger to the mother's life would not really be the only allowable reason for therapeutic abortion and from this statement, Dr. Freehof later draws other conclusions, more liberal than the other denominational positions.

Rabbi Jackobovits also finds that Jacob Emden "has considered the case of an adulteress to be different insofar as she had been guilty of a capital offense," since in Jewish law her execution would involve also the death of her child.[26] Rabbi Jakobovits, however, adds, "But in later Responsa work, the abortion of an illegitimate embryo is distinctly forbidden."[27]

On the question of whether the possibility or certainty of deformity as a result of German measles, or other drug use, might allow abortion, there is a strong difference of opinion. The Orthodox, stressing the principle that therapeutic abortion is permitted only when there is a risk to the life of the mother, does not grant abortion in the cases under question. Rabbi Jacobovits says:

All the authorities of Jewish law are agreed that physical or mental abnormalities do not in themselves compromise the title of life, whether before or after birth. Cripples and idiots, however incapacitated, enjoy the same human rights (though not necessarily legal competence) as normal persons.

Human life being infinite in value, its sanctity is bound to be entirely unaffected by the absence of any or all mental faculties or by any bodily defects; any fraction of infinity still remains infinite.

The absolute inviolability of any human being, however deformed, was affirmed in the first responsum on the status of monster-births. Early in the nineteenth century, a famous rabbinical scholar advised a questioner that it was forbidden to destroy a grotesquely misshapen child; he ruled that to kill, or even to starve to death, any being born of a human mother was unlawful as homicide . . .

Based on these principles and precedents, present-day rabbis are unanimous in condemning abortion, feticide, or infanticide to eliminate a crippled being, before or after birth, as an unconscionable attack on the sanctity of life . . .

These considerations would be valid even if it were known for certain that the expected child would be born deformed. The almost invariable doubts about such a contingency only strengthen the objections to abortion in these circumstances, especially in view of the Talmudic maxim that in matters of life and death the usual majority does not operate; any chance, however slim, that a life may be saved must always be given the benefit of the doubt.

A similar attitude was adopted in a recent rabbinical article on the celebrated trial in Liege (Belgium) in which a mother and others were acquitted of guilt for the confessed killing of a thalidomide baby. The author denounced abortion for such a purpose as well as the Liege verdict. 'The sole legitimate grounds for killing a fetus are the urgent needs of the mother and her healing, whereas in these circumstances the mother's efforts to have the child aborted are based on self-love and plain egotism, wrapped in a cloak of compassion for this unfortunate creature, and this cannot be called a necessity for the mother at all.'[28]

Rabbi David Feldman quotes a Rabbi Unterman responsum dealing specifically with the question of rubella and the latter rules out an abortion saying "we have no law that permits us to deny one who is wounded."[29]

46

Rabbi Jacobovits presented the same position, more concisely, in another volume: "The Jewish view unanimously affirms that the title of an unborn child to life is not compromised by any physical or mental abnormalities, however crippling, even if such defects were definitely ascertained before birth. The deliberate killing of such a child therefore constitutes "an appurtenance of murder," although feticide is not technically regarded as a capital offense in Jewish law."[30]

> . . . Nothing can justify recourse to abortion, not even radiological evidence that the child will be born deformed, except the safety of the mother.
>
> He adds: "Rabbi Zweig found support for this view among leading doctors and jurists, too, and he adds: 'Even the Church has expressed its disapproval of killing any unborn child, however deformed; hence, there would be the additional element of Hillul Hashem (desecration of God's name) in any permissive ruling given by us.' "[31]

The position of the Conservative movement can be illustrated from a number of sources.

Dr. Morris S. Fond, President of the New York Metropolitan Region of the United Synagogue of America, testifying on behalf of Jewish organizations, including the United Synagogue, the synagogue arm of the Conservative movement, and in the presence of Rabbi David Feldman, spiritual leader of Congregation Shearith Israel and an authority on the subject, and with authorization from the Chairman of the Law Committee of the Rabbinical Assembly of America, presented a statement to the Joint Hearings of the Health and Codes Committee of the State, considering an act to amend the Public Health Law in Relation to Therapeutic Abortion, in which the following statement on the specific issue is included:

> The possibility of deformity when a child is born has also been given a legal hearing in the Responsa. For possible deformity the rulings have not been permissive; for a certain deformity abortion would be warranted.

The statement calls for the enactment of amendments which would permit abortions in the four cases mentioned above.[32]

Rabbi Feldman reaches the following conclusion:

> The principle that a mothers' pain 'comes first' however, is the most pervasive of all factors in the consideration of the abortion question. It produces the following *fundamental generalization:* if the possibility or probability exists that a child may be born defective and the mother would seek an abortion on ground of pity for the child whose life will be less than normal, the Rabbis would decline permission. Since we don't know for sure that he will be born defective, and since we don't know how bad that defective life will be (in view of the availability of prosthetic devices, etc.) and since no permission exists in Jewish law to kill born defectives, permission *on those grounds* would be denied. If, however, an abortion for that same potentially deformed child were sought on the grounds that the possibility is causing *severe anguish to the mother*, permission would be granted. The fetus is unknown, future, potential, part of 'the secrets of God'; the mother is known, present, alive, and asking for compassion.[33]

This view may also be deduced from a review by Rabbi Seymour Siegel:

"A very important *teshuvah* (Responsum) is presented from the pen of the late Rabbi Yehiel Weinberg of Switzerland. It involves the permissibility of abortion in a case where it is almost certain that the child will be born defective. This leads Rabbi Weinberg to investigate the prohibition against aborting fetuses in general. The prohibition seems to be based more on the general feeling that it is wrong to destroy life which has begun, than on any specific *issur*, (prohibition). His concrete conclusion is the following:

> "That which emerges for the whole discussion about a woman who has contracted German measles during her pregnancy, and who, according to the physicians, will give birth to a child who will be missing an organ or will be mentally deficient, is that during the first forty days it is "only water" (*maya balma)* and therefore not considered an *ubar* (fetus) . . . And after forty days there is in the Responsa Sh'elot Yabetz, a tendency to permit (abortion) where the child causes the mother pain or illness.' "[34]

The position may be noted by the calls issued by a number of Conservative rabbis, urging state legislatures to amend the state laws to permit, though not demand, abortion in cases of pregnancies arising out of rape, incest, adultery or rubella.

The Reform position, published in the Central Conference of American Rabbis Yearbook, 1958, presented by Dr. Freehof as chairman of the Responsa Committee, deals with the case of a woman who had had German measles in the third month of pregnancy, leading some doctors to believe that her child would be deformed. Dr. Freehof responds that since there is a preponderance of medical opinion that the child will be born physically and even mentally, imperfect, then, for the mother's sake, (i.e., the mental anguish now and in the future) she may sacrifice this part of herself. He follows the liberal interpretation of Jacob Emden that "to save a mother excessive physical pain" abortion is permissible, and also is in line with Rashi's view that an unborn fetus is actually not a *nefesh* (living being or soul) at all, and that it has no independent life and is a part of the mother. Just as one may sacrifice a limb to be cured of a worse sickness, so may this fetus be destroyed for the mother's benefit. Dr. Freehof also notes that Rabbi Bachrach in the 17th century shared the same view when he said the fetus was not really a *nefesh*, (that is, a person).

## THE ORTHODOX POSITION

*In summation*, the general Orthodox position may be seen from the following passage:

There are four distinct legal phases in the development of man:

1.  Up to the moment when the first signs of parturient labor set in, the fetus is an organic part of the mother. While, according to the consensus of rabbinic opinion, its life is not protected by any definite legal provisions, the artificial termination of a pregnancy is strongly condemned on moral grounds, unless it can be justified for medical or other reasons of due gravity.

2.  During the process of birth, and until the child's head or the greater part of its body has emerged, its life is still of inferior value, although vested nevertheless with a certain measure of human inviolability. Its claim to life may (and must) be set aside in the mother's interest only if it is the child (and not some illness) that threatens her life. During these two phases it would be a criminal violation of the sanctity of human life to let the mother die by refusing to destroy her fruit.

3.  From the moment the major part of the child is born, it

assumes human status in most respects, and the value of its life is practically equal to that of any adult person. But, unless conclusive evidence exists to show that it was carried for a full term of nine months, the child's viability is not fully established or presumed until the thirty-first day of existence. That uncertainty frees the person who terminates the life of such an infant from capital guilt. It also confers the right to save the mother at the expense of the child, when the failure to sacrifice the child would lead to the loss of both lives, but not when it would otherwise be expected to survive the mother's death.

4. A child born definitely after a full term pregnancy, or else following the first thirty days of its life, enjoys human rights in every respect. It must not be sacrificed for the preservation of one or even more lives under any circumstances (except those applicable to the surrender of normal adult lives.)[35]

The unborn child, particularly after the 40th day of conception, has a right to life which cannot be denied him. Even if the fetus is the product of rape or incest, or even if an abnomality of any kind is foreseen, the right to life is still his.

The only condition under which this right may be denied is when it threatens the life of another, namely, the mother. Under the principle which permits taking the life of a human being in defense of another human being attacked by the first, an abortion can be permitted if the mother's life is endangered.

It is for a competent religious authority, upon consultation with medical authorities, to determine whether a threat to a mother's well being is sufficient to warrant an abortion.

"Jewish law sanctions abortions only when continuation of pregnancy is a grave hazard to the mother. Such hazards include psychiatric disturbances that may be caused or aggravated by the continued pregnancy, if e.g., these disturbances express themselves as suicidal tendencies. Under such conditions, an abortion must be carried out since the life of the mother is considered to be distinctly superior to that of her unborn child. The fear that a child may be born deformed because the mother contracted Rubella (German measles) or other virus diseases, or took drugs suspected of affecting the child's normal development, does not in itself justify recourse to abortion. Both during and after birth, an abnormal child — whether the defects be mental or physical — enjoys the same title to life as a healthy child. This consideration is quite apart from the chance that an abortion might eliminate a perfectly normal child. The sole indication for terminating a pregnancy under these conditions must therefore be the health of the mother, as previously defined.

"In all cases where an abortion is being considered, rabbinic authority must be consulted. This becomes all the more necessary because of liberalized state laws and the recent permissive Supreme Court decision. The moral liability in such momentous judgments is so great that it is strongly urged that one or more religious advisors be included in the formal decision making process."[36]

The Orthodox position may be understood from the first sentence of an article in Tradition by Rabbi Shalom Carney: "For me, as for most readers of Tradition, abortion on demand is prohibited because *Halakhah* says so; and that's that."[37]

A similar strong posture was asserted by Rabbi Moshe Feinstein, one of the most recognized of authorities, in his telegram to Israeli Prime Minister Menahem Begin in February, 1978:

"We are stirred to the depth of our souls, from the painful and frightening report, which grieves all Jews, that the Knesset accepted and affirmed the immoral law, which legalizes abortion, even where, in the opinion of expert physicians, there is not danger to life.

We hereby state with absolute finality, that a law which says you can abort a child prior to its birth, is tantamount to murder and according to Halakhah it amounts to the taking of a Jewish life for which the penalty is very grave.

How vast and deep is the storm inside the Jewish soul to behold that in the Holy Land, laws are passed approving of murder. It is a law which soils the good name of Eretz Yisrael and also the name of all Jews who stood at Sinai, heard and accepted, the commandment, "Thou shall not Murder."

Eretz Yisrael must serve as a model to the whole world how to conduct a sacred and pure family life and not, God forbid, the reverse.

Under no circumstances will we make peace with this bitter reality and we will not be silent until this shame is eliminated.

We will be most happy to receive your reply and to advise us what your plans are, as head of the Government, to void this disgraceful law.

We write and sign this message with pain and deep concern and with hope to God, that peace will come to the Holy Land, and not, God forbid, an evil place which allows the legalized taking of a human life, but instead, a peace of Blessing.

> Agudath Harabanim
> Union of Orthodox
> Rabbis of
> U.S.A. and Canada
> Moshe Feinstein,
> President"

These words repeated an earlier stand:

"The statement of the special Jewish Committee (composed of leaders from the Conservative and Reform movements) for the legalizing of Abortion — which states that the practice of Abortion is also according to Jewish tradition — is a senseless, open falsification of Jewish Law.

"Agudath Harabanim (Union of Orthodox Rabbis of U.S.A. & Canada) has already declared, and reiterates, that the holiness of a human-being begins even before it is born. ABORTION IS PROHIBITED ACCORDING TO JEWISH LAW. EVERY ACT OF AN ABORTION IS AN ACT OF MURDER. Only in a case when the life of the mother of the unborn child is endangered, then, after determining how dangerous it is, you can consider it a matter of "Pikuach Nefesh" (a matter of life or death); and as in all questions of "Pikuach Nefesh," the rav (Rabbi), must make a thorough investigation,before issuing a verdict.

We repeat: the fundamental Halakhah, the basis for the existence of the Jewish nation, does not permit, God forbid, Abortion. And this is so, not because the Jewish people lost millions of Jews during the Holocaust, and we are in need of more Jewish births. Abortion is prohibited BECAUSE THE HALAKHAH (JEWISH LAW) SAYS SO. Even if, today, there would be millions of Jews, the abortion of one single Jewish child, would also be strictly prohibited."

## THE CONSERVATIVE POSITION

The Conservative position, while more divergent than the Orthodox stand, and hence, less clear, may be generally found in the following statement issued "to enable congregations in the New

York Metropolitan Region of the United Synagogue to address themselves to the issue of abortion which is the subject of a bill introduced in the current session of the New York State Legislature."[38] (1966-1967), a statement which was reaffirmed at the 1975 convention:

"Jewish law grants the mother theoretical power over the fetus as part of herself. She must however, have valid and sufficient warrant for depriving it of potential life. Talmud and Rabbinic Responsa through the ages have ruled on what is or is not adequate warrant.

In so-called therapeutic abortion, Jewish law not only permits, but requires abortion. That her life takes precedence over that of the fetus, up to the minute of its birth, is an unequivocal principle. A threat to her basic health, when well established, is on an equal footing with a threat to her physical health. Although the definition and determination of the seriousness of these threats are subject of detailed and specific discussion, the principle is nonetheless clear.

The tendency of Jewish law is to permit abortion in other grave situations as well. While one ruling forbids it when the pregnancy results from an adulterous union — because to 'permit such would open the flood-gates of immorality' — another ruling would clearly allow termination of a pregnancy resulting from rape.

The question has arisen concerning the abortion of a child who might possibly be deformed. In this case, the rulings have not permitted abortion; but where deformity is a certainty, abortion would be warranted. Since contraception by means of approved methods, to protect the fundamental health of existing infants has precedent in the Talmudic case of the nursing mother, abortion, for similar reasons has been judged permissible.

In sum, Jewish law teaches a reverent and responsible attitude to the question of abortion: reasons of convenience are inadmissible; reasons affecting basic life and health may sanction, or even require abortion; public policy ought to protect the basic human moral sense that is threatened by easy abortion, while at the same time safe-guarding the well-being of mother and child, when adequate justification for birth control prevails."

Rabbi Isaac Klein, following a comprehensive responsum, summarizes:

"When abortion is therapeutic, there can be no objection to it because like any other surgery, we sacrifice the part for the whole.

This is the attitude the rabbis have taken. Abortion is forbidden. Though it is not considered murder, it does mean the destruction of potential life. If, however, the purpose is therapeutic this objection is removed.

Our conclusion, therefore, must be that abortion is morally wrong. It should be permitted only for therapeutic reasons."[39a]

The view of the Conservative movement may be extrapolated from the following paragraphs:

What is the status of the unborn fetus? In the current debate we have representatives of two extreme views. One segment of our society believes that the fetus is to be considered as a child who is already born. In this view, killing a fetus is equal to murder. On the other extreme, we find advocates of the view that the fetus is no different than any other part of the mother. Just as a woman has the right to cut her hair or fingernails, she has a right over her body and may remove the fetus whenever she wishes to do so.

The Jewish view rejects both of these extreme positions. The fetus is not the same as a born child. In a famous passage in the *Mishnah* the rabbis say that if a woman is giving birth and the fetus threatens her life, it is permissible to destroy the child: her life takes precedence. This is not the case in Jewish law where the child has already been born.

However, as potential human life, the fetus is not like a fingernail or gall bladder. It has the right to our protection and care, as long as it does not threaten the life of a living woman. The fetus enjoys the benefit of our *bias for life*. As *potential* life, it is not the same as a born baby. As potential *life*, it should be protected and allowed to realize its destiny; that is, to be born as a human being. The fetus as life-in-process cannot be destroyed except where it threatens the life of the mother.

In a *responsum* on abortion written by Rabbi Isaac Klein for the Committee on Jewish Law and Standards of the Rabbinical Assembly it is stated: "Our conclusion, therefore, must be that abortion is morally wrong. It should be permitted only for therapeutic reasons." Of course, the question as to what is "therapeutic" is still being debated. Does it refer only to the physical health of the mother? Can it be interpreted to cover situations where the economic health or social health of the family is involved? These are questions that have not as yet been solved.[39b]

A group of Conservative rabbis from the St. Paul-Minneapolis area declared "that the following instances of abortion would in no way be objectionable to Conservative Jewish practice:

1. *A woman who has become pregnant but has a serious illness, such as cardiac disease, cancer, tuberculosis, etc., and her pregnancy is medically determined to be a danger to her life.* This follows the principle of Maimonides, who in turn bases his ruling on the principle that the fetus becomes a 'pursuer', meaning a threat to the life of another, and 'every effort should be made to prevent another organism from aggressively destroying the life of a person.'

2. *A woman who becomes pregnant as a result of rape.* Rape is a criminal act of violence against the person. If the child resulting from this crime be brought to term, against the will of its mother, it would further violate human rights. This is also an instance where the sinner is rewarded through his participation in the creation of life. (The principle of not rewarding the sinner as cited in the Talmud, deals with instances of rape and seduction). It is thus unthinkable that a woman be forced to bear a child conceived through a criminal and violent act perpetrated upon her.

3. *A woman who becomes pregnant through an act of incest.* Incest is a violation of a primary Scriptural injunction. The law prohibiting incest is basic to the family and to all morality. Denying abortion in this case would result in the further evil of a child being born under outrageous circumstances.

4. *A woman who had contracted Rubella (German measles) or who has taken thalidomide during pregnancy or who has ingested any drug in which medical authorities state that there is a substantial liklihood that the fetus will be born with permanent and severe damage.* An abortion in this situation would be justified on two counts. Firstly, this might be considered an instance of *tikun olam* (righting the wrongs of the world or creating a healthy and stable society). In the thirteen instances that this principle is cited in the Talmud, it is always in connection with an ambivalent situation and the possibility of

non-performance of mitzvot and abuse of human situations. A deformed child would certainly place parents and itself in this kind of situation. Secondly, a mother asked to rear such a child would be faced with untold anguish, pain, and suffering. All the previous rabbinic writers on this subject consider this to be a crucial factor in making a decision on abortion. In a similar manner, our hearts go out to pregnant women who must face such a situation. Even as we justify a therapeutic abortion in this instance, we plead with society to refrain from commenting on the mother's decision in the rabbinic words of 'do not judge anyone else until you have stood in that person's place.'

5. *A mother who is severely mentally ill (psychotic).*
Such a mother is not capable of rearing a child. This child would be thrust into a situation of such madness and crushing conditions that it would cause great and grave emotional destortion of the child and the future generations to come. To prevent this and using again the principle of *tikun olam*, (righting the wrongs of the world or creating a healthy and stable society) permission for abortion must be granted.[40]

## THE REFORM POSITION

The Reform position concurs with the pressures of society allowing therapeutic abortions not only for grave danger to the mother's life, but also to her health. Pregnancy resulting from rape, incest, German measles, or serious physchological affection would grant permission for abortion.

In Recent Reform Responsa, Dr. Solomon Freehof states:

Since there is strong preponderance of medical opinion that the child will be born imperfect physically, and even mentally, then for the *mother's* sake (i.e., her mental anguish now and in the future), she may sacrifice this part of herself.[41]

The Committee on Judaism and Medicine of the Central Conference of American Rabbis reported at the convention in 1964:

Today the hazards to the unborn child of a pregnant woman who contracts the so-called German measles are well known. In most states, the abortion of such a fetus is permitted by law. In 1958, this question was submitted to the Committee on Responsa. In his reply, Dr. Solomon B. Freehof stated that 'permission to destroy a child to save the life of a mother is cited in all the codes and is finally fixed as law in the Shulhan Arukh and he concluded, 'In the case which you are discussing, I would, therefore, say that since there is strong preponderance of medical opinion that the child will be born imperfect physically, and even mentally, then for the mother's sake, (i.e., her mental anguish now and in the future), she may sacrifice part of herself.'[42]

The Union of American Hebrew Congregations at its convention in 1967 adopted the following resolution:

We commend those states which have enacted humane legislation in this area and we appeal to other states to do likewise and permit abortions under such circumstances as threatened disease or deformity of the embryo or fetus, threats to the physical and mental health of the mother, rape and incest, and the social, economic and psychological factors that might warrant therapeutic termination of pregnancy.[43]

## SUMMARY

The New York Board of Rabbis issued a statement in which the views of the three groups within Judaism are recorded:

1.    Orthodox Judaism

The unborn child, particularly after the 40th day of conception, has a right to life which cannot be denied him. Even if the fetus is the product of incest or rape, or an abnormality of any kind is foreseen, the right to life is still his.

The only condition under which this right may be denied is when it threatens the life of another, namely, the mother. Under the principle which permits taking the life of a human being in defense of another human being who is being attacked by the first, an abortion can be permitted if the mother's life is endangered.

It is for a competent religious authority, upon consultation with medical authorities, to determine whether the threat to a mother's well-being is sufficient to warrant an abortion.

2.  Conservative Judaism
    Rabbinic law holds that "the mother has theoretical
    power over the fetus as part of herself." She must,
    however, have valid and sufficient warrant for depriving
    it of potential life. The Talmud and subsequent rabbinic
    responsa through the centuries have ruled on what is or
    is not adequate warrant.

    In all cases, "the mother's life takes precedence over that
    of the fetus" up to the minute of its life. This is to us an
    unequivocal principle. A threat to her basic health is
    moreover equated with threat to her life. To go a step
    further, a classic responsum places danger to one's
    psychological health, when well established, on an equal
    footing with a threat to one's physical health. Although
    the definition and determination of the seriousness of
    these threats are subject to detailed and specific discus-
    sions, the principle is none the less clear.

    The tendency in Jewish law is to permit abortion in other
    grave situations as well. While one ruling forbids it
    when the pregnancy results from an adulterous union,
    because "to permit abortion would open the floodgates
    of immorality", another ruling would clearly allow ter-
    mination of the pregnancy resulting from rape.

    In sum, Jewish law teaches a reverent and responsible at-
    titude to the question of abortion — reasons of con-
    venience are inadmissible. Reasons affecting basic life
    and health may sanction, or even require abortion.
    Public policy ought to protect the morality threatened by
    easy abortion, and, at the same time, the well-being of
    mother and child when adequate justification for control
    of birth prevails.

3.  Reform Judaism
    Many state legislatures are in the process of revising
    their laws concerning abortion and are seeking the
    counsel of religious bodies on this question. Each year
    more than one million American women, many of them
    married, obtain abortions. Existing state statutes do not
    provide sufficiently for social and medical reasons to ter-
    minate a pregnancy. Existing laws penalize the poor who
    cannot afford services available to the more affluent.

The hazards of illegal abortions take a tragic and needless toll of life.

Dr. Solomon B. Freehof, in a responsum in 1958 . . . recommended leniency in a specific abortion case. In a letter of May 12, 1962, he unqualifiedly endorsed a statement that "Reform Judaism extends the position of Orthodox Judaism to this degree: When the preponderance of medical opinion is that the child will be born physically and/or mentally imperfect, then for the mothers sake, i.e., her mental anguish now and in the future, she may sacrifice the part of herself which is the unborn fetus, just as a person may sacrifice a limb in order to be cured of a worse illness."

To establish the position of the Conference, we propose the following resolution:

Whereas, many state legislatures are attempting to revise antiquated statutes dealing with abortion, and whereas, there is a pressing need to reduce radically the present menace of illegal abortion with its frightful human toll, but without in any way condoning illegal or immoral conduct that leads to the desire for abortion, and whereas, we believe additional concern for the mother and for society should enter into formulation of carefully guarded procedure to make abortion available under proper conditions: Therefore be it resolved that:

1) The CCAR considers as religiously valid and humane such new legislation that: a) recognizes the preservation of a mother's emotional health to be as important as her physical well-being; and b) properly considers the danger to anticipated physical or mental damage; and c) permits abortion in pregnancies resulting from sexual crime, including rape, statutory rape, and incest.

2) We strongly urge the broad liberalization of abortion laws in the various states, and call upon our members to work towards this end.[44]

NOTES

1a. Immanuel Jakobovits, "*Jewish View on Abortion,*" in Abortion and the Law, David T. Smith, editor, *Western Reserve University*, Cleveland, 1967, page

125. See also "When Should Abortion be Legal, *Public Affairs Pamphlet*, No. 429, Public Affairs Committee, 1969, N.Y. See also Fred Rosner and Seymour Grumet, The Morality of Induced Abortion, *Jewish Life*, Vol. 38, No. 3, Jan.-Feb. 1971, p. 5.

2a. For an excellent analysis of the Mishnah on which this is based, see David Feldman, supra note 19.

2b. See, Abortion: A Challenge to Halakhah, Blu Greenberg, Judaism, American Jewish Congress, New York, Spring, 1976. Ms. Greenberg is an Orthodox Jew and a feminist.

3. *Reconstructionist*, Society for the Advancement of Judaism, New York, March 17, 1967.

4. The *"Humanist,"* American Humanist Association, Yellow Springs, Ohio, September/October 1966, p. 148.

5. Immanuel Jakobovits, *Jewish Law Faces Modern Problems*, Studies in Torah Judaism, Yeshiva University, Leon D. Stiskin, Editor, New York, 1965, p. 73.

6. For a discussion of the Protestant view see Ralph B. Potter, Junior, "The Abortion Debate," in *The Religious Situation*, Donald R. Cutler, Editor, Beacon Press, Boston, Mass., 1968, p. 112.

7. Exodus 21:22-23.

8. The rabbis were divided on this law of retaliation, some holding that it was to be acted upon literally, while others maintained that it signified monetary compensation, since there was no intention to kill. The man is free from paying compensation for the loss of the child . . . since the former punishment is larger than the latter. See Immanuel Jakobovits *Jewish Medical Ethics*, Bloch Publishing Co., New York, 1959, p. 180.

9. Exodus 21:12.

10. *Rashi, Pentateuch With Rashi, Commentary*, Edited by A.M. Silberman, Shapiro, Vallentine and Company, London, 1930, p. 110a.

11. *Midrash Rabbah Exodus*, Translated by Rabbi Dr. S.M. Lehrman, Soncino Press, London, 1951, p. 353.

12. See Seymour Siegel, "Some Aspects of the Jewish Tradition's Views of Sex," in, *Jews and Divorce*, Ktav Publishing House 1968, p. 183: "The Jewish interpretation of this passage understands that if the woman does not die, then the aggressor should pay for the unborn children. But if the woman does die, then he does not pay for the children as a man cannot be made legally to pay two punishments. (In this case execution and monetary payment.) However, the *Septuagint* understands the passage as involving a distinction between a formed embryo and a non-formed embryo. According to the Jewish interpretation it would seem that the unborn children have monetary value, whereas the Septuagint would endow even the unborn with life." See also, David Feldman, *Birth Control in Jewish Law*, New York University Press, New York, 1968, p. 257.

13. Mishnah, Oholoth, VII, 6.

14. Tosefta Yebamoth IX, 114.

15. Sanhedrin 72B.

16. See, *Time magazine*, Time Essay, "The Desperate Dilemma of Abortion," Time and Life, New York, October 13, 1967, "Many Jews accept abortion because

60

they regard a fetus as an organic part of the mother and not as a living soul until its birth."

17. See, Seymour Siegel, ibid, p. 184.

18. Immanuel Jakobovits, *Jewish Medical Ethics*, Bloch Publishing Co., New York 1959, p. 182.

19. David Feldman, *op. cit.*, p. 273. See also, Abortion and Ethics, Conservative Judaism, Vol. 29, No. 4, Summer 1975, Rabbinical Assembly, New York, page 31.

20. Sanhedrin 91b.

21. Philo's view is quoted by Feldman, ibid, p. 258.

22. *'ubbar yerekh immo hu'* (Gittin 23b, Hullin 58a), literally the fetus is the *thigh* of its mother, or, the fetus is regarded as one of her limbs.

23. Immanuel Jakobovits, "Jewish Views on Abortion", in *Abortion and the Law*, David Smith, Editor, Western Reserve University Press, Cleveland, 1967, p. 134. *See also*, David Feldman op. cit. note 12, pp. 285-286.

24. Morris S. Fond. "Testimony on an Act to Amend the Public Health Law In Relation to Therapeutic Abortion," at *Joint Hearings of Health and Codes Committees of New York*, Feb. 10, 1967, on behalf of United Synagogue.

25. Solomon Freehof, "Recent Reform Responsa," *Hebrew Union* College Press, 1963, New York, p. 191. *See also*, Seymour Siegel, note 12, p. 184. ibid. Also, Isaac Klein, "Is Abortion Permitted According To Jewish Law?" mimeographed: also, Teshuva on Abortion, Conservative Judaism, Fall, 1959, Rabbinical Assembly, pp. 47-51. Rabbi Klein's Teshuva is quoted completely in Conservative Judaism and Jewish Law, Seymour Siegel, editor, The Rabbinical Assembly, New York, 1977, p. 258-263. See also, Isaac Klein, Responsa and Halakhic Studies, Ktav, New York, 1975.

26. Lev. 20:20.

27. Isaac Halevi, Lehem Hapanim, Kuntres Ahron, No. 19.

28. Immanuel Jakobovits, Views on Abortion, ibid., p. 132.

29. David Feldman, *Birth Control in Jewish Law*, ibid., p. 292.

30. Immanuel Jakobovits, *Journal of a Rabbi*, Living Books, New York, 1966. p. 164.

31. Immanuel Jakobovits, *Jewish Law Faces Modern Problems*, Also, *Tradition*, Rabbinical Council of America, New York, Vol. 6, No. 2, p. 115.

32. Morris S. Fond, ibid., note 24.

33. David Feldman, op. cit., p. 292.

34. Seymour Seigel, Conservative Judaism, Vol. IX, p. 74, Rabbinical Assembly, New York, Reviewing NOAM, a forum for the clarification of Contemporary Halakhic Problems.

35. Immanuel Jakobovits, op. cit. p. 191, note 19. See also, Judah Dick, "The Proposed Abortion Law and the Jewish Position, March 1968, "The Jewish Press," New York, p. 28.

36. Medical Ethics, Rabbi M.D. Tendler, Editor, Federation of Jewish Philanthropies, New York, 1975, p. 3.

37. Shalom Carney, Halakhah and Philosophical Approaches to Abortion, *Tradition*, Rabbinical Council of America, Vol. 16, No. 3, Spring 1977, p. 126. See also, Rabbi Abraham Scheinberg, "What is the Halakhah?" Jewish Press, Nov. 30-

Dec. 6, 1974, New York. Also, The Halakhic View of Abortion, London Jewish Chronicle, England, quoted in Jewish Exponent, Philadelphia, Nov. 19, 1976 and in The Jewish Digest, Bridgeport, Conn., Nov. 1976.

38. The New York Metropolitan Region, United Synagogue of America, New York, Statement on The Jewish Attitude Toward Abortion. The author has paraphrased this statement somewhat but the complete statement appears in the summation as published by the New York Board of Rabbis, supra.

39a. Isaac Klein, op. cit., p. 9.
Rabbi Klein reports a responsum by Rabbi Yitzhak Oelbaum of Czechoslovakia on the question of a woman who has a weak child who according to doctors, needs to be breast-fed by the mother to live. She has been pregnant for four weeks, and felt a change in her milk. May she destroy the child she is carrying for the sake of the child she is feeding? The rabbi concludes that if there is expert evidence that danger might result if there is no abortion, it is permitted. Rabbi Klein notes that "a new issue is introduced here. Until now we have spoken of danger to the mother. Here there is no danger to the mother but to another child. This opens new possibilities which we shall not pursue here."

39b. Seymour Siegel, The Ethical Dilemmas of Modern Medicine, United Synagogue Review, Fall, 1976, p. 4. *See also* "Conservative Judaism," Rabbinical Assembly, Vol. XIII. Fall, 1959, New York, pp. 47-51. See also, David Novak, *Law and Theology in Judaism, A Jewish View of Abortion*, Ktav, New York, 1974, p. 114. See Also Jordon Ofseyer, Liberalized Abortion Laws, *The Jewish Spectator*, Vol. 36, March, 1971, New York, p. 11.

40. *Beth Din Shel Arba*, A group of Conservative rabbis, St. Paul-Minneapolis, 1967. Also, Jewish Telegraphic Agency release, entitled "Minnesota Rabbis Would Modify Abortion Bill", February, 9, 1967.

41. Solomon Freehof, op. cit., page 193. See also, Solomon Freehof, *Reform Responsa For Our Time*, Hebrew Union College Press, New York, 1977, p. 256. Also, William B. Silverman, Remember Us Unto Death, C.C.A.R. Journal, New York, Vol. 21. No. 2, 1974, p. 2.

*Yearbook*, C.C.A.R. Vol. LXXIV, 1964, Atlantic City, New Jersey, Report of Committee on Judaism and Medicine, p. 73.

43. Union of American Hebrew Congregations Convention, Montreal, Canada, 1967. Quoted by Albert Vorspan, Jewish Values and Social Crisis, p 212.

44. Quoted in The Jewish Family, A Compendium, Norman Linser, editor, Commission on Synagogue Relations, Federation of Jewish Philanthropies, New York, p. 57.

# ADOPTION

Cases of adoption have been rapidly on the increase over the past generation. In keeping with the modern liberal ethic, there has been an unprecedented rise in the number of illegitimate children and interracial births, creating many problems of an entirely new kind. Many states and countries are considering the updating of old laws so that the religion of the adoptive parents and of the child should be the same.[1a]

What is the attitude of Judaism towards adoption, both from a moral and from a legal standpoint? Can the legal process legitimizing an artificial relationship entirely substitute for the natural bond between parent and child? What rights do or do not accrue to an adopted child? Are there varying Jewish views on this whole subject?[1b]

The process by which an attempt is made to imitate by legal means the biological bond between parent and child is unknown to Talmudic and Biblical law. Indeed, *ametz*, the Hebrew for adoption, is a modern coinage, although there are cases in the Bible which bear a resemblance to the general concept.

There is, for instance, the case of the childless wife who gives her maid to her husband, raising the child that is born of that union as her own. Here are two examples: 1. Sarai, the wife of Abram, was childless, so she advised her husband to take her Egyptian maid, Hagar. 'Look, the Lord has kept me from bearing. Live with my maid: perhaps I shall have a son (be built up) through her.'[1c] 2. "When Rachel saw that she had borne Jacob no children she became envious of her sister; and Rachel said to Jacob, 'Give me children, or I shall die.' Jacob was angry with Rachel, and said, "Can I take the place of God, who has denied you fruit of womb?" She replied, "Here is my maid Bilhah. Consort with her, that she may bear on my knees, and that through her I too may have children."[2]

There is another case of a man with no sons who wants to marry off his daughter to a servant so that her son should be considered his: "Now Sheshan had no sons, but daughters. And Sheshan had a servant, an Egyptian, whose name was Jarha. So Sheshan gave his daughter to Jarha his servant as a wife; and she born him Attai . . ."[2a]

The legal process of change of status is non-existent in Jewish sources.

To establish a Jewish position toward adoption we can search the Bible, take note of cases which resemble this entirely modern idea, and develop them into legal principles. There are a number of events in biblical and talmudic times which project a legal principle enunciated in the Talmud that "he who raises an orphan, Scripture ascribes it to him as though he had begotten him."[3]

The Talmud[4] elaborates on a number of such occurrences, including such historic Jewish personalities as Moses, and the sons of Michal, Ruth and Esther.

The excerpt from the Talmud reads as follows:

> Concerning the sons of Michal, daughter of King Saul,[5] Rabbi Joshua ben Korha answers you: Was it then Michal who bore them? Surely it was rather Merab who bore them. But Merab bore and Michal brought them up; therefore they were called by her name. This teaches you that *whoever brings up an orphan in his home, Scripture ascribes it to him as though he had begotten him.*

> Rabbi Hanina drew the same doctrine from Ruth:[6] And the women her neighbors gave it a name saying: "There is a son born to Naomi." Was it then Naomi who bore him? Surely, it was Ruth who bore him. But, Ruth bore and Naomi brought him up; hence he was called after her (Naomi's name).

> Rabbi Johanan drew the same doctrine from Chronicles:[7] And his wife, Ha-Jehudiah (the Jewess[8]) Bithia, daughter of Pharaoh, (who is referred to at the conclusion of the verse) bore . . .all these are the names of Moses. Bore? But was he (Moses) born of Bithia and not rather of Jochebed: But, Jochebed bore and Bithia reared him; And the child grew, and she brought him unto Pharaoh's daughter, and he became her son."[9] Therefore, he was called after her.

Rabbi Eleazar, quoting Psalms "You have with Your arm redeemed your people, the sons of Jacob and Joseph.[10] Did then Joseph beget them? Surely, it was rather Jacob? But, Jacob begot and Joseph sustained; therefore they are called by his name."

A similar idea is expressed regarding Mordecai and Esther in the Purim story:

And he (Mordecai) brought up Hadassah, that is, Esther, his uncle's daughter; for she had neither father nor mother, and the maiden was of beautiful form and fair to look on; and when her father and mother were dead, Mordecai took her for his own daughter.[11]

There are other such variations on the idea of adoption. "Ephraim and Manasseh are mine ... as Reuben and Simeon, they shall be mine."[12] Or "one born in my house is mine heir."[12a] Or the account in the Midrash where, elaborating on the verse of Isaiah, "You, O God, are our Father,"[13] the scholar notes in explanation that "whoever raises the child is called father, not the one who begets it."[14] Or the statement in the Talmud that "he who teaches the son of his neighbor Torah, Scripture ascribes it to him as though he had begotten him."[15] A famous Talmudic scholar, Abaye, orphaned at birth, was adopted and taught by his uncle, Rabbi Bar Nahamani, and is frequently referred to as Nahamani, in his honor.

So that there is a substantial literature which we might draw on for a Jewish concept of adoption. From these accounts can be elicited a number of legal principles so as to provide a perspective from which a position can be established:

The legal principles are:

1. The Code of Jewish Law, Shulkhan Aruch, notes that "a legal document bearing the name of an adopted person as the child of the adopting father is valid."[15a] Greater care is, however, required where the document is that of marriage and divorce.

2. The question of the legitimacy of the child or a foundling is discussed in the following context. In Jewish law, a child born of a forbidden relationship is illegitimate. On the other hand, where marriage could have been concluded even if it was not, the child is legitimate. Therefore, a child born out of wedlock is not automatically illegitimate. Jewish law in this respect is much more liberal than Christian doctrine.

This subject is relevant because of the Biblical injunction that "a bastard shall not enter into the assembly of the Lord."[16]

So, the Talmud discusses the status of abandoned children and tries to create presumptions in favor of legitimacy.[17] Many conditions had to be fulfilled before the Rabbis were willing to declare a foundling illegitimate. There were, for example, the circumstances in which the child was found. Did external evidence show that the mother was or was not concerned with the fate of her child? If there was reason to think that the mother did have her child's welfare at heart, then the child was considered legitimate. If, on the other hand, the mother seemed to want to rid herself of it, there were grounds for thinking it was illegitimate.

In case of adoption, the tendency is to assume that the mother (or parents) who makes contact with potential adoptive parents or agencies, is concerned with the welfare of the child. A child in such an instance is, therefore, deemed legitimate and can be included within the Jewish community. The other presumption here is that the infant is of a Jewish mother who, in Jewish law, determines the religion of the child. No further act of conversion is necessary.

If the child is of a non-Jewish mother, it is not officially Jewish until converted. (Circumcision and ritual immersion in the case of a boy, and ritual immersion for a girl.)

Apart from the question of Jewish identity of the child, for the Orthodox and Conservative groups the problem arises of the child's status vis-a-vis the special class of priests. The child might, for instance, be born of a father who is a *Kohen* (member of the priesthood), or she might, on the other hand, have originally been born a non-Jew — and since, according to Jewish law, a proselyte may not marry a *Kohen*, the problem might arise as to whether the adopted child can marry into this elite.

## THE ORTHODOX POSITION

The Orthodox position on adoption may be summed up in the following quotations, and can be understood only in the explanations which follow. To accept these statements as the official position without getting down to what is their practical significance, is to do them an injustice.

Legal adoptions in the Jewish view merely represent obligations which the parties involved have agreed to assume, implicitly or otherwise. Such obligations may also result in some privileges as defined by the courts. But no court can create the full equivalent of natural family relations or replace them.[18]

A recent review of responsa from Israel states:

"Several articles are devoted to adoption. It is pointed out that the concept of adoption is foreign to Judaism. Nevertheless, it is meritorious to undertake the support of children, who are helpless. Ties to natural parents can never be severed completely."[18a]

The essence of this idea can be extracted from the following:

"The *Halakhah* does not regard an adopted child as a flesh and blood member of his adoptive family."[19]

This general position can be understood only as it affects the following practical considerations:

1. *In terms of his name.*

Reference here is to the Hebrew name of the father. In documents used to draw up contracts for marriage or divorce a man or woman's Hebrew names are used together with the name of their natural father. He or she is known as _____ son/daughter of _____, the natural, and not the adoptive, father's name being used. If the father's name is unknown, the child is called son/daughter of *Abraham*, as in the case of a proselyte, or, as another authority notes, he may be called by the "adoptive father's name . . . to avoid embarrassing the son."[19a]

2. *In terms of privileges and restrictions applying to the Kohen.*

Deference for the *Kohen*, the priestly class, has been retained in Jewish tradition, though the Holy Temple in Jerusalem has been destroyed, and therefore the whole ritual of Temple worship is no longer in use. The Priest still officiates at the redemption of the first born, joins with the other priests in offering the Priestly Benediction in the Orthodox synagogue on festivals, and leads in the recitation of Grace after meals. His choice of people he can marry is even more restricted than that of the ordinary Jew, and he is not allowed to participate in funerals except for very close relatives.

The adopted child retains only the status with which it was born. If he is born a *Kohen*, that is, if his natural father is known to have been one, all the privileges and limitations of that state automatically devolve upon him, no matter what the status is of his adoptive father.

3. *In terms of the duty of circumcision and redemption of the first-born.*

Jewish tradition imposes the duty to have child circumcised in the presence of the father. If a father is not present, a Beth Din, Jewish Court, assumes the responsibility. An adoptive father, having assumed the responsibility of raising the boy, and acting on behalf of the Beth Din, is required to arrange for the boy to be circumcised. The duty of performing the ceremony of *Pidyon Ha-ben*, Redemption of the First Born, also rests on the adoptive father. (The assumption here is that the mother is not the daugher of a *Kohen* or *Levi*.) The adoptive father is not required to recite the traditional blessing of redeeming the child, since the child is not his. He may, however, recite the customary blessing of joy, *Shehecheyanu*, because it is a prayer of gratitude for a joyous occasion.

4. *In terms of relationship of child to parents and parents to child.*

According to the Rabbis, the Biblical command to honor father and mother applies equally to an adopted, as to a natural, child. There are, however, occasions, in which this is not the case: An adopted child may recite the *Kaddish*, memorial prayer, for adoptive parents, but is not required to keep the laws of mourning, *K'riah*, *Shiva*, etc. which are applicable only to the natural child. From this point of view, too, if an adoptive father is a *Kohen*, since the latter is only allowed to take part in the funeral of a near blood relative, he is therefore forbidden to attend the funeral of his child by adoption.

5. *In terms of laws of consanguinity, forbidden marriages.*

An adopted child, for the purposes of prohibited marriages, is in the same category as a stranger, or non-family member. Thus, an adopted person may marry a member of his adoptive family, since no blood relationship would forbid such marriage.

6. *In terms of inheritance.*

An adopted child does not from the Jewish legal point of view, automatically inherit from an adoptive parent, unless provision for this is specifically made in the form of an agreement. On the other hand, an adopted person may inherit from his natural father as next of kin. The issue here is academic since in Jewish law the principle of *Dina d'Malchuta Dina*, (the law of the land, i.e., civil law) prevails.

The Orthodox position is contained in the following statement.

> . . . adoption is not recognized as legal in Jewish law and the question of a child does not relieve the adopting parents of the consequences of childlessness (exempting the mother from levirate marriage of *halitzah* in the case of the death of the husband) nor can such a child legally claim inheritance should his foster father die

intestate. In modern Israel a form of adoption has evolved whereby without overcoming the religious difficulties, the rights of the child to care, maintenance and inheritance are legally assured.[20a]

The *Chabad*-Lubavitch movement has stated its opposition to formal legal adoption on additional grounds: that parents lavish a great deal of physical affection upon their children, and by doing the same to their adopted children, a couple would automatically have forbidden contact with a member of the opposite sex to whom they were not blood relatives.[20b]

## THE REFORM POSITION

The Reform position on adoption comes from a Responsum which appeared in the *Yearbook of the Central Conference of American Rabbis* in 1956.[21] The following are the passages that stand out:

> Since nowadays, however, the majority of the people in the cities are Gentile, such a child (a foundling . . . having been put where someone could pick it up . . .) is presumably Gentile, and therefore must be converted, or accepted in some ways into the community . . . What process is to be followed? . . . On the question of conversion of children (not specifically for adopted children, but it applies fully), the Central Conference of American Rabbis came to a definite decision in the report on marriage and inter-marriage. There it was decided that such children need go through no other process than to attend our religious schools, and that the confirmation service that ends the school course shall be deemed sufficient as a ceremony of conversion. Naturally, an adopted boy would be circumcised. Generally now most boys are circumcised. In that case, a more observant family might want to take the drop of blood of the covenant . . .

> What is the status of an adopted child in a Jewish family? . . . It is clear that race or religion of parents has no bearing with us. A child who is adopted is accepted in Judaism according to the practices of the branch of Judaism to which the adopting family belongs. Such a child is absolutely and completely a member of the family, a full child of the parents.

To fully appreciate the differences of opinion, one must also read the statement which follows:

Reform Judaism does not regard as binding the Biblical law prohibiting the marriage of an Aaronide (the name of the priestly group since they derive from Aaron the High Priest) to a divorced woman, or the law which prevents an Aaronide from coming into contact with the dead through visiting a grave or attending a funeral.

Reform Judaism has dispensed with the custom of *Pidyon Ha-ben*, by which a first born male child is redeemed by the father through payment of a sum of money to a *Kohen*.[22]

## THE CONSERVATIVE POSITION

The Committee on Marriage and the Family of the Rabbincial Assembly of America presented its position in a statement on adoption, prepared by Rabbi Sidney Steiman.[23]

Jewish law and tradition have always emphasized the importance of family life. To make a home for a homeless or an unwanted infant is certainly a great Mitzvah. Our tradition recognizes two aspects of parenthood. First, there are the father and mother who give physical life to a child and then there are those "parents" who rear a child even though they may not be the physical parents. The Talmud (Sanhedrin 19b) records the following statement quoted by Rabbi Samuel ben Nahmani in the name of Rabbi Jonathan: "He who teaches the son of his neighbor the Torah, Scripture ascribes it to him as if he had begotten him." While we do not find laws on adoption in the Scripture and the Talmud such as the *adrogatio* of the older Roman law (by which a man can create legally a relationship of father and child with a person not his child by birth), there is a strong feeling that the man and the woman who rear a child should be *honored* as parents. "Whoever rears an orphan in his own house is, in the word of the Scripture, deemed its parent."

In the spirit of this tradition, the Committee on Marriage and the Family looks favorably upon the practice of adoption by Jewish couples of a child who is homeless or orphaned. Especially in the case of Jewish couples who are not blessed with offspring of their own, it is our hope and prayer that, through adoption, they will find family happiness and bliss as adopting parents. Cognizant of the many complications involved in the process of adopting, we urge prospective adopting parents to consult the authorized civic, welfare, and family agencies which are equipped to counsel and process adoption in the respective communities throughout the country. It is our deep conviction that the Jewish home and the Jewish way of life can help to develop a continuing spirit of love, devotion, and family fulfillment between parents and child.

In order to aid the adopting parents in fulfilling the requirement of Jewish law in cases of adoption, the Commission presents the following procedures based on the decisions of the Committee on Jewish Law and Standards.

In cases where the child being adopted is the offspring of a Jewish mother, the child is treated in most matters as the physical offspring of the adopting parents.

If a Jewish child is adopted before reaching eight days of age, the adopting father may recite the benediction *al ha-milah* (for circumcision) and the child may be named as the son of the adopting father.

When a child born of a Jewish mother is adopted before the eighth day and the whereabouts of the real father is unknown, there is no *Pidyon ha-Ben* (Redemption of the First Born) when the child reaches its thirty-first day.

The rabbi is able to state in court, in cases of adoption where the infant was born to a non-Jewish mother, that the child is Jewish once the process of conversion has begun (i.e. a ritual circumcision or naming, or attending Hebrew School, etc.)

The circumcision of a male child born to a non-Jewish mother is performed ritually with the intention of conversion. In the case of a boy born to a non-Jewish mother who is adopted before the eighth day, the infant is to be circumcised *le-shaim gairut* (for the purpose of conversion) on the eighth day. He is to undergo *tevilah al daat bet din* (immersion by the authority of the court) at some later date.

In cases involving the adoption of a female child born to a non-Jewish mother, the child is "to undergo *tevilah al daat bet din* (immersion by the authority of the court) before the age of twelve and is named in the synagogue only after *tevilah"* However, she may be named at a home ceremony before *tevilah* (immersion,.

According to Jewish law, the conversion of a minor is possible with the consent of the parent. "When no parent is available to consent to the conversion of an adopted non-Jewish infant, the conversion is done *al daat bet din,*" (by authority of the court).

An option is to be given an adopted non-Jewish girl or boy before ages of twelve and thirteen respectively to enable them to voluntarily remain Jewish or revert to their ancestral faith.

In the State of Israel adoption is governed by the Adoption of Children Law which empowers the district court and, with the conset of all the partners concerned, the rabbinical court, to grant an adoption order in respect of any person under the age of 18 years . . . Such an order has the effect of severing all family ties between the child and his natural parents. On the other hand, such a court order creates new family ties between the child and the adopter to the same extent as are legally recognized as existing between natural parents and their child . . . Thus, an adoption order would generally confer rights of intestate succession on the adoptee, who would henceforth also bear his adopter's name. However, the order does not affect the consequences of the blood relationship between the adoptee and his natural parents so that the prohibitions and permissions of marriage and divorce continue to apply. On the other hand, adoption as such does not create new such prohibitions or permissions between the adopted and the adoptive family.[24]

## NOTES

1a. See Justine Wise Polier, *Adoption and Religion*, Louise Wise Services, New York: Also, Frances A. Koestler, The Adoption Revolution, National Jewish Monthly, Washington, D.C., October 1966. Also, Werner J. Cahnman, 'The Interracial Jewish Children,' Reconstructionist; New York, June 9, 1967, p.8.

1b. For a detailed analysis on Adoption see *Encycolpedia Judaica Yearbook*, Jerusalem, 1974, p. 300. See also Solomon B. Freehof, *A Treasury of Responsa*, Jewish Publication Society, Philadelphia, 1963, p. 211.

1c. *Gen.* 16:1-3.

2. Ibid. 30:1-2.

2a. I Chronicles 2:34.

3. *Sanhedrin* 19b.

4. *Ibid.* See also, Universal Jewish Encyclopedia, Vol. 1, 1939, p. 100.; Also, Sholom Klass, *Responsa of Modern Judaism*, The Jewish Press, Vol. 11, 1966, p. 146.

5.II *Samuel* 21:18.

6. *Ruth* 4:17.

7. I *Chronicles* 4:18

8. *Megillah* 12a.

9. *Exod.* 2:10.

10. *Ps.* 77:16.

11. *Esther* 2:7.

12. *Gen.* 48:5.

12a. *Ibid.* 15:3.

13. Isaiah 64:7.

14. *Megillah* 13a.

15. *Sanhedrin* 19b.

15a. *Shulhan Arukh*, Hoshen Mishpat, 42:15, quoted by Solomon Freehof, *Yearbook CCAR*, Vol. LXVI, Atlantic City, p. 109.

16. *Deut.* 23:3.

17. *Sanhedrin* 23a.

18. Immanuel Jakobovits, *Jewish Law Faces Modern Problems*, Yeshiva University, Studies in Torah Judaism, New York, 1965, p. 91 (discussing presentation of Rabbi Mordecai Cohen).

18a. Seymour Siegel, 'Responsa from Israel,' *Conservative Judaism*, XIX, No. 2, Rabbinical Assembly, New York, 1963.

19. Hyman Tuchman, 'Adoption Review of Recent Halakhic Periodical Literature,' *Tradition*, Rabbinical Council of America, Volume II, Fall, 1960, (discussing position of Rabbi S. Hibner) p. 74. See also, *The Jewish Family, a Compendium*. Norman Linzer, Commission on Synagogue Relations, New York, quotes Walter Wurzburger, as follows:

> ... naturally the child owes an abiding debt of gratitude to his adoptive parents ... but the fact that someone else assumes the preogatives of spiritual parents does not negate or supersede the natural relationship to one's biological parents, who, after all is said and done, are still responsible for one's very existence and whose genes have formed one's very being. Professor Linzer records "halakhic differentiations between biological and adoptive parents" and practical implications of the difference.

19a. Immanuel Jakobovits, *Journal of a Rabbi*, Living Books, New York, 1966, p. 241.

20a. *Encyclopedia of Jewish Religion*, Werblonsky and Wigoder, Editors, Holt, Rinehart and Winston, New York, 1966.

20b. 'The Lubavitch Movement,' in *Encyclopedia Judaica Yearbook*, p. 302, Jerusalem, 1974.

21. Yearbook, *CCAR*, Vol. LXI, Responsum. Also in Solomon Freehof, *Reform Judaism*, Hebrew Union College Press, Cincinnati, Ohio, 1960, p. 200. Selections of above quoted also in Rabbi's Manual, Central Conference of American Rabbis, New York, p. 113.

22. *Rabbi's Manual, p. 136, according to Rabbinical Conference, Philadelphia, 1869. See also, M. Mielziner, The Jewish Law of Marriage and Divorce, p. 59.*

23. Rabbinical Assembly, New York, 1960.

24. Ibid., Encyclopedia Judaica, *Adoption*, Yearbook, p. 302.

# ARTIFICIAL INSEMINATION

The birth of a child resulting from artificial insemination rather than normal sexual intercourse is a new phenomenon that has opened problematic areas for religious leaders and legal experts alike.

The legal questions arising from the increasing number of this type of birth (150,000 in the United States alone) include those of adultery, the legitimacy of the children, and property and inheritance laws.

Moral concerns arise because of the question of the sexual relationship between the marriage partners.

Religious questions abound, especially from the Jewish point of view. Has the donor fulfilled his duty of procreation? Or has he infringed the prohibition not to waste seed? By submitting herself to the seed of a stranger, has the wife committed adultery and, if so, may she continue living with her husband?

Does this artificial means of procreation satisfy the Biblical command to "be fruitful and multiply?" Does it make a difference whether the sperm was procured from the husband or an anonymous donor? Is it indeed permissible for male seed to be collected in this way? Can the child resulting from such a process be included in the community of the people of Israel?

Even from the point of view of the civil law, which has been very much influenced by Roman Catholic and Protestant rulings on the subject, A.I.D., the method by which the semen is supplied by a donor, is considered adulterous, and the child resulting illegitimate.

Russia has refused to recognize children born in this way. Germany has legalized A.I.D. with the proviso that donors have the right to know the name of their offspring and claim paternity. In England, while A.I.D. is disapproved of, it is not prohibited. Court decisions in "Cook County and in Illinois and in Ontario, Canada declared that A.I.D. constitutes adultery." Where, however, the semen is taken from the husband, a more lenient view is taken. The Roman Catholic Church is, however, even opposed to this method (known as A.I.H.); when, in certain cases, they do permit it, the insemination must take place only as a part of the natural intercourse between marriage partners. The Protestant Church permits A.I.H., and does not concern itself with the way in which the semen was procured. Courts of law consider the child resulting from A.I.H. legitimate.[2]

In the main, Judaism morally frowns upon the whole procedure, especially A.I.D. It does not, however, hold the union to be adulterous, nor the child of such an union illegitimate. So, while there may be strong opposition to this transaction, Judaism is not as negative as either the civil law or the Roman Catholic Church.

There are, however, many different approaches which Jewish authorities apply to A.I.H. and the following traditional sources have been considered relevant:

**First, From the Bible:**

Leviticus details the duties and restrictions laid upon the priests and details their rite of service in the Tabernacle and in the sanctuary. Among the injunctions connected with the High Priest is mentioned that he should take a wife in her virginity.[3]

**Second, From the Talmud:**

Discussing a related issue, the rabbis of the Talmud note this Biblical passage and elaborate upon it. (Most authorities look to this as the basic source for an analysis of the contemporary issue of artificial insemination).

"Ben Zoma was asked: May a High Priest marry a maiden who has become pregnant? (The question here is: If the girl claims that, despite her pregnant condition, she is still a virgin, may the High Priest marry her?)

"Do we (in such a case) take into consideration Samuel's statement, when he said, "I can have repeated sexual connections without (causing) bleeding," i.e., without the woman losing her virginity. Or is perhaps the case of Samuel rare (exceptional cases

are not taken into account; the marriage would therefore be illegal)."
He replied: "The case of Samuel is rare, but we do consider (the possibility) that she may have conceived in a bath (into which a male had discharged semen)."[4]

### Third, From the Midrash:

The Midrash says that Ben Sirah was conceived in this way, by his mother having bathed in water fertilized by a male. Legend continues to suggest that the father was the prophet Jeremiah, and the mother, his daughter.[4a]

What is important here is not whether legal principles are deduced from this illustration. Halakhah, Jewish law, rarely depends on Aggadah, narrative or illustrative materials, for legal bases. Rather, here the point is made that offspring can result from insemination without the natural act of intercourse. Authorities differ on this issue. Some, citing this story, infer that, even without physical intercourse, the person from whom the actual semen is derived is the real father. In fact, they press this point to the extent of asserting that, though the birth is only indirectly attributable to him, he has fulfilled the Biblical injunction of procreation. So, if he already has a daughter, and a boy is born from the process of insemination, he has fulfilled his duty to have a boy and girl.

The extent to which this line of thinking is followed is revealed by another authority who says that a child born in this way is not illegitimate even if, had its mother and natural father engaged in normal sexual relations with each other, they would have committed an act of incest.

### Fourth, From Responsa:

A thirteenth century authority, Perez ben Elijah states in a note that a woman must be very careful about the sheet she sleeps on.

"A menstruous woman may lie on the sheet of her husband, but not on that of a stranger, lest she become pregnant from the seed of a stranger emitted on the sheet. But why should she not be afraid of her husband while she is menstruating, and thus produce a child of a menstruous woman, which is prohibited?" *The answer:* "Since there is no prohibited intercourse, the child is entirely *kasher* (legitimate for all purposes, and no stigma attaches to him), even if she became pregnant (in such a way) by a stranger, since Ben Sirah was *kasher* (no stigma attached to him). Yet, if it is a stranger, we have to be cautious (i.e., she must not lie on his sheet) because of the possibility that the resulting child might marry his own sister by his father (whose identity is unknown).Bet Shemuel (the School of Samuel) concludes from this note that the child resulting from such insemination is that of the emitter of the seed in every respect."[5]

Again, the deductions and the lessons to be learned are far more important than the facts of the case itself. One learns that the union is not adulterous, that the child is *kasher*, legitimate, with no stigma attached to him, that physical intercourse of parents is not absolutely necessary to establish a relationship of father and child, and that "on the other hand . . . the legal consequences of incest illegitimize a child only if the forbidden union between the parents was natural."[6]

A more recent responsum actually deals with the question whether, on the advice of a physician, a barren woman may, by law, be artificially inseminated by her own husband. The answer:

> . . . I find three doubts: one, as to whether it is permitted to take the seed from the man on the assurance of the doctor that the wife will thereby surely be impregnated; second, whether the insertion of the tube into the womb may not produce blood; and third, whether by means of such an artificial impregnation, the child who would be born, should be considered his child, so he may be deemed to have fulfilled thereby the commandment, "increase and multiply." Perhaps it should be argued that the child would not be considered completely his son, to be part of his family, unless the child is born from normal sexual relationships.
>
> As for the doubt about whether it is permitted to follow this prohibition against "bringing forth seed in vain," if we follow the earlier sages, it seems that the Talmud agrees that doctors are to be trusted even in cases where prohibitions (of religious law) are involved. If, then, the doctors' words are correct, that by this procedure (of taking seed) it will be easier for her to become pregnant, since this is the physical nature of this woman, then this procedure (of taking the seed) is not in vain at all. On the contrary, it is for the purpose of achieving pregnancy more easily. The rabbis forbade bringing forth seed in order to destroy it, but here there is no destruction; it is placed into the womb of the wife in order that she shall be impregnated. Then, clearly, there is nothing wrong with this procedure . . .[7]

## THE ORTHODOX POSITION

Orthodox authorities are unanimous in their condemnation of A.I.D., since it leads to too many *halakhic* complications. For example, a widow who had a child by the A.I.D. method might not be required to undergo Levirate marriage (marriage with her brother-in-law) on the false assumption that her deceased husband had left a child behind. There is also the question as to whether the child born of such a process is the heir of the donor or of the legal father. Nor is it clear whether the mother can have sexual relations with her husband while pregnant with another man's child.

Certain rulings have been made concerning A.I.D.: a) a girl born through A.I.D. must not marry a *Kohen;* b) a woman on whom A.I.D. has been performed must not marry a *Kohen;* c) a married woman who has used this method does not become forbidden to her husband unless he is a *Kohen;* d) A.I.D. can be a ground for divorce if perfomed without the husband's consent.[7a] It is these kinds of complications that motivated the Orthodox authorities not to allow A.I.D.

The difficulty that arises in the question of A.I.H. — insemination from the husband — is connected with the prohibition that a man should not waste his seed. The authorities have also been perplexed by the means through which the semen is collected. Even in order to fulfill the commandment of procreation, according to some extremist views, the act of masturbation is forbidden. More liberal authorities, however, hold that the method by which the semen is collected is not relevant here because the intent is to fulfill the commandment of procreation.[8a] Even so, blanket authorization is not given; each individual case is judged on its own merits.

One authority suggests how semen might be obtained without breaking the law; like the Catholics, he advocates that the semen be "banked" during the natural act of intercourse between marriage partners, either by use of a perforated condom or of a specially invented instrument called a "cervical spoon."

> The instrument is a concave lucite spoon, inserted into the vaginal canal before coitus and withdrawn an hour later with its contents which can be used for a seminal test or for the renewed insemination.

The same authority discloses that experiments have been car-

78

ried out in Israel which well may eliminate the entire problem of A.I.D. by creaming the seminal plasma of the sperm cells of the donor through a centrifugation process, and then resuspending it with the spermatozoa of the husband "much like blood-transfusions and skin-grafts from one to another." The final result would, in Halakhic opinion, be the equivalent of A.I.H.[9]

> In summary, then, Judaism condemns A.I.D. in any form as an utter abomination, though we are less concerned with the intrinsic immorality of the practice than with the abuses to which it lends itself. Such human stud-farming exposes the society to the gravest dangers which can never be outweighed by the benefits that may accrue in individual cases . . . On the other hand, the consensus of Halakhic opinion disagrees with the law of the state and the church as it now stands in regarding the offspring produced by A.I.D. as illegitimate, and the operation, itself, as adulterous. Such an offspring, according to Jewish law, is the legal child of the donor (that is, if he can be identified with absolute certainty); the child cannot inherit his putative father nor free his mother for the levirate law in case of her husband's death. There are weighty reasons for imposing marriage restrictions upon such product of A.I.D. No final opinion can be expressed on A.I.H. or the procuring of semen for examination purposes; but there is every probability that, under certain circumstances, and with suitable safeguards, a *Heter* (permission) for this practice can be found in individual cases.[10]

A guide to Jewish moral and religious attitude can be summarized by the following:

> While in the Jewish view, heterogeneous artificial insemination does not constitute adultery, and the resultant offspring is not branded as an illegitimate child, Jewish law registers the strongest moral revulsion against such insemination . . .
>
> Where penetration is impossible or post-coital tests are unsatisfactory in showing living sperms in the cervix, artificial insemination with the husband's semen is permitted, but this operation should not be performed within the seven day period following the cessation of menstruation. Where short cycles occur ovulation may be delayed medically to conform with this latter requirement. Semen required for insemination or testing purposes should not be obtained by normal methods.[11]

## THE REFORM VIEW

In general, Reform Judaism permits the practice of artificial insemination, even in the case of A.I.D. Although authorities may differ in their analysis of the whole issue, the decision they arrive at is as liberal as they can make it.

The Reform position is described in a Responsum reported in 1953 by the Responsum Committee of the Central Conference of American Rabbis. The basic Talmudic text about the restrictions imposed upon the marriage of the High Priest develops into the position of recognized authorities who maintain that, in any event, the child is legitimate, and that the woman has not committed adultery, and therefore is not forbidden to her husband, and it is upon this last that the Reform position depends. There are conflicting views as to whether the child is that of the donor or of the mother. If the former is the case, there exists the remote possibility that some day there might be an incestuous union between the son and daughter of the same father.[11b]

Another authority adds that for the purpose of inheritance and the levirate law, the child is not to be considered the child of the donor. Furthermore, since the child is not that of the donor, he has committed the violation of wasting seed.

> ... inasmuch (as this authority) concludes that the woman is not immoral and not forbidden to her husband, he seems to incline toward permitting the procedure at the recommendation of the physician, although he hesitates to do so.

> My own opinion would be that the possibility of the child marrying one of his own close blood kin, is far-fetched, but that since, according to Jewish law, the wife has committed no sin, and the child is *kasher*, then the process of artificial insemination should be permitted.[12]

The same Responsum also gives the view of Professor Alexander Guttman who questions the appropriateness of using the Talmudic text as a basis for dealing with the whole question, since the description in the Talmud deals with accidental insemination which brought about an undesired pregnancy, and not with planned and premeditated insemination. One of the problems that has been raised is whether or not the emission of seed for artificial insemination would fall into the prohibited category of "wasting seed."[13]

Guttman quotes an authority who equates both accidental and planned insemination, stressing, however, that the emission of seed is forbidden. While he thinks that there is a real difference between the sperm of the stranger and that of the husband, it is possible, if the doctors find this to be the only method by which he is capable of begetting a child, that it is allowed.

His summary is as follows:

> Artificial insemination, as understood and practiced today, is not mentioned in Rabbinic source literature. What we find here is merely accidental, indirect insemination. We must also keep in mind that the bath insemination of the Talmud is not merely an ex post facto case, but it also involves the concept of Onus, meaning, accident. Jewish law, mostly, though not always, clearly distinguishes between accidental and premeditated deed. I do not believe that we do justice to Jewish Law or to Judaism by disregarding its concepts and principles in an effort to force certain conclusions, one way or other.

> Also, the fact that the laws and discussions of the rabbis with regard to bath insemination, are of a theoretical nature, is of importance. Not one incident of actual bath insemination is attested to in Jewish literature. What we find, including the Ben Sirah case, is mere Agaddah. Had such an incident actually occurred, the rabbis might have found a solution entirely different from the known theoretical considerations. Noteworthy is the fact that the Sages never recommend bath insemination, even if this were the only means of saving a marriage which ranks high with the rabbis. A case in point is in incident in Yabamot 65b.[14]

> I do not claim that the last word has been said on artificial insemination in its relation to Jewish life and practice. It is hardly possible to draw safe conclusions from the theoretical accidental insemination found in Jewish sources to the artificial insemination of our day. While indications strongly point to a negative answer (particularly if the seed of a stranger is to be used), other aspects of Judaism should be explored as well, in order to arrive at a conclusion reflecting Judaism at its best.

> Whereas I do not see sufficient evidence for recommending the issue of a prohibition against artificial insemination, I should like to caution against a hasty Hetter, permit, for which I found no backing worth the name in our Jewish teachings.[14a]

A later responsum recalling that the issue had been presented in 1952 and had been accorded the suggestion that "these decisions of the Conference [should] not . . . of course, . . . govern the members and their congregations (in any legal sense), but are intended as guidance and counsel," states:

> In general, the liberal attitudes on this subject are not affected by the negative mood of recent Orthodox opinion, but are based upon what is deemed to be the fundamental principles of the law and tradition. Artificial insemination is therefore favored if both husband and wife wish it. It is preferable, of course, for the seed to be taken from the husband, but even if a stranger is the donor, there is no objection.[15]

In 1964, the Commission on Judaism and Medicine summed up these two final positions.[16] In passing, a member of the Commission let fall the interesting idea that A.I.D. would not be objectionable even if the donor was not Jewish.

> Actually, there may be some advantage in that fact. For while legally the resulting child is not deemed to be the child of the donor, but of its mother, nevertheless, there would be some biological, hereditary kinship between that child, and the children of the donor in his own marriage. In that case, if the donor is Gentile, the liklihood is far less that the child born of the insemination might some day marry one of his blood kin.[17]

An Orthodox authority, however, had already stated that:

> Although these disabilities may not exist if the donor was a non-Jew, the use of his semen for the insemination of a Jewess would meet with even greater moral objection.[18]

## THE CONSERVATIVE POSITION

In 1959, Rabbi Isaac Klein, analyzing the various issues related to both AID and AIH, concludes as follows:

> Jewish tradition is thus at variance with those persuasions that condemn all artificial insemination as unnatural and therefore forbidden, as well as with those who while permitting AIH would condemn AID as adulterous.

That does not mean, however, that Jewish authorities permit AID. There are a number of other considerations legal and moral that complicate matters. There is the question of the legal paternity of the child. There is also the question of the chances of mating of brothers and sisters. If these considerations should cause us concern for the family with a totally sterile husband, we can find solace in a report of the Israel Medical Association which tells of a new method of insemination developed by Dr. Rozin of the Hadassah Hospital in Jerusalem. This would make it possible even for a sterile husband to become a true biological father. This would avoid many of the complex legal and religious problems involved because the husband supplies the fluid while the donor gives cell-free plasma which acts only as a chemical aid to fertilization.[19]

A letter written in 1967, taken from the Archives of the Committee on Jewish Law and Standards, records:

The Committee on Jewish Law and Standards has taken a position against artificial insemination by an anonymous donor.

If the transfer of the semen is not from the husband but from another man, there are a number of Halakhic objections: 1) The child born of such an act might be considered to be a *mamzer* since his mother conceived from a man other than her husband. 2) There is a possibility that the child would eventually marry a brother or sister or other forbidden relative. These are the two major objections, and neither of them would exist were the semen to come from the husband of the woman involved.

The letter repeats the report from the Israel Medical Association quoting verbatim from Rabbi Klein's earlier statement.

Rabbi David Feldman, an expert in Jewish law and a member of the Law Committee of the Rabbinical Assembly, has written:

Procuring the husband's seed for the purposes of artificial insemination, for example, would be declared proper if this is deemed the only way of effecting procreation; hence it is not "brought forth in vain" . . . Still, the manner of its procurement is restricted to one which is relatively indirect . . .[21]

Offering his own opinion, Rabbi Seymour Siegel has written recently:

My own personal opinion is that AID would not be ojectionable. My reasons are the following: 1) The accepted procedure is to mix the semen of the husband with the donor's. There is, therefore, no certainty that the husband has not been the biological father. 2) There is certainly no unanimity on the fact that the mother would be considered an adultress or the child a *mamzer* through AID. . . 3) There is only a far-fetched chance of incest. This is especially true, as Rabbi Moshe Feinstein points out, since donors tend to be non-Jewish. 4) I do believe that AID should be undertaken only with the consent of the husband and should not be considered for single women.[22]

## In Vitro Fertilization — Test Tube Babies

The subject of Artificial Insemination attracted world attention in June-July, 1978, with the startling announcement by two reputable physicians in Great Britain, Robert G. Edwards and Patrick Steptoe, that they had successfully achieved *in vitro* (in glass or test tube) fertilization and that the first medically authenticated birth of a baby conceived in a laboratory would occur on July 24, 1978. The healthy, normal baby girl was born by Caesarean section.

(A recent book entitled *The People Shapers* by Vance Packard, contains a fascinating chapter, *Starting Man in a Test Tube*, which discusses the many aspects of the subject including revelations of earlier cases of *in vitro* fertilization, references to the two doctors as being among leaders in this frontier field of experimentation, and the 'ban' on such research by the National Institute of Health in November, 1973, which while not a law, severely restricted the experimentation).[23]

The method — withdrawing a ripe egg from a woman whose Fallopian tubes are blocked or damaged, placing it *in vitro*, in a dish containing blood serum and nutrients and then exposing the egg to the husband's sperms. Once fertilized, the egg is transferred to another dish of blood serum and sustaining nutrients. The fertilized egg divides into a cluster of cells. The egg is then implanted in the uterus, where the nine month gestation period begins.

Scientists, ethicists, and religionists responded to this historic feat. To the scientists, it was a brilliant medical breakthrough. Many hoped that the experimental restrictions would now be lifted or at least modified. To the ethicists, many ethical issues arose pondering the vast ramifications of the new technique, overpopulation, the rights of the child/fetus, responsibilities of physicians, the possibility of host or surrogate mothers, virgin births, storing and freezing of the eggs, embryo banks, or hatcheries as Aldous Huxley warned in his novel (1932) *Brave New World*. Religionists responded, basing their views on their own religion's attitude toward artificial insemination. The Roman Catholic Church leaders viewed the incident as illicit since conception took place outside the body. Protestant churchmen hailed the birth. Rabbis of all denominations reacted positively, asserting that so long as third parties, i.e. donors, were not involved, this was a case of artificial insemination by the husband (A.I.H.) and therefore permissible.

The Jewish Week-American Examiner issue of August 8, 1978, carried a full page in which leading rabbinic authorities responded to queries about the historic incident. While side-issues and mis-use, such as the possiblity of sibling incest, the question as to how semen is obtained, host and surrogate mothers, the number of ova from the woman chosen for fertilization, etc., concerned all, there was general agreement about the Halakhic permissibility. Indeed, a feeling of exhilartion and gratitude was sensed in the responses.[24]

## NOTES

1. Only once has a child resulting from artificial insemination been held to be legitimate. This happened in New York in 1948 (Strand vs. Strand). Whether the husband gave his consent or not, all other cases on record seem to rule in favor of illegitimacy. Bills are at present being introduced to legalize artificial insemination and give full legal protection to all parties involved. See also Vance Packard, *The People Shapers*, Little, Brown, Boston, 1977, p. 178.

2. In 1967, Oklahoma became the first state in the nation to legalize artificial insemination of human beings, and to legitimatize the offspring of the procedure. Written consent of both husband and wife are required.

3. *Lev.* 21:13.

4. Hagigah 14b, 15a. See also, H.J. Zimmels *Magicians, Theologians, and Doctors*, Edward Goldstein & Son, London, Philip Feldheim, New York, 1952, p. 65.

4a. See Alexander Guttman, CCAR Vol XII, 1952, page 126. See also Immanuel Jakobovits, *Journal of a Rabbi*, Living Books, New York, 1966, p. 484, note 321.

5. *Ibid.* Alexander Guttman, page. 126.

6. Immanuel Jakobovits, *Journal of a Rabbi*, Living Books, New York, 1966, p. 209.

7. Solomon Freehof, *A Treasury of Responsa*, Jewish Publication Society of America, Philadelphia, 1962, p. 307. Dr. Freehof describes the decision as that of Aaron Walkin (1863-World War Europe rabbi of Pinsk-Karlin and the Responsum in *Zekan Aharon.*)

7a. See 'Artificial Insemination,' *Encyclopedia Judaica Yearbook*, Jerusalem, 1974.

8a. *Ibid.*, Immanuel Jakobovits, page 485, note 346. Frozen semen banks have been established, See *Readers Digest*, report, October 1971, page 172, Pleasantville, New York.

9. Immanuel Jakobovits, *Jewish Medical Ethics*, Bloch Publishing Co., New York, 1959, p. 250.

10. Immanuel Jakobovits, *Journal of a Rabbi, ibid.*, p. 212.

11. Jakobovits and Sharfman, *A Hospital Compendium*, Commission of Synagogue Relations, Federation of Jewish Philanthropies of New York, New York, 1965, p. 19.

A recent JTA release (1977) stated "A Haifa Rabbinical Court has ruled that artificial insemination with sperm from an anonymous donor is not adultery if the woman's husband had consented in writing for the procedure to take place. The same court had ruled a few years ago that a woman was committing adultery by receiving artificial insemination unless the donor was the husband.

"The new ruling involved a divorce case in which the husband claimed his wife had committed adultery by having a child through artificial insemination. He said that since the child was not his he should not have to support the child. The court ruled that his wife did not commit adultery since he had consented to the procedure after he found out that he was sterile and ordered him to pay."

11b. "*Newsweek* reports a case in which a doctor urged two young people to call off their marriage plans. He knew that they had both conceived by artificial insemination and that the same man had supplied semen for both. Thus they were half sister and half brother and their marriage would embody a new kind of incest. Wedding plans were cancelled." Vance Packard, p. 178. Similarly, the article in *Encyclopedia Judaica* (see note 72) records this possibliblity as a concern of the Rabbis.

12. Solomon Freehof, CCAR, Vol. LXII, 1952, p. 125.

13. *Gen.* 1:28.

14. The case deals with a woman who desired to be divorced on the ground that she had not given birth from her husband and came to R. Johanan at the Synagogue of Caesarea.

14a. CCAR Vol. LXII, 1952, p. 128.

15. Solomon Freehof, *Reform Responsa*, Hebrew Union College Press, Cincinnati, 1960, p. 128.

16. CCAR Vol. LXXIV, Atlantic City, 1964, p. 75.

17. Solomon Freehof, *Ibid.*, p. 218.

18. Immanuel Jakobovits, Jewish Medical Ethics, *Ibid.*, p. 359, note 41.

19. Isaac Klein, Science and Some Ethical Issues — The Jewish View, *Conservative Judaism*, Rabbinical Assembly, Summer, 1959, pp. 41-43.

20. Jules Harlow, for the Committee on Jewish Law and Standards, April 11, 1967. Letter to the author, May 15, 1978.

21. David Feldman, Birth Control in Jewish Law, New York University Press, New York, 1968, p. 123. See also, Isaac Klein, Responsa and Studies in Jewish Law, Artificial Insemination, Ktav, New York, 1975, p. 166.

22. Letter to the author, May 15, 1978.

23. See note 1.

24. See also, David Gross, Judaism and the New Biology, *Jewish Exponent*, Phila., Aug. 4, 1978.

# AUTOPSY

Autopsy, the dissection of a deceased person to determine cause of death or for the purposes of physical experiment, is more an emotional issue than a sharply-drawn legal one. The deep feelings that the whole question has aroused often surpass the rational considerations involved.

The major issue that has aroused controversy recently in Israel has more to do with the alleged abuses of family consent than with legal, Halakhic, considerations. In 1945, the Chief Rabbinate and the Hadassah Hospital authorities agreed to a number of provisions which might allow for the performance of autopsies. Permission for autopsies would be given where:

a) they were legally required,

b) the cause of death could not otherwise be determined, provided there was certification to such effect given by three doctors,

c) the lives of other existing patients, either in or out of the hospital, might be helped, provided there was certification by three doctors,

d) hereditary diseases were involved and the health of surviving relatives might be safeguarded,

e) in all cases and under all circumstances, the operations had to be carried out with proper reverence for the dead, and the corpses had to be delivered to the burial society afterwards for dignified interment.[1a]

Dealing with a related issue, the use of bodies for medical teaching purposes, Dr. Isaac Herzog, the late Chief Rabbi of Israel, stated that:

> The Plenary Council of the Chief Rabbinate . . . do not object to the use of bodies of persons who gave their consent in writing of their own free will during their life-time for anatomical dissections as required for medical studies, provided the dissected parts are carefully preserved as to be eventually buried with due respect to Jewish law.

Jewish attitudes toward autopsies, however, hardened owing to the growing incidence of the procedure due to an increase in the number of medical schools. Jewish medical students had been excluded from some Euorpean universities on the grounds that the Jewish authorities had refused to deliver the corpses of members of their community for dissection. Occasionally the policy had been adopted to allow the donation of Jewish bodies where necessary. When the National Jewish Hospital in Denver requested bodies for anatomical dissection in the study of tuberculosis, however, Rabbinic leaders refused their permission. The whole issue had already been discussed in relation to the establishment of a medical school in Palestine at one of the earlier Zionist Congresses held in Vienna.

Objections to the performance of autopsies include the desecration to the body of the dead and the opportunities opened up for unlimited abuse, the delay incurred, while dissection takes place, in the performance of the *mitzvah* to bury the *whole* body, and infringement of the laws of defilement and mourning, especially where priests are concerned. Also, it is considered reprehensible that anyone, and doctors especially, should derive material benefit or consolidate their careers at the expense of the dead.

To determine Jewish attitude toward this issue, one must go to the official pronouncements.

The basic sources for this, as for any other halakhic problem, are to be found in the Bible, the Talmud, the Codes, and the Responsa.

## A. From the Bible

1. The prohibition not to disgrace or disfigure the dead, derives from the Biblical law, which forbids the infliction upon the dead of any change which might be considered degrading:

> If a man is guilty of a capital offense and is put to death, and you impale him on a stake, you must not let his corpse remain on the stake overnight, but must bury him the same day. For an impaled

body is an affront to God; you shall not defile the land that the Lord your God is giving you to possess.[1b]

The Talmud deals with this statement in the following way:

Whence is it inferred that whoever keeps his dead unburied overnight transgresses thereby a negative commandment?. . . .

From the verse: You must bury him (the infinitive indicates that command concerns *all* dead, not only those executed by the court.[2]

The Talmud expands upon the nature of this principle:

If the body of a sinner must come to burial on the same day, then a righteous man must assuredly be laid to rest within twenty four hours.[3]

What is more, while, under certain circumstances, the requirement to bury the body within a twenty four hour period may be waived, the burial of the entire body, with no bodily part or organ missing, is a serious positive commandment of the Torah.

2. However, the duty to preserve the physical well-being of a person is a Biblical requirement:

"You shall keep My laws and My rules, by the pursuit of which man shall live."[4]

From this the Rabbis of the Talmud deduce that human-beings are intended to live and not *die* by keeping the Torah. They go on to draw the conclusion that, in the case of saving life, all laws except those dealing with idolatry, incest and murder, are abrogated. This principle is noted in the following statement:

". . . We may cure (i.e., save) ourselves with all (forbidden things), except idolatry, incest, (which includes adultery) and murder."[5]

3. "If you see your fellow's ox or sheep gone astray, do not ignore it; you must take it back to your fellow. If your fellow does not live near you or you do not know who he is, you shall bring it home and it shall remain with you until your fellow claims it; then you shall give it back to him."[6]

On this point, the rabbis of the Talmud ask: "Whence can it be derived that it is obligatory to restore the body of a fellow man when in danger just as it is obligtory to restore him his lost chattels? Because it is said: 'And you shall give it back to him,' implying him himself, i.e., his person"[7]

4. "He who touches a dead body . . . or the bone of a man . . . who died . . . shall be unclean seven days."[8]

From this Bible source is derived the principle of safeguarding the sanctity of the dead.

5. "By the sweat of your face shall you eat bread, till you return to the ground; for out of it were you taken, for dust you are and to dust you will return."[9]

From here derives the principle that burial applies to the whole body, and then if any part is missing the *mitzvah* has not been completed.

### B. From the Talmud:

Many of the principles mentioned above are elaborated upon in Talmudic literature in episodes which reveal an intimate knowledge of the human body.

1. "There is nothing that comes before the saving of life, except idolary, incest, and bloodshed only."[10]

2. "Rabbi Johanan said in the name of Rabbi Simeon ben Jehozadak: By a majority vote, it was resolved in the upper chambers of the house of Nithza in Lydda, that in every other law of the Torah, if a man is commanded: 'Transgress and suffer not death,' he may transgress and not suffer death, excepting idolatry, incest (which includes adultery) and murder."[11]

3. "If one has a pain in his throat, he may pour medicine into his mouth on the Sabbath (the dispute here concerns not the principle whether one *can* take medicine on the Sabbath but the efficacy of the particular treatments in question) because there exists a possibility of danger to human life and every risk to human life suspends the laws of the Sabbath."[12]

4. ". . . the possibility of danger to human life renders inoperative the laws of the Sabbath . . ."[13]

The following are Talmudic sources which reveal the extensive knowledge of the human body necessary before any position on the issue of autopsy could be formulated.

1. A story is told about Cleopatra, Queen of Alexandria, 68-30 B.C.E., that when she had sentenced her handmaids to death, they were subjected to a test (fertilization, and dissection after the death sentence had been carried out), and it was found that both (a male and a female) were fully fashioned on the forty-first day . . .[14]

2. "Rabbi Judah related in the name of Samuel: The disciples of Rabbi Ishmael once dissected (some insist that the word here should be 'boiled hard' or 'cooked') the body of a prostitute who had been condemned to be burnt by the king. They examined it and found two hundred and fifty two joints and limbs. They came and inquired of Rabbi Ishmael: 'How may joints has the human body?' He replied to them: 'Two hundred and forty eight.' Thereupon they said to him: 'But we have examined and found two hundred and fifty two.' He replied to them: 'Perhaps you made the post-mortem examination on a woman, in whose case Scripture adds two hinges (in her sexual organ) and two doors (the muscles) of the womb.'[15]

3. "It was taught: Abba Saul stated, 'I was once an undertaker, when I made a practice of carefully observing the bones of the dead. The bones of one who drinks undiluted wine are burned; those of one who drinks wine excessively diluted are dry; and those of one who drinks wine properly mixed are full of marrow. The bones of a person whose drinking exceeds his eating are burned; those of one whose eating exceeds his drinking are dry; and those of one who eats and drinks in a proper manner are full of marrow.' "[16]

4. "There are two hundred and forty eight members (bones) in the body of a man; thirty in the foot, six in each toe, ten in the ankle, two in the lower leg; five in the knee, one in the thigh, three in the hip, eleven ribs, thirty in the hand, six in every finger, two in the forearm, and two in the elbow, one in the upper arm, and four in the shoulders (and so there are thus far) one hundred and one on one side of the body and one hundred and one on the other side; and there are further eighteen vertebrae in the spinal column, nine members in the head, eight in the neck, six in the chest, and five in the openings. (Thus 202 plus 46 equals 248) . . .[17]

The following extracts from the Talmud deal with physical mutilation, and are the basic sources of the autopsy prohibition.

1. Whence is derived the principle which the rabbis adopted, viz: "Follow the majority? . . .? Rabbi Kahana said: It is derived from the case of a murderer, for whom the Divine law prescribes

death. Now why do we not fear that the victim may have been *trefah* (a person afflicted with a fatal organic disease, whose killing is not considered as serious an offense as murder, and therefore, does not entail the death penalty )? Is it not because we follow the majority? It is not allowed (to dissect the body of the victim) because it would thereby be mutilated! And should you say that, since a man's life is at stake, we should mutilate the body, and that there was a hole (in the victim) in the place (where he was struck) by a sword. (The murderer may have killed the victim by striking him in a place where he was already suffering from a fatal wound, and his blow may have removed all traces of the previous wound.) In such a case it is clear that no amount of post mortem examination would show that the victim was *trefah*: hence it is proved that we follow the majority.[18]

2. . . . It once happened at Bene Berak that a person sold his father's estate and died. The members of the family thereupon protested that he was a minor at the time of his death (and therefore not old enough to sell any of his father's estate. The property he had sold should belong by right to the surviving members of the family). They came to Rabbi Akiva and asked him to have the body examined (so as to ascertain the age of the deceased by a post-mortem). He replied to them: "You are not permitted to dishonor him; and furthermore, (the) signs (of maturity) usually undergo a change after death. (And so the autopsy could not produce any reliable evidence of his age.) . . . When he (Rabbi Akiva) said to them, "You are not permitted to dishonor him," they remained silent. If it is taken for granted that the *members of the family protested, one can well understand why they remained silent; (They had consideration for the honor of their relative;) if, however, it is assumed that the buyers protested, why, (it may be asked,) did they remain silent? They should have replied to him: 'We paid him money; let him be dishonored!"* (Would strangers consent to lose their purchase-money out of consideration for the body of a man who had appropriated what belonged to them?) If (only) because of this (if this argument had been the only proof that it was the relatives who protested) there would be no argument, (for Rabbi Akiva may) have said to them (the buyers) thus: "In the first place (a post mortem must not be held) because you are not permitted to dishonor him; and, furthermore, in case you might say, 'He took our money, let him be dishonored,' the signs (of maturity) usually undergo a change after death."[19]

## C. From the Codes:

Jewish legal codes of all periods have reflected principles originating in the Talmud. Special stress is laid particularly on the following:

*Met Asur B'hanah*, it is forbidden to enjoy or derive benefit from anything belonging to the dead.[20]

This idea is best summed up in the following text:

"It is not permitted to let the body of the dead remain (unburied) overnight, for it is written: 'His body shall not remain all night . . . but you shall, whatever the circumstance, bury him on the same day." If, however, one let the body remain overnight, for the sake of honoring the dead, e.g., to procure a coffin or shrouds, or to await for the arrival of relatives or people who will deliver the funeral orations, in these circumstances it is permitted (to postpone) burial, as the Torah forbade only that delay which leads to contempt for the dead, as we find in the case of a person who was hanged, (and whose body was left overnight).[21]

## D. From the Responsa:

There are rabbinic responsa dealing with autopsies that date back to the seventeenth and eighteenth centuries. The first modern authority to have been confronted with this issue was Rabbi Jacob Emden (1697-1776). In 1737, he was asked by Wolf Ginsberg, a student, at the University of Goettingen, whether he might participate in the dissection of a dog on the Sabbath. Rabbi Jacob Emden answered that there were many prohibitions involving the Sabbath in the performance of autopsies, and that in any event there was no distinction between the dissection of a human being or of an animal. Furthermore, Jewish law did not allow any benefit to be derived from human corpses.

The first of the two primary sources always referred to when examining this issue, and one directly in line with the position of Rabbi Emden, is that of Rabbi Ezekiel Landau (1713-1793), known as the *Noda Be-Yehudah* (the name of his volumes of responsa). He was asked whether an autopsy might be performed on a Jew who had died of gall stones in order to learn how such cases should be dealt with in the future. Rabbi Landau, detailing Jewish legal principles dealing with disfigurement and the degradation of the human body concluded that, while except in cases of idolatry, adultery, and murder, all laws were waived where there was even a possiblity of saving life, in this case this did not apply, because there was no "reasonable or immediate prospect" of saving a human life. There was no patient *at hand* who was in immediate need of such knowledge, and it was only particular individual need which would permit the law dealing with *Pikuah nefesh*, the saving of life, to become operative. He concluded:

> The principle that even a possiblity of saving a life waives all Biblical commandments except in three cases applies only when there is before us concretely such a possibility as for instance a sick person with that same ailment. In our case, however, there is no patient whose treatment calls for this knowledge. It is only that people want to learn this skill for future possibility of a patient who will need this treatment coming before us. For such a slight apprehension we do not nullify a Biblical commandment or even a Rabbinic prohibition.[22]

The second of the two sources is that of Rabbi Moses Schreiber (1763-1839) known as the *Hatham Sofer* (also after the title of his book) . . . who supports Rabbi Landau's conclusion. Permission for dissection on the grounds of saving life can be given only when the specific person is at hand who has exactly the same disease as the deceased and can therefore gain immediate benefit from an autopsy. A *remote* possibility of saving life is highly insufficient to permit the desecration of the body. Rabbi Schreiber introduced new factors into his responsum. He wondered whether the prohibition against benefitting from the dead might not apply also to the dissection of non-Jewish bodies, and he also was very strongly opposed to the bequeathing of his body by a Jew for medical research.

These two latter positions have predominated, with occasional variations, over the past two centuries. In the main, what seems to hold is that autopsies are forbidden unless there is an immediate possibility of saving life. This does not mean that later rabbis might not have arrived at their various conclusions, for or against the use of autopsies, on different grounds.

Rabbi Jacob Ettlinger, for example, a leading German rabbi of the 19th century, was even more extreme in his opposition to autopsies, maintaining that, even though there might be a sick person with the same disease as the deceased and the physician might believe that a cure would be discovered for him if the body of the dead were dissected, even then an autopsy could not be performed. Rabbi Ettlinger bases his extreme stand on the Talmudic statement that "it is forbidden to rescue oneself through the destruction of another's property."[23] He declares further that the duty of saving life is imposed only upon the living and does not obligate the dead. The corpse is under no legal obligation to save anyone's life. The rabbi does agree, however, that if the deceased had, during his lifetime, sold his body to be used after his death, then an autopsy was permissible. If this was what he wanted to do, why should we oppose it?

Still another rabbi living in the same time, Rabbi Moses Schick, known as the *Maharam Schick*, disagrees with Rabbi Ettlinger. He is of the opinion that one cannot sell one's body since burial is a Biblical requirement, the purpose of which is to prevent human degradation, and a person is not free to renounce the respect due to his body. In other words, a person cannot decide for himself that he is not to be buried; it is not up to him to make that decision.

In the twentieth century there is a disagreement over the last point. The Chief Rabbi of the British Empire, Hermann Adler, notes in a memorial address that:

> His selflessness (Fredric David Macotta) is proved by a remarkable instruction he gave to his physician. He directed that, in the event of his dying of an obscure disease, after death examination be made, the cost to be borne by his estate, for the advancement of medical science and for the benefit of those who might suffer hereafter from a similar ailment.[24]

Rabbinic authorities, it seems, found different reasons for their various positions. Rabbi Hayyim Hirshenson, for example, concluded that autopsy should be permitted when doctors believe that they might find the cause of a disease, thus helping to find a cure for humanity in general and for those who were immediately suffering from the disease in particular. He reached his conclusion by reexamining what is meant by the mutilation of the dead. Mutilation was only a degradation of the dead when such was the underlying intention. Where that was not the intention, however, the practice could not be classified in the same category as mutilation at all. Rabbi Hirshenson proceeds to recall the Talmudic assertion that where certain measures have to be taken in honor of the dead, there is no violation if burial does not take place immediately:

If he kept him overnight for the sake of his honor, to procure for him a coffin or a shroud, he does not thereby transgress.[25]

The Talmud continues:

When did the Merciful One say, "His body shall not remain all night upon the tree? Only in a case similar to that of the hanged: where it (the keeping of the corpse) involves disgrace.[26]

An autopsy for the purpose of finding a cure, he concludes, cannot be called a disgrace to the dead, and therefore is permitted. He does not, however, go so far as to permit dissection for medical purposes. He cannot imagine that the dead could be honored by devoting their bodies to medical research.

An Israeli medical authority quotes Rabbi Hirshenson:

As a result of investigation and post-mortem examinations, the doctors have learned more during the last century than in the previous two thousand years. It is now accepted as an important rule that one cannot investigate the true nature of diseases and changes in the body of a patient, except through the post-mortem examination of those whose lives have come to an end as a result of one illness or another. Accordingly, post-mortems are a vital need of the community.[27]

Rabbi Ben Zion Uziel, Chief Rabbi of Israel, went further. He saw no objection to the medical dissection of Jewish bodies, provided that the operation was performed with dignity and reverence. He did not, however, approve of people selling their bodies before death. He settled the arguments of those who maintained that autopsy could be permitted only if there was a person present suffering from the same disease who could derive immediate benefit from such an examination, by asserting that there must indeed exist people who could so benefit since they had the same disease, *even though they were not present.* He approved autopsies not only for purposes of cure by also for medical research. What he opposed, however, was the practice of willing away one's body in exchange for money, which he felt was really a form of self-degradation. He insisted, moreover, upon proper burial for the body on which an autopsy has been performed. Rabbi Hirshenson seems to view his own line of thinking as purely academic, and advises that competent rabbis be consulted before it is followed in practice.

A more right-wing view is offered by Rabbi Eliezer Meir Prail. He is more concerned that so many restrictions have been liberalized and declares that it is "forbidden to dissect the dead bodies of Jews for the purpose of learning the nature of the disease, even if there are sick people present, because the cure is clearly not known. Even when the cure is clear, nevertheless, according to Rashi and Meiri, it is forbidden since one is not permitted to save himself by causing a loss to others. If because of the autopsy the body of the dead will be kept overnight, there is the additional transgression of delaying burial. It is certainly forbidden for a physician who is a *Kohen*, an Aaronide, to participate in an autopsy because there is the issue of becoming unclean."[28]

Rabbi Joseph Zweig voices a more liberal view, when he says that to study anatomy by observation does not constitute a forbidden "benefit" derived at the expense of the dead, and that any intrinsically prohibited act performed for study purposes was exempt from the original prohibition; that it was no disgrace to the dead when the welfare of the living was at stake; that a ban on anatomical studies would close the door to medical science, and that hospitals everywhere were full of patients actually awaiting the findings of anatomical research so that, with the speed of modern communications, the objections of Rabbi Landau no longer applied.

The pendulum swings from one extreme to another, and Rabbi Yekuthiel Greenwald in his recognized volume *Kol Bo*, expresses strong objections both to autopsies and to anatomical experiments. He insists that, since after an autopsy burial would be performed piecemeal, this is an extreme form of degradation of the dead. He brings up the problem of medical schools entrance by suggesting that a parent who wants his son to attend medical school ought himself to will his body for dissection. He repeats many of the traditionally known objections to autopsy; a) disgrace to the dead, and b) the prohibition of deriving benefit from the dead.

Any possible benefit, suggests Rabbi Greenwald, is, at best, superficial. Medicine, he says, is not certain; many thousands have been examined by autopsy and cures have not yet been found. Furthermore, the temperaments of people are different, and the mere fact that a sought-for discovery may be made, does not necessarily prove that it will benefit another person. Indeed, precisely because of the differences in the bodies of particular individuals, the reverse might be true. Rabbi Greenwald touches upon another and newer issue by recalling a Talmudic statement that:

> . . . the flesh of the dead does not feel the scalpel. But that is not so, for did not Rabbi Isaac say, "Worms are as painful to the dead as a needle in the flesh of the living, for it is said, 'But his flesh upon him has pain, and his soul within him mourns:' "[29] Say: The dead flesh in a living person does not feel the scalpel.[30]

Rabbi Greenwald continues: "But, in truth, the flesh of the dead does feel. If so, certainly it is prohibited to cut and cause pain on the doubtful assumption that good for others may be produced by such examination." In addition, he goes back to an earlier objection, that of the obligation to save life, reiterating that the duty rests only with the living, not the dead. So, the dead are not to be used for such a purpose. On the other hand, if a man agrees to an autopsy before his death, or even if he makes an agreement to sell his body, it is allowed. An interesting exception to his strict interpretation involves the danger of hereditary disease.[31] Where such a disease can be transmitted to survivors and doctors feel that an autopsy might afford insight into a cure for the children, it is permitted, provided that the body is buried with dignity. The exception applies even if the children or survivors have not contracted the disease, and there is only a possibility that they may. Especially is this true, he notes, if the father agreed, during his lifetime, to the examination.[32]

Rabbi Yitzhak Arieli, a member of the Israeli Ministry of Health and member of Commission on Autopsy, speaking at the Sixth Annual Congress on Oral Law in Jerusalem, in 1963, theoretically would allow autopsy "even to patients who are not locally at hand, but who, through modern means of communication may benefit from the finding of autopsies elsewhere, provided that the ailment is widespread enough to warrant the assumption that another sufferer *at the same time* may be cured from these findings. In fact, however, since the liklihood of a cure being discovered as a result of any particular autopsy is very remote indeed, one is not justified in setting aside the ban on disfiguring the dead." Rabbi Arieli also rejects autopsies for the purpose of cause of death, since he regards the link between such operations and the saving of life as too remote. He does allow an exception to be made in the case where someone has given his consent during his lifetime. A review article summarizes Rabbi Arieli's views.[33]

The well-known Orthodox leader, Rabbi Moshe Feinstein, recognized for his leniency in various areas of Jewish law, permits a post-mortem examination which involves the taking of "some fluid to investigate the cause of death or to remove blood from the corpse. Therefore, the procedure of inserting an electric needle into the corpse, thereby making it possible to know whatever sickness there is," is permitted.

Rabbi Joseph Soloveitchik of Boston is quoted by Professor Kalman Mann, Director General of the Hadassah Medical Organization as saying:

> According to Halakhah, autopsies may be performed if medicine is likely to be advanced thereby and if they lead to the saving of life. In our day, the question of whether the life to be saved is that of a person in the same place, has not Halakhic significance, since all discoveries in medical science become known immediately in all parts of the world.[34]

In a lengthy responsum entitled 'Post Mortem Examination for Medical Purposes in Jewish Law.' Rabbi David M. Shohet writes, condensing various positions:

> The question as to whether Jewish law permits the opening and examining of a deceased body in order to ascertain the cause of death did not so far authoritatively engage the attention of Jewish scholarship. In the Bible, the Talmud, and in the vast post-rabbinic literature we almost find no discussion having a direct and practical bearing on the subject . . .
>
> There is no direct biblical or rabbinic authority that prohibits post-mortem examination . . . it is clear that dissection is not only not contrary to Jewish law, but that the teachers of the law themselves practiced autopsies and post-mortem examination. How could they otherwise have acquired that knowledge of the human structure, which, as we have seen, they so frequently display and which in so many essentials agree with the findings of modern medical science . . . The question of mutilation or indignity cannot enter when medical examinations are made for purposes of ascertaining the causes of death whereby life and health among the living is concerned. The dead are thus rendering a service to mankind . . . We thus see that the intent of the law is to prevent abuse by making use of the lifeless remains of a human being for mean and private purposes . . .

There is no basis in the Bible for the law prohibiting the use of a
dead body. The rabbis infer it in a very indirect and cir-
cumlocutory manner . . . There can be no doubt that such an indirect inference is hardly strong enough to stand in the way of
saving the life of a person . . .[35]

## THE ORTHODOX POSITION[36]

After all the necessary structures have been made, such as the
avoidance of undue pressure upon the family to gain consent and
the limitation of the autopsy to the absolute minimum required, the
following may be considered the Orthodox position on autopsy,
bearing in mind that there are widely varying views.

All Jewish religious authorities agree that any sanction of dissection can be contemplated solely on the grounds of its immediate, if
only potential, contribution to the saving of life; that the number
and extent of autopsies must be limited to an irreducible
minimum, that a sense of reverence must be preserved during and
after the operation; and that all the remains must be buried as
soon as possible with due respect. Prior consent for an autopsy
should also be obtained from the subject during his lifetime or his
family. Ideally all operators should themselves be God-fearing or
fully conscious of the dignity with which every human body is en-
dowed as a creation "in the image of God."[37]

The same authority, addressing the Sixth Annual Congress on
Oral Law in Jerusalem, 1963, stated the position in detail as follows:

The consensus of rabbinic opinion today will permit autopsies
only on the basis of the famous responsum of the *Noda Be-
Yehudah* (Rabbi Landau, above), viz., if they may be expected to
help directly in saving the lives of other patients *at hand* . . . But in
applying this ruling, the following new circumstances must be
taken into account:[38a]

1. With the speed of present-day communications such patients
are in fact at hand all over the world, and the findings of an
autopsy in one place may aid a sufferer in another immediately.

2. Without autopsies some of the worst scourges still afflicting
mankind cannot be conquered. Indeed, any autopsy nowadays,
when medical science is so advanced, is more likely to help in the
saving of life than the case permitted by the *Noda Be-Yehudah*

under the relatively primitive conditions of two centuries ago.

3. Autopsies now bear a relationship to the saving of life not only for finding new cures for obscure diseases, but also in testing the effects and safety of new medications and in demonstrating errors of diagnosis and treatment.

4. On the other hand, the very frequency of autopsies increases the danger that they will become a sheer routine, without any regard for their urgency, and without proper safeguards for the respect due to the dead.

5. With some patients refusing to be admitted to hospitals for fear of autopsies, the consideration of the saving of life now also operates in reverse.

The author (Rabbi Immanuel Jakobovits) concluded with these practical proposals:

1. While no general sanction can be given for the indiscriminate surrender of all bodies to post-mortem examinations, the area of the sanction should be broadened to include tests on new drugs and cases of reasonable suspicion that the diagnosis was mistaken; for autopsies under such conditions, too, may directly result in the saving of life.

2. In the place of the existing Israeli law requiring the signature of three physicians to authorize an autopsy, each hospital should establish a special board consisting of two (preferably religious) doctors and one rabbi who should unanimously approve of every post-mortem operation.

3. Any permission for an autopsy is to be given only on condition that operation is reduced to a minimum, carried out with the greatest dispatch, in the presence of a rabbi or religious supervisor if requested by the family, and performed with the utmost reverence and with the assurance that all parts of the body are returned for burial.

4. Just as it is the duty of rabbis to urge relatives not to consent to an autopsy where the law does not justify it, they are religiously obliged to ensure that permission is granted in cases where human lives may thereby be saved, in the same way as the violation of the

Sabbath laws in the case of danger of life is not merely optional but mandatory.

5. But relatives must be warned that the precept to bury their dead has not been carried out unless all parts of the body have been interred, and that the laws of mourning, cannot be observed until then. If they are of priestly descent, they should also be advised that they must not defile themselves for bodies subjected to autopsies.

The position of Orthodox Judaism has remained constant. In 1975, in Medical Ethics, published by the Federation of Jewish Philanthropies of New York, Rabbi Moses Tendler, notes:

> . . . an autopsy is condoned in Jewish law when it is needed to obtain information that is life-saving. When alive, a Jew has the obligation to do all he can to save his fellow man from certain death. The submission to autopsy, when it can bring immediate benefit, is assumed to be with the deceased's acquiescence if his immediate relatives grant permission for such a procedure. In the absence of such permission, or in the presence of known objections of the patient to autopsy, his body remains inviolate, protected by all the rights and privileges due him when alive.
>
> The dominant consideration in permitting an autopsy is the immediacy of the constructive application of the findings. This "here and now" principle, once limited to the medical needs of a local community, is now extended through the excellence of communication and scientific reporting, to the whole medical world. Results of autopsies in New York can be available in London in a matter of minutes. However, autopsies that are not directed to the quest for an answer to a specific problem with immediate application, cannot receive rabbinic approval. The routine autopsy cannot be sanctioned although great benefit may accrue at some distant future time.
>
> Autopsy in Jewish law is permitted only to answer a specific question. The knowlege gained would then contribute to the immediate improvement of care of patients.[38b]

On February 16, 1978, Rabbi Moshe Feinstein, issued a *Psak* (Rabbinic Decree) on the new Plutonium 238-powered cardiac pacemaker, reflecting Halakhic dispensation for its use. One of the guide lines, under strict Nuclear Regulatory Commission procedures, because of radiation underground, requires morticians to retrieve the device and return it to the manufacturer.

Rabbi Moshe Sherer, of Agudath Israel of America, forwarded the following question:

"I asked Rabbi Wolpin, our editor, to convey to Reb Moshe Feinstein, Shlita, our concern about the regulation on a new Plutonium cardiac pacemaker made by the U.S. Nuclear Regulatory Commission, which requires the device to be retrieved from the body after death. We asked the Rosh Yeshiva to define for us the Halakhic dimensions of this requirement, in order to determine whether Agudath Israel has to take action with the government if this situation violates our autopsy laws. The patient who receives this nuclear pacemaker must always have on his body information informing others of the nature or the device, such as a medallion or bracelet . . ."

Rabbi Feinstein replied in Hebrew. Following is the official translation:

"In regard to his question about the new pacemaker which is sold on the condition that it be returned after the death of the recipient (i.e. removed from his body after death), it is my opinion that initially one should not put such a pacemaker in his body. However, if the pacemaker was already inserted, or the doctors recommed that this particular pacemaker be used, it is permissible to use it even though there is a slight defilement of the body. Also in regard to the identification tags which must be worn by one who has this pacemaker installed, if one can walk outside without it, it is preferable. However, if it is forbidden for him to go without it, he should make an ornament of it, just as it is permissible to make an ornament of a key in order to go with it on Shabbos. If a bracelet specifically is necesary, the way many sick people wear, it is permissible since it is considered their personal ornament."[38c]

## THE CONSERVATIVE POSITION

Conservative Judaism's position on autopsy may be gleaned from the statment of the Committee on Jewish Law of the Rabbinical Assembly:

> The Committee is inclined to permit autopsy when medical science looks for some information that may help other human beings and reasonably expects to find all or part of that information by means of that autopsy; but is inclined to prohibit autopsy for general advancement of medical science. The Committee is sympathetic to

scientific research, but combats the idea that a human corpse is a laboratory guinea pig . . . The performance of an autopsy as a general routine in order to increase the prestige of the hospital concerned is incompatible with Jewish law. But wherever it would aid in establishing a doubtful diagnosis or help to discover a cure for a baffling disease, it should permitted.

In addition, a leading Conservative rabbi, Isaac Klein, in a scholarly and detailed responsum on the subject, writes:

> There is a whole literature around this question because it involves a number of problems posed by the developments in the medical field. It involves the use of bodies for dissection in medical schools. It involves the transplanting of tissue from a deceased into a living body, as well as post-mortem examinations performed to study a disease with the purpose of furthering medical knowledge, i.e., to ascertain the exact manifestations of the disease from which the deceased died with a view to more efficient treatment of other causes of the same disease; or for judicial purposes, i.e., when there is suspicion of crime, to ascertain whether the condition of the body, particularly internal organs, corroborate the suspicion.[39]

Rabbi Klein puts the development of the traditional views in a historical perspective. He notes the basic positions of Rabbis Landau and Schreiber as well as later sages, and reaches the conclusion:

> We can permit all (these) uses of the bodies of the deceased where there is an obvious help to other people and where the general public considers such uses as Pikuah Nefesh, saving of life. If medical science claims that these may save lives, then we should add that in such cases it is not only permitted but is actually a Mitzvah, duty. There should always be, however, a respectful attitude to the human body, and burial should be piously performed wherever feasible.

## THE REFORM POSITION

In 1925, Professor Jacob Z. Lauterbach, issued a responsum on the autopsy question. In it he discusses the legal prohibitions put forward by Rabbinic sages, evaluates Talmudic descriptions of anatomical dissections, and concludes:

104

To my knowledge no law or regulation expressly forbidding the practice of autopsy can be found in the Bible or the Talmud or the Shulhan Aruch (Code of Jewish Law). It may safely be stated that in case the autopsy would not unduly delay the funeral, one could not find the least support for any objection to it in these authoritative sources of Jewish law. In case the autopsy would unduly delay the burial, one might object to it on the ground that the ancient Jewish law recommended burial on the same day in which the death occurred . . . But the practice of autopsy as such one cannot find any express objection to in the Talmud. On the contrary, one could cite the Talmud in support of the practice, since it is evident from Talmudic reports that some of the Rabbis of the Talmud, no doubt prompted by their interest in the science of medicine, acutally performed an autopsy . . .

Dr. Lauterbach recalling the stricter views of Rabbis Landau and Schreiber, states:

Their reasons for permitting the autopsy are very cogent. Since by the autopsy the physicians may learn to understand better the nature of the disease and thus be enabled to save the life of the other person afflicted with it, it is a case of *Pikuah Nefesh*, saving of life. And according to the Talmudic Rabbinic law, all the laws of the Torah, except those against idolatry, incest, and murder, may and should be violated if necessary for the saving of a human life. And according to the Talmudic-rabbis, then, even if there could be found an express law in the Torah prohibiting the dissecting of a human body it would have to be ignored in favor of autopsy which might lead to the saving of human life. Thus far we can fully agree with these two great Rabbinical authorities. But with all due respect to them, we cannot see any reason for limiting, as they do, the permission for autopsy only to cases where there is then and there another person suffering from the same disease who might immediately be benefited by the findings of the physicians.[40]

Dr. Solomon Freehof, another leading scholar of the Reform movement, has written:

Reform Judaism has no religious objection to autopsy. Whether an autopsy is to be performed or not is left to the decision of the family.

In a responsum, Dr. Freehof wrote:

> . . . In general, Jewish law prohibits delay in the burial of a body and also mutilating a body. On either one of these two grounds it is possible to declare autopsy and dissection forbidden by Jewish law. However, as is well known, the Talmud has such knowledge of anatomy as could have been obtained only from the dissection of bodies . . .

> The two great Orthodox authorities, Ezekiel Landau and Moses Sofer, permit autopsy when there is in the same locality a person suffering from the same disease; in other words, when the autopsy would permit the physician to save a life . . . Dr. Lauterbach in his complete responsum on the matter quite properly argues that nowadays the discoveries made by one physician are broadcast all over the world and may result in the saving of innumerable lives. Therefore, there is no need to insist, as Ezekiel Landau and Moses Sofer insisted, that, there should be present an invalid with exactly the same disease whose life depends upon this particular autopsy . . .

Dr. Freehof concludes:

> General Reform practice is to base the question of autopsy upon the desire of the family. If the family is willing , there is no objection to it.[41]

In 1964, the Committee on Judaism and Medicine of the Central Conference of America Rabbis reaffirmed its position on autopsy.[42]

## NOTES

1. See Aryeh Newman, 'The Post Mortem Impasse in Israel,' *Jewish Life*, New York, Sept.-Oct. 1966, p. 28. See also 'The Facts About Autopsies in Israel'. Ruth Seligman, *Hadassah Magazine*, New York, April 1972, p. 7.

1a. See, Encyclopedia Judaica, Yearbook 1974, article on Autopsies and Dissection, Jerusalem 1974, p. 932. See also, The Second Jewish Catalogue, Sharon Strassfield and Michael Strassfield, Editors, Jewish Publication Society, Philadelphia, 1976, p. 135.

1b. Deut. 21:22-23.

2. Sanhedrin 47a.

3. Sanhedrin 45b, 46a.

4. Lev. 18:5.

5. Pesahim 25b.

6. Deut. 22:1-2.

7. Baba Kamma 81a, Sanhedrin 71b.

8. Num. 10:11.

9. Gen. 3:19.

10. Kethuvoth 19a.

11. Sanhedrin 74a.

12. Mishnah Yoma, VIII:6.

13. Yoma 84b.

14. Niddah 30b.

15. Bekhoroth 45a.

16. Niddah 24b.

17. Mishnah Oholoth 1:8.

18. Hullin 11b.

19. Baba Bathra 154a.

20. Yoreh De'ah 349:1, 167:11.

21. Yoreh De'ah 349:3.

22. Quoted by Rabbi Isaac Klein, *Responsa*, "Should Autopsy be Permitted?"
See, Isaac Klein, Autopsy, in *Responsa and Halakhic Studies*, Ktav, New York,
1975, p. 34.

23. Baba Kamma 60b.

24. Adler, *Anglo-Jewish Memories*, London, 1909, p. 137.

25. Sanhedrin 47a.

26. Ibid.

27. Kalman Mann, Director General, Hadassah Medical Hospital in the
*Jerusalem Post*, March 27, 1967.

28. Quoted by Rabbi Isaac Klein. Note 22.

29. Job 14:22.

30. Shabbath 13a.

31. See, *Sefer Hayovel* (Jubilee Volume) HaPardes, New York, 1951; Rabbi
Yitzhak Levin (Minneapolis, Minnesota), *Autopsy*.

32. See, 'Autopsies With Consent of the Deceased,' *Tradition*, Vol. 12, No. 3-
4, R.C.A. New York, p. 121, in which Rabbi Greenwald's view is expanded on.

33. Book Review, *Conservative Judaism*, Rabbinical Assembly, New York,
1965, Vol. 19, Number 4.

34. *Jerusalem Post Weekly*, Jerusalem, March 27, 1967.

35. *Conservative Judaism*, Vol. 4, No. 3, May, 1948.

36. The positions here assume family consent except as required by legal
authority.

37. Immanuel Jakobovits, *Jewish Medical Ethics*, Bloch Publishing Company,
New York, 1959. See also, 'The Dissection of the Dead in Jewish Law,' *Tradition*,
Rabbinical Council of America, New York, Vol. 1, No. 1, Fall, 1958, pp. 77-103.

38a. See also *Petahim*, Jerusalem, Israel, 1969, where Rabbi Jakobovits' summary is quoted at a public discussion on Religion, Medicine, and Research, Tel
Aviv, July 31, 1969.

38b. Medical Ethics, Rabbi Moses D. Tendler, Editor, Federation of Jewish Philanthropies of New York, 1975, p. 59. See also, Contemporary Halakhic Problems, Rabbi J. David Bleich, Ktav-Yeshiva University, New York, 1977, p. 125.

38c. Agudath Israel of America, Flatbush Coordinating Committee, Nissan 5738, New York, p. 1-7.

39. Isaac Klein, *What is the Attitude of Jewish Law to Autopsy?* Proceedings of Rabbinical Assembly.

40. C.C.A.R. Yearbook Vol. 35, New York 1925, p. 130.

41. Solomon Freehof, Reform Jewish Practice, Hebrew Union College Press, Cincinnati, 1944, p. 113. See also Freehof, Solomon, Modern Reform Responsa, HUC Press, 1971, p. 278.

42. *Yearbook*, C.C.A.R., Vol. LXXIV, Atlantic City, New Jersey, 1964.

# BIRTH CONTROL

Family planning and planned parenthoood may sound like contemporary issues, whereas in fact, from the beginning of recorded history, religious law has been dealing with the problems arising from contraception.

For millennia the issues discussed here remained the preserves of academies of learning and elite groups. The fact that, in the Eisenhower Administration, the Draper Commission, reexamined the foreign aid policies of the United States, and recommended that our government aid the peoples of Africa and Asia to control their population problem, and also the rise of a more permissive and open society, have brought the entire subject onto the market palce. The question of contraceptives and "The Pill" has quickened discussion and forced sociological and religious confrontation.

The Roman Catholic Bishops of the United States, maintaining unequivocal opposition to the use of birth control other than the rhythm or safe method, a position underscored by Pope Paul's Encyclical, "Of Human Life," expressed vigorous dissent to the Draper Commission's proposals; and President Eisenhower, submitting to pressure, stated that population control was a strictly religious, and not a political matter.

The United States, he stressed, did not, and would not use funds for such purposes. Religious groups in America have rushed forward to present their own positions, drawing upon their own religious sources to do so.

An article in the London *Jewish Chronicle* recently began with the words: "If you are a member of a religious faith, your decision about whether to use contraceptives will probably involve your spiritual leader as well as your doctor."[1]

Which leads us to the question as to what Judaism has to say about birth control.[2] Is there a difference whether the contraceptive is used by the man or the woman? May contraceptives be used rather in some circumstances than in others? Is the diaphragm a better or worse method than "The Pill"? Are the major religious denominations in Judaism in agreement on this issue? If there are differences, in what do they consist?

Basic to an understanding of the subject is the fact that Jewish law regards the procreation of children as a cardinal duty any interference with which constitues a violation of man's primary responsibility.

## Biblical Sources

The duty to have children is clearly defined in the Bible:

> And God blessed them; and said to them, Be fruitful and multiply, and replenish the earth . . .'[3]

The commentary on this simple injunction, made up of only two words in Hebrew "Peru u-r'voo," "be fruitful and multiply," states that "this is the first precept given to man." The duty of rearing a family figures in the rabbinic codes as the first of the 613 mitzvoth recorded in the Bible. This obligation, therefore, has an overwhelmingly strong religious basis, and all else stems from this premise.

What "duty" means is elaborated in the Mishnah as follows:

> A man shall not abstain from the performance of the duty of the propagation of the race, unless he already has children (as to the number). Beth Shammai ruled: two males, and Beth Hillel ruled: male and female, for it is stated in Scripture, "male and female created He them."[4]

The view of the School of Hillel is generally regarded as the official position in Jewish tradition. Thus, the duty of being fruitful is legally fulfilled, technically speaking, when one has had a son and a daughter. This does not mean that one's *moral* obligation to go on having children has come to an end. It is the legal aspect we are presenting here. Many Talmudic rabbis give support to the moral aspect of the duty by such striking dicta as: "he who does not engage in propagation of the race is as though he sheds blood," or, behaves "as though he has diminished the Divine Image."[5] From the technical point of view, however, a man has fulfilled his religious obligation when he has fathered a son and a daughter, thus reproducing himself and his wife.

## Contraception in the Bible

The only biblical reference to contraception is found in the account of Judah and his sons.[6] Judah, fourth son of Jacob, took a wife, Tamar, for Er, his first-born son. The Bible notes:

> And Er, Judah's first-born, was wicked in the sight of the Lord; and the Lord slew him.

Judah then instructed his second son, Onan, to take Tamar as his wife, on the basis of the traditional practice of the levirate, the law which says that where a brother dies without children, his brother must marry his widow in order to perpetuate the family name.

The account proceeds:

> But Onan, knowing that the seed would not count as his, let it go to waste (spilled it on the ground) whenever he joined with his brother's wife, so as not to provide offspring for his brother. What he did was displeasing to the Lord and He slew him also.

From the passage it seems that Onan practiced contraception by the means of withdrawal, or coitus interruptus. Some commentators deduce from the word *also* that Onan was slain for the same crime as that committed by his brother who also had practiced that form of contraception. The commentator Rashi notes that the word *also* places both brothers in the same category of sin. The reason for Er's action, says Rashi, was that Er wanted to prevent a pregnancy which might injure her beauty.[7]

The term "Onanism" derives from this account, meaning the prevention of procreation by withdrawal, or coitus interruptus.

The Midrash's version of the story tells us that Er's wickedness consisted in the fact that "he ploughed on roofs . . . a delicate expression for unnatural intercourse, so that his wife should not conceive."[8]

In addition, expatiating on the phrase "he spilled," the Midrash comments, "He cohabited naturally but scattered it without. Therefore, He slew him also."[9]

To continue the thesis, another Biblical passage in an entirely different context, also shows opposition to onanism. Describing the events which led up to the flood, the Bible records:

> And it came to pass when men rebelled . . . And began to multiply on the face of the earth . . .[10]

The commentator says:

> This teaches that they spilled their semen upon the trees and stones, and because they were steeped in lust, the Holy One, blessed be He, gave them many women . . .[11]

The Universal Jewish Encyclopedia, on the subject of Birth Control, explains:

> Simlarly, according to the rabbis, the destruction of the generation of Noah, was to a large extent in punishment for their practices which artificially prevented conception.[12]

Opposition to birth control is, therefore, already indicated in the Bible itself.

## Talmudic Basis

The first Biblical commandment, "be fruitful and multiply," has been interpreted by the rabbis to apply primarily to the man, and only indirectly to the woman. Hence, according to the strict principle of the law, a man may not practice contraception because, whatever the means, no artificial barrier is permitted. All Jewish authorities accept this principle.

The only reason offered for the discrimination implicit in this first commandment has been put forward by Rabbi Immanuel Jakobovits. He suggests that, since it is the woman, after all, who is the "mother of all life," she has been implanted with the unalterable instinct of motherhood and there is therefore no "need to reinforce her natural impulses by divine legislation."[13]

Whether a woman is permitted to use contraceptives and under what circumstances is touched upon only once in the Talmud, and within a legal context. All authorities begin from the text:[14]

Rabbi Bebai recited before Rabbi Nahman: Three (categories of) women *may* use an absorbent (hackled wool or flax) in their marital intercourse (to prevent conception); a minor, a pregnant woman and a nursing woman. The minor (may use an absorbent) because (otherwise) she might (literally, perhaps) become pregnant, and as a result (perhaps) might die. A pregnant woman, (may use an absorbent), because (otherwise), she might (perhaps) cause her fetus to degenerate into a *sandel* (lit., a flat fish-shaped abortion due to superfetation). A nursing woman (may use an absorbent) because (otherwise) she might have to wean her child prematurely (owing to her second conception) and this would result in his death. And what is the age of such a minor (who is capable of conception but exposed thereby to the danger of death)? From the age of eleven years and one day until the age of twelve years and one day. One who is under (when no conception is possible), or over this age (when pregnancy involves no fatal consequences) must carry on her marital intercourse in the ususal manner. This is the opinion of Rabbi Meir. The Sages, however, say, "The one as well as the other carries on her marital intercourse in the usual manner, and mercy will be vouchsafed from heaven (to save her from danger), for it is said in Scriptures, *The Lord preserves the simple.*"[15] (Meaning: those who are unable to protect themselves.)

Whether the reasons promoted by this text for the use of con-.raception are medically sound is not germane to this chapter. One modern authority, commenting on this Talmudic passage, has written:

In biblical times, a girl reached majority when she became twelve years and one day old and she was free to marry. A daughter under twelve could legally be given in marriage by her father, which was not uncommon. Then she was permitted to use a contraceptive tampon until she reached her majority at twelve years and one day.

*Sandal* is a perfect description term for fetus papyraceous, or a fetus as thin as papyrus paper, for in Hebrew the word sandal means flat fish (like a flounder),which such a generating embryo resembles. No doubt, it was observed in Talmudic times that in occasional twin pregnancies, a normal infant had a sandal as a co-twin.

113

Hebrew medical scholars concluded that a sandal was caused by conception occurring in the midst of an already existing preganany (superfetation), a phenomenon which modern medical opinion generally rejects. Today, we know that in fetus papyraceous both twins are conceived during the same insemination; as one continues to develop, the other dies at some time during the first several months, and the expanding sac of the developing twin compresses the gelatinous remains of its dead co-twin.

As to the third instance cited in the Talmud, I am uncertain whether pregnancy during lactation suppresses milk production; it is more likely that the hormonal influence which promotes lactation is already waning sufficiently to release its inhibitory influence on ovulation. Therefore, from present medical knowledge, contraception would be useless in preventing a *sandal* and probably of little value first, in promoting the safety of early adolescent by eliminating the increased risk of occasional very immature motherhood; and second, by practicing contraception throughout lactation, the interval was probably somewhat prolonged between one pregnancy and the next.[16]

There is a basic disagreement among legislators underlying the question of whether women are allowed to use contraceptives. The difference of opinion is about the meaning of the term "may." When it says that women in the three categories mentioned *may* use absorbents, does it mean that they have the *choice*, or is there a nuance of *obligation*?

Rashi holds that the decision is up to the woman. She *may*, if she desires. Rabenu Tam, Jacob ben Meir, holds that these three *must*, that they are required to use tampons.

In addition, there is the question as to whether the tampon may be inserted before, and used during intercourse, or whether it can only be used *after* cohabitation, to eliminate as much of the semen as possible so as to prevent conception.

Women are permitted to use contraceptives only for medical reasons, where there is danger to the life and health of the woman concerned.

This explains why nearly all the relevant responsa raise the question of whether women are allowed to use contraceptives. The woman whose life is certified to be in grave danger if she became pregnant employ contraceptives, and, if so, what method should she use?[17]

114

It should also be understood that the Talmud permitted special methods of contraception to be used where the health of the child was involved, or where the children already born of a marriage are physically or mentally defective and there is danger that further births may bring similar defectives into the world.

### Responsa Literature — Applying the Law

From Talmudic times until the era of responsa literature, surprisingly little was codified into law. The past two centuries have seen a spate of responsa on this issue. The pronouncements that have been forthcoming, ranging from liberal to conservative, are based on the presentations of the individual cases offered for adjudication.

One liberal position goes back to Rabbi Solomon Luria, recognized authority of the sixteenth century: a woman *may* use a tampon *before* intercourse if there is danger to her health or child if pregnancy occurs. Many authorities agree. A more stringent position is held by Rabbi Akiva Eger (1761-1837). He holds that no impediment may be used *during* intercourse, no matter the danger or fear. Such a barrier interferes with the normal conjugal relationship. *After* intercourse, however, where there is danger to the life of either mother or child, a tampon may be used.

Although authorities may differ, there are two principles on which all agree. First, the male is never allowed to use contraceptives because the semen which is wasted is life-giving. Hence, the condom method and Onanism, or coitus interruptus, is forbidden by Jewish law. Second, women may use contraceptives under certain circumstances, each case standing on its own merits, and each requiring the decision of a competent rabbi, according to the Orthodox position.[18]

### Contraceptive Methods and Their Uses

Contraceptives for use by women have been the subject of many discussions.

The *diaphragm method* is considered by some as resulting in the "casting of the seed on wood and stones," a form of onanism, and hence forbidden. "Even if life-threatening medical consideration demands contraception," according to Moses D. Tendler, the view of Rabbi Akiva Eger forbidding the use of the diaphragm remains firm. Other authorities, in serious medical cases, permit the use of the method.

In the periodical *Tradition*, Professor Tendler responds to a questioner regarding the use of the diaphragm, citing 19 references to authorities who permit use of the diaphragm only in cases of grave danger.[18a] He also quotes his father-in-law, Moshe Feinstein, a leading halakhic expert, on the question as to whether the tampon and diaphragm can be placed in the same category. Halakhically, "the rubber that a woman places in her uterus" clearly has the Halakhic status of "mokh," the tampon mentioned in the original Talmudic text on contraception.

The *Rhythm* method, or the "Safe" period, described by the Ogion-Knaus calculation made by Professor Ogino in Japan, in 1924, and by Knaus in Austria, in 1929, shows "that the fertility of a normal woman varies in regular cycles, and that there is a monthly period, lasting about seven days, during which conception is not likely or altogether impossible."[18b] This type of calculation was anticipated by Talmudic knowledge two thousand years ago. Here only the question of abstinence from normal conjugal relations arises. Rabbi Jakobovits notes that:

> The question of the "safe period" has not received unfavorable treatment in any of our modern responsa, and it would not seem wrong to advise young people to seek medical guidance along these lines in circumstances which morally and religiously justify such negative precautions.[19]

He also explains in his notes, that a rabbi of the last century, "advises women whose pregnancy may endanger them to restrict intercourse to the infertile period. They may also use a tampon to ensure their safety, since conception at that time is, in any case, unlikely."[20]

A Talmudic scholar at the Rabbi Isaac Elchanan Theological Seminary writes:

> . . . the rhythm method wherein conception is avoided by abstaining from sexual intercourse for a calculated "fertile period" during which fertilization may occur, is not construed as per se contrary to Halakha. Assuming that the couple have fulfilled the Torah commandment of "be fruitful and multiply," the minimal fulfillment being by way of a son and daughter, they may, by mutual consent, refrain from further sexual relations. They may also take such measures as are not forbidden by the Torah to prevent conception.[21]

Dr. Alan Guttmacher writes:

> The rhythm technique is used by some Orthodox Jewish women. Dr. Sobrero, Director of the Sanger Bureau in New York City, informs me that the Bureau has quite a large rhythm clinic, and its clientele is all Jewish; no Roman Catholic women attend. The constant recourse to the rhythm method is not approved by many rabbinical authorities because it creates an obstacle to normal sex life between husband and wife.[22]

An additional problem has arisen in connection with Intra-Uterine Devices:

> The use of I.U.D., intra-uterine contraceptive devices, such as the Grafenberg rings of the 1920's or their modern counterparts designed by Margulies and others, presents unique problems to Halakhic authorities. If the evidence we now have proves accurate, contraception is accomplished by increasing uterine or tubal contractions. The resulting expulsion of the fertilized ovum is actually an early abortion. Abortions prior to 40 days of conception are halakhically differentiated from true abortion unless there be adequate justification based on medical or other equally valid grounds. The recently proposed post-coital contraceptive pills must be equated with the I.U.D., since their effectiveness is a result of abortivicant action.[23]

In his article Dr. Guttmacher states:

> The new intra-uterine devices are also under scrutiny by modern Orthodox Jewry. An Orthodox hospital in Jerusalem is using I.U.D. as the preferred method of contraception in indicated cases. They believe that, among all methods, it interferes least with the physiology of the coital act, since undamaged spermatozoa reach the tube, and the ovulatory-menstrual process is unaffected. However, the I.U.D. is too recent for Orthodox Jewry to have developed a broad consensus concerning its use.[24]

An additional problem related to I.U.D. is connected with the Orthodox law of *niddah*, a term appied in Biblical and Rabbinical literature to a menstruating woman, who, in Jewish law, is subject to certain restrictions during her period and for a number of days afterwards. The use of the I.U.D. may, it is held, provoke spotting which, in turn, may induce the state of *niddah* and bring into play the many restrictions on conjugal relations.[24a] While the latest version of I.U.D. may have been perfected to avoid or lessen this possibility, Orthodox law holds that "no observant Jew can consider their use except under the constant supervision of a halakhic authority."[25]

The use of chemical spermicidals which repress ovulation, offers, from the traditional point of view, a lesser violation. The relationship itself is not affected nor is an artifical barrier imposed. Jewish law does not, therefore condemn this method:

> The use of chemical spermicidals or the yet experimental induction of immunological infertility, or the use of injected high dosage progeterones which appear to inhibit ovulation with the problem of intermenstrual spotting, offer the best possibilities for halakhically acceptable contraception for the family that must use artificial contraceptive techniques.[26]

The development of the Pill or oral contraceptives, has brought about a new challenge to rabbinic scholarship. Authorities have not completed studies nor issued specific decisions. It is clear, however, that its availability has opened the way for a "new appraisal of birth control in the light of Jewish Law."

There are fewer objections to the employment of oral contraceptives than to any other method.

Some physicians have indicated that the pill "may cause breakthrough-bleeding perhaps half way through the safe period. This may be just inconvenient to any couple, but to Orthodox couples, it becomes useless."[27]

Rabbi Moshe Feinstein urges extreme caution in the use of the pill because it disturbs menstruation and therefore might introduce complications in the observance of the laws of niddah.[28]

Authorities are quick to point out that oral contraceptives were not unknown to the rabbis of the Talmud. The availability of a potion called in Hebrew *kos shel ikkarin* (cup of roots) which produced temporary sterility, or, with other dosages, fertility, is referred to in the Talmud in the following text:

> A man is not permitted to drink a cup of roots to render himself sterile, but a woman may drink such a potion so that she will not bear children.[29]

> A woman is permitted to drink the cup of *ikkarin* in order to render her incapable of bearing children. It is not permitted to administer such a potion to a man, but he who does is not culpable.[30]

> A woman may sterilize herself to avoid excruciating pain in childbirth as did the wife of a prominent rabbi, Rabbi Hiyya, who drank a cup of sterilization.[31]

> All women may drink such a cup of sterilization.[32]

The reasons offered are clear. For the man, no contraceptive device is permissible. For the woman, there is no direct impairment of the productive organs, nor is the physical relationship affected nor is a physical barrier utilized.

Dr. Alan Guttmacher writes:

> In our day of oral contraception, it is interesting to note that contraceptive 'root potions' are mentioned several times in the Talmud. The cup of roots described by Rabbi Johanan ben Napha, was a mixture of Alexandrian gum, liquid alum, and garden crocus. It was primarily prescribed as a cure for jaundice, but it was noted that two-thirds of a cup mixed with beer will sterilize permanently.[33]

Another statement:

> There are fewer objections to the employment of oral contraceptives, frequently referred to in rabbinic literature since the time of the Talmud, nearly 2,000 years ago, as a 'cup of sterility,' or a 'potion of roots.' Interestingly enough, this drink to prevent conception, known to the ancient rabbis, could also be used to induce greater fertility, a remarkable anticipation of the present-day hormone preparation, which can likewise serve both to promote and to suppress ovulation. Jewish law prefers this means to achieve temporary, or even permanent, sterility, to surgical or other contraceptive procedures, on the grounds that it does not directly impair the reproductive organs or constitute a physical impediment to the generative act.[34]

The Talmud tells us that Judith, the wife of R. Hiyya, having suffered agonizing pains in childbirth, appeared before her husband in disguise after her recovery and asked whether women were commanded to propagate the race. "No," he replied. Relying on this decision, she drank a sterilizing potion.[35] As late as 1949, Rabbi Dr. J. Horovitz "satisfied himself by obtaining medical evidence from qualified physicians that such a drink was 'no longer known in our time' and that it had 'surely been forgotten in the course of time.' "

The cup of roots has been referred to repeatedly over the past centuries. Rabbi Isaac Unterman has written:

> Today we have no idea how this *kos shel ikkarin* worked, for there is no potion today which renders one sterile by drinking . . . But, very likely, even in those days, the *kos* achieved its effect through functional changes in the nervous system rather than by actual means.[37]

Little has been written by the Rabbis specifically on the Pill. What there is, has been described in a book by David Feldman.[38a] Rabbi Moshe Feinstein was one of the first to deal with the issue. He at once recognized it as an effective method and, aside from the spotting it causes in some women rendering them subject to the laws of Niddah, he noted prophetically, that it might cause dangerous side effects, in which case it would be prohibited because of the principle of "Hamira sakhanta meissura." The fact is that regulations concerning danger to life are more stringent than ritual prohibitions. Apart from this issue, he says, the Pill might well be permissible from a Halakhic point of view.

Rabbi Feldman notes a book from Israel which accepts use of the Pill and aside from the risk of spotting and hazards to health, cautions against its use only on the grounds of the ideal of fruitfulness. In addition, Rabbi Feldman quotes Rabbi Eliezer Waldenberg of the Jerusalem Court as saying: "If they (oral contraceptives) are indeed perfected so that they do no evil, this will be the best method of birth control. They merely prevent sperm and egg from meeting but involve no *hash-hatat zera* (waste of seed)..." nor do they cause active or permanent sterilization."[38b]

A recent article by the same author entitled "Judaism and the Pill" concludes:

> An oral contraceptive . . . is free of the twin liabilities of onanism and of diminution of the wife's gratification. The Pill and its analogue in the Talmud — the 'cup of roots' — was therefore permitted much more readily. While the Church would oppose the Pill on grounds that the primary purpose of the sex act was being

deliberately frustrated, the Rabbis could have no such objection. The sex act is allowed to follow its natural course, and, despite the deliberateness in depriving it of one of its functions, still retains its other co-equal function.

The Pill, then, assuming its safety from a medical point of view — is the most acceptable of applied contraceptive methods. That means that as a *method*, it is acceptable; its use for any specific sex act does not require weighty justifications. But its use in principle is based not on method but on motive and programme. It could certainly not be used to nullify 'be fruitful and multiply' entirely, except for reasons of health. The legal factors involved and their disposition in rabbinic literature, however, do suggest that the Pill could be used *consistent* with 'be fruitful and multiply' — which includes family planning[38c]

## THE VIEWS OF ORTHODOX JUDAISM

Generally, the Orthodox stand may be phrased as follows:

> Contraceptive devices may never be used by the male, and even the females may resort to them only on pressing medical grounds. Concerned to insure the minimum interference with the normal function of the male, Jewish law grades methods of prevention of conception in the following order of preference: oral contraception (provided they cause no unduly irregular bleeding or staining), chemical spermicides, and physical impediments (e.g., diaphragm). The first method is the least objectionable because it does not involve any operation on, or in, the reproductive organs at all. (The religious attitude to the uterine ring, lately again more widely used as an effective contraceptive device, remains to be elucidated, as its precise manner of operation has not yet been scientifically ascertained.)[39]

Dr. Joseph Hertz, former Chief Rabbi of England, has noted: "Contraceptives permitted to women are allowed in cases where considerations of health make such action necessary." Dr. Jacobovits, adds that this statement may be accepted, for practical purposes, "had its author added the proviso that the practice of contraception cannot be sanctioned by Jewish law, unless the conditions prevailing in each individual case have first been submitted for rabbinic judgement."[40] In addition, "birth control generally involves a grave religious offense. Such measures can be justified before our conscience only in cases of serious danger to health. In no case, however, can the individual allow personal considerations to determine the issue without seeking the objective halakhic advice of his rabbi."

A noted Orthodox scholar summarized the Orthodox view:

The Halakhic basis for a decision on the question of contraception is the Biblical story of Onan, son of Judah. Two factors are emphasized in this Biblical narrative: the method of preventing conception, and the intent of reason for wanting to prevent conception. In the biblical case cited, both the method and the intent were objectionable to God.

The development of this law is the Talmud and in later Responsa literature reveals the following trends:

a. Some contraceptive methods are, whatever the circumstances, totally forbidden. The withdrawal method as practiced by Onan, or the use of the equivalent contraceptive device by the male which prevents the implanting of the sperm is prohibited under the sanction of *vayerah b'eyne' Hashem asher assah vayimath gam otho* (What he did was displeasing to the Lord, and He took his life also.)[40a]

b. The use of a mechanical barrier by the woman (diaphragm method), too, is considered by the vast majority of Halakhic authorities to be forbidden under all circumstances, for here too the husband 'casts his seed on wood and stones.' Some of the greatest rabbis of the last generation have prohibited the use of a diaphragm device even if cogent medical reasons made the prevention of conception absolutely essential. Abstinence by mutual consent was the only solution they would offer. Other authorities of equal reputation have disagreed with the interpretation. The concept of intent inherent in the Biblical injunction has been given greater weight. Since natural cohabitation is not interfered with by the use of the diaphragm, *then when significant medical reasons are presented to a competent rabbinic authority, permission may be* granted for its use during the duration of the medical emergency.

A decidedly minority group of rabbinic scholars have refused to consider the diaphragm contraceptive method as Onanism. These rabbis felt that the letter of the law is not violated when the diaphragm method is used even in the absence of significant medical considerations as long as the reason for preventing conception is not of "evil intent."

c. The use of non-mechanical contraceptive devices such as chemical spermicidals or the still experimental hormonal repressors of ovulation is not in direct conflict with the letter of the law. Similarly the rhythm method wherein conception is avoided by abstaining from sexual intercourse for a calculated 'fertile period' during which fertilization may occur, is not construed as per se contrary to Halakhah. Assuming that the couple have fulfilled the Torah commandment of 'be fruitful and multiply' — the minimal fulfillment being the bearing of a son and daughter — they may by mutual consent refrain from further sexual relations. They may also take such measures as are not forbidden by the Torah to prevent conception.[41]

These summaries would indicate that from the Orthodox point of view, birth control for reasons other than the medical ones of hazards to life or health is not in keeping with Jewish law. The pressures of today's society, or any economic reason are not sufficient ground for the practice of contraception.

It must be immediately stated that authorities in Halakhah unanimously agree that family planning in this sense, in the absence of significant medical consideration, is a violation of the spirit of our Torah.[42]

In another article Moshe Tendler states dramatically:

. . . on the question of population control. If reduction in the birth rate of the famine-threatened population of the world is indeed the proper response, then the Jew as a world citizen should join in the world-wide effort of providing contraceptive materials to those desirous of limiting family size. The Jew as a Jew must, at this time, reject the suggestion that he, too, limit the size of his family. We have unique problems created for us by world citizenry. Six and one half million Jews destroyed at the hand of world citizenry in one generation represents a staggering loss. When calculated on the Malthusian geometric tables, it represents an astronomical loss of our life blood. Only a total lack of moral and historic responsibility can explain the present statistics which show our brethren leading the list of ethnic groups with the lowest birth rates in America. Their motivation is that of an egotist hedonist, rather than of a world citizen sleepless from nights of Malthusian nightmares. Reduction of family size must be justified only on a personal, familial basis, not as part of the demographic problem.[43]

In an article which appeared in the Israel series, *Noam*, a Dr. Jacob Levy opposes any form of contraception, even oral methods, not only on Halakhic, but also on demographic grounds. "The Jewish birthrate in Israel fell from 32.96 births per thousand people in 1950 to 22.21 in 1961, while the Arab birth-rate in Israel rose from 48.8 per thousand in 1954 to 55.2 in 1960. If the rate continues, within fifty years the Arab population in Israel will overtake the Jewish." On these grounds, Dr. Levy is opposed to birth control.[44]

"The philosophy of the Halakhah is clearly opposed to any limitation of family size."[45]

Judaism regards propagation as a proper natural fulfillment of the divine creative plan . . . Birth control on a universal scale can never be condoned as an ethical practice. Even when faced with the prospect of teeming billions, it is not the moral prerogative of a preceding generation to designate the numerical limits of future offspring . . . Birth control and planned parenthood are transgressions against the divine commandment of human propagation.[46]

It is not for men to determine who is fit to survive and whose life and birth should be preserved. But Judaism is also emphatic in condemning the economic argument as a valid indication for contraception . . . This explains why nearly all of the innumerable relevant responsa raise the question from the medical point of view only. The question is: May a woman whose life is certified to be in grave danger if she became pregnant, employ contraceptives, and, if so, in what form? Motives other than these were not even worth considering . . .[47]

On this issue, another source asserts:

On the side of modern social and moral factors, the Jewish opponents of birth control, in addition to invoking the authorities, advance the following opinions. They regard birth control as only a step to race suicide, as a permission to the selfish and the luxury-seeking among married couples for a life of ease, free from the burdens of childbearing and child-caring. They insist that, even in such cases where considerations of health may necessitate a limitation of offspring, it is dangerous for any individual to be allowed to take the law into his own hands, or to act without consulting a competent religious authority. They point out that Judaism has a definite ideal of marital relationship, and that if this is properly followed, it will result in conjugal happiness; to introduce into this harmony the universal sense of sin and shame which is implanted in the conscience of men and women who practice birth control, is to disrupt the very marriage bond itself. Furthermore, they maintain, woman reaches her highest and most exalted function in the role of motherhood, and when deprived of this is punished by nature with an unstable and neurotic psyche as well as by possible physical suffering.

The opponents of birth control deny the argument that it is necessary to limit the number of births for economic reasons. They hold that there is no danger of overpopulation, and they point to the fact that it is precisely among those parts of the population that are most favorably situated from the economic point of view that birth control is most frequently practiced. They contrast the self-reliance, generosity and responsibility engendered by the large family with the petted, self-opinionated and self-seeking members of a smaller family, and still more with the artificial life in small expensive apartments. Finally, they appeal to the idea of Divine Providence, and declare that men and women, instead of striving for selfish ease, should trust in the goodness of God.[48]

A tragic responsum of the war period allowed women in the Nazi ghettos, whose lives were doomed if found pregnant, to resort to birth control, especially since any child she might conceive would also be doomed and could thus be regarded as unviable.[49]

There is precedent in Jewish law for sanctioning birth control because of perilous conditions confronting the general community. Jewish women in the ghetto, under the Nazis, were permitted to maintain normal marital relations with their husbands while using a contraceptive to prevent conception because of the hazards confronting the pregnant women at the time.[50]

In our own day, Rabbi Ephraim Oshri permitted Jewish couples entombed in the hell of Nazi ghettos normal sexual relations with contraceptives in the belief that it would be sinful to bring children into such a world but equally wrong to prevent husband and wife from enjoying sexual love. (The Nazis on May 7, 1942 "had promulgated a decree stating that any Jewish woman found to be pregnant would be put to death immediately.")[51]

## THE VIEW OF REFORM JUDAISM

The position of Reform Judaism is that "according to the main decisions of Jewish law, birth control is permitted, especially if the husband has already fulfilled the duty of having children.'[52]

A well-known responsum by Dr. Jacob Z. Lauterbach, prepared in 1927, was presented to the Central Conference of American Rabbis in Cape May, New Jersey, and adopted in "determining the policy in 1930."[53]

The responsum concludes as follows:
1. The Talmudic-Rabbinic law does not consider the use of contraceptives, as such, immoral or against the law. It does not forbid birth control but it forbids birth suppression.
2. The Talmudic-Rabbinic law requires that every Jew have at least two children in fulfillment of the Biblical command to propagate the race which is incumbent upon every man.

There are, however, conditions under which a man may be exempt from this prime duty: (a) when a man is engaged in religious work like the study of the Torah, and fears that he may be hindered in his work by taking on the responsibilities of a family. (b) when a man because of love or other considerations marries a woman who is incapable of having children, as an old or sterile woman. (c) when a man is married to a woman whose health is in such a condition as to make it dangerous for her to bear children. . . In this case, then, the woman is allowed to use any contraceptive or even to permanently sterilize herself in order to escape the dangers that would threaten her at childbirth.

3. In a case where a man has fulfilled the duty of propagation of the race, when he has already two children, he is no longer obligated to beget children and the law does not forbid him to have intercourse with his wife in such a manner which would not result in conception. In such a case, the woman certainly is allowed to use any kind of contraceptive . . .

Of course, in any case, the use of contraceptives or of any device to prevent conception is allowed only when both parties, that, is, husband and wife, consent.

Dr. Lauterbach asserts that while there are a number of Aggadic sayings, (Aggadah refers to the illustrative parables of the Talmud), which speak against the practice of self-abuse and forms of birth control, from the Halakhic point of view, there can be no doubt that birth control is within the mainstream of Jewish tradition. He approaches the problem with a sweeping question:

> Does the Talmudic-rabbinic law permit cohabitation between husband and wife in such a manner or under such conditions as would make conception impossible; and if so, what are the conditions under which such cohabitation is permitted:

Bringing varied sources to substantiate his position, he concludes:

> From all this it is evident that the act of cohabitation, even when it cannot possibly result in conception, is in itself not only not immoral or forbidden, but in some cases even mandatory. Hence, we may conclude that the discharge of sperm through sexual intercourse, even though it does not effect impregnation of the woman, is not considered an act of 'wasteful discharge of semen' which is so strongly condemned by the Aggadic sayings of the Talmud.

He shows that the Halakhah does not restrict the husband's gratification of his sexual desire and does not forbid intercourse so long as he does not become accustomed to these practices:

> And I cannot see any difference between the protection of a minor from a conception which might prove fatal to her and the protection of a grown up woman whose health is, according to the opinion of physicians, such that a pregnancy might be fatal to her. Neither can I see any difference between protecting a child from the danger of being deprived of the nourishment of its mother's milk, and protecting the already born children of the family from the harm which might come to them due to the conception of a larger number of sisters and brothers. For the care and comfort which the parents can give to their children already born, will certainly be less if there be added to the family other children claiming attention and care.[54]

Dr. Lauterbach provides sources to explain that, especially if the duty to propagate had been fulfilled, women may take potions which induce sterility if they have experienced great pain in child-birth, if they are concerned about bringing into the world children who are likely to turn out to be morally corrupt. He further notes that even where the duty of procreation has not been fulfilled, if there is a high "moral" purpose, as, for example, the desire to study Torah, birth control may be practiced.

> Since we have seen that the act of having intercourse with one's wife in a manner not resulting in conception is in itself not against the law, there can be no difference between the failure to fulfill the commandment of the propagation of the race by abstaining altogether from marriage and the failure to fulfill the command-ment by practicing birth control. The considerations that permit the one permit also the other. It would seem that the other, that is, the practice of birth control, should be preferred to the one of total abstention.[55]

The Reform view also holds that there is no difference between protecting children from the danger which might come to them from health hazards and those which inhere in poverty, overcrowding, disease and deprivation or other economic or practical reasons.

Thus, the Central Conference of American Rabbis, maintaining that birth control is not incompatible with Judaism, included into its social justice program in 1929, the following:

> We recognize the need of exercising great caution in dealing with the delicate problem of birth regulation in view of the widespread disregard of the old sanctions affecting the institution of marriage and of the family. We earnestly desire to guard against playing into the hands of those who would undermine the sanctity of these time-honored insitutions through reckless notions and prac-tices. We are especially mindful of the noble tradition obtaining among the Jewish people with respect to the holiness of domestic relations; but, at the same time, we are keenly aware of the many serious evils caused by a lack of birth regulation among those who, by reason of lack of health or of a reasonable measure of economic resources, of intelligence, or all of these, are prevented from giving to their children that worthy heritage to which all children are entitled. We, therefore, urge the recognition of the importance of intelligent birth regulation as one of the methods of coping with social problems.[56]

In 1958, the Union of American Hebrew Congregations, at its convention in Miami Beach, stated:

> We fully recognize the right of all persons for religious reasons or otherwise, to abstain from or to practice birth control as they see fit. However, the failure of large section of our population to plan their families effectively is due neither to conscience nor to free choice, but rather to legal and official obstacles imposed upon many Americans with the result of depriving them of knowledge and medical assistance in this field . . .

> When government responds to the theological beliefs of any religious group by interfering with the dissemination of birth control information to all who desire it, such interference represents an improper imposition of such religious beliefs upon the community at large. Therefore, be it resolved that:

> A. We favor the elimination of all restrictions and prohibitions against the dissemination of birth control information and of rendering birth control assistance by qualified physicians, clinics, and hosptials.

> B. We favor the wider dissemination of birth control information and medical assistance, both by private groups, such as the Planned Parenthood Association, and health agencies of local, state and the federal government as a vital service to be rendered in the field of public health.[57]

In 1960, the Commission on Justice and Peace of the Central Conference of American Rabbis, included the following in its report:

> As Jews, we take pride in our historic emphasis upon the values of family life. We believe that it is the sacred duty of married couples to 'be fruitful and multiply,' unless child-bearing is likely to impair the health of the mother or the offspring. This is the position which we took in 1929 and which has support in traditional sources. We believe, moreover, that a righteous God does not require the unlimited birth of children who may, by unfavorable social and economic circumstances, be denied a chance for a decent and wholesome life. Therefore, we declare that parents have the right to determine the number, and to space the births of their children in accordance with what they believe to be the best interests of

their families. We hold, moreover, that apart from its procreative function, the sex relation in marriage serves positive spiritual values. Contraceptive information and devices should be legally and inexpensively available to married persons.

The problem of population has today taken on worldwide significance and urgency. A number of nations are suffering from what has been termed, 'explosive population growth,' where the birth rate is outrunning their resources and living space and makes a decent living standard unattainable. Means should be placed at the disposal of the United Nations, through the World Health Organization, to enable it where requested, to provide education techniques and materials. The effort to solve this problem must not be delayed, for the penalites will be famine, increased poverty, and the unrest which leads to conflicts.[58]

## THE VIEW OF CONSERVATIVE JUDAISM

The position of Conservative Judaism may be gleaned from the following statements:

A. In 1935, the Rabbinical Assembly of America adopted the following resolution:

> As rabbis, we are deeply concerned with the preservation and extension of the human values inherent in the institutiion of the mongamous family. Careful study and observation have convinced us that birth control is a valuable method for overcoming some of the obstacles that prevent the proper functioning of the family under present conditions.

> Hence, we urge the passage of the legislation by the Congress of the United States and the State Legislatures to permit the dissemination of contraceptive information by responsible medical agencies. We maintain that proper education in contraception and birth control will not destroy, but rather enhance, the spiritual values inherent in the family and will make for the advancement of human happiness and welfare.

B. In 1955, a leading Conservative Rabbi, writing on the Jewish concept of marriage and the family noted that in Judaism, marriage has two purposes, the fulfillment of the commandment to be fruitful and multiply, and second, companionship and happiness. He says:

It is clear that Rabbinic Judaism regarded limitation upon the procreation of children as permissible or even as obligatory, in cases where the mother's health was in danger or she was exposed to extraordinary pain, or where the health of the child, born or unborn, would be jeopardized by this pregnancy. Finally, it reckoned with the danger of a poor heredity or environment.

In sum, Judaism regards the procreation of children as a God-given duty. It may, however, be set aside when it conflicts with the supreme divine imperative, 'He shall live by them — and not perish by them,'[59] which commands us to preserve existing human life and enhance it. Hence, Judaism does not regard mechanical and chemical methods as more objectionable per se than abstinence from sexual relations. As long as the means employed do not deprive the act of its natural satisfaction, these means are as legitimate as continence.[60]

Rabbi Gordis evaluates the reasons of the shifting of the rabbinic authorities from leniency to stringency, explaining that during the Middle Ages, from the sixth to the eighteenth centuries, the Jewish people were constantly threatened, and many tragedies decimated the people.

Faced by these perils, medieval Jewry saw its preservation dependent on a high birth rate, without restriction or qualification. The imperious demand for group survival showed no consideration for individual desires or family welfare. Only through children and more children could the Jew hope to overcome the tragic mortality rate. Thus, the instinctive wish for progeny was intensified by overpowering religio-national motives.

Hence, the view of the Halakhah that the birth of two children fulfills the requirements of the Law was ignored . . . A deep-seated opposition to birth control became dominant among traditionally-minded Jews, in spite of Jewish tradition. Nevertheless, in the Rabbinic Responsa of the eighteenth and nineteenth centuries, more liberal viewpoints are met with, side by side with more rigorous ones. Today, modern Judaism unequivocally reaffirms the obligation to perpetuate the human race through the medium of the family as a basic and general goal, but it recognizes also that family planning is a basic necessity of modern life, in view of the complex, moral, hygienic and economic factors.[61]

C. Another leading Conservative rabbi has written:

> If there is room for doubt whether the use of contraceptives is permissible when it concerns planned parenthood, there can be no doubt that it is permitted where the absence of its use will bring the evils accompanying overpopulation.[61a]

D. In 1960, the Committee on Jewish Law and Standards of the Rabbinical Assembly, adopted a Statement on Birth Control, prepared by Rabbi Ben Zion Bokser,[62] following the nationally raised issue of the dissemination of birth control information. The statement poses the question:

> Is it right for a couple to maintain normal relations as husband and wife while interfering with the conception and birth of children that are otherwise destined to derive from their union?

The statement holds that while the primary duty of procreation is imposed upon the male, the woman is not completely divested from the duty-sharing on the principle "He did not create it to be a waste; He formed it to be inhabited."[63] God created the world to be a home for human life, and it is incumbent on man and woman to further God's work by bringing children into the world and raising them to continue the work of creation.

The growth of a tradition extolling parenthood is indicated while it is admitted that, in some circumstances "it was considered right to curtail childbirth."

> In the face of peril to the life or health of the mother or the child, permission was granted by rabbinic authorities to the woman on the advice of a physician, to use a contraceptive in order to avoid pregnancy; some rabbis went beyond the permission in such cases and declared the use of a contraceptive obligatory . . .

Responsibility for the determination of peril to life and health, which should have been placed within the hands of the doctor is here given to rabbinic authorities. There are other occasions in Jewish life, however, where the final determination rests with the competence of the individual, on the principle, "The heart knows its own bitterness."[64] The statement concludes:

We are, therefore, justified in sanctioning birth control as a precaution against a danger to the life or health, physical or mental, of the mother or her children, on the advice of a physician, or on the personal conviction expressing the private conscience of the individuals involved.

It is especially in the realm of mental health that we must reckon with the subjective factor. There are various circumstances which may produce pressures on a family dangerous to mental health. In some cases, the wife must share in the securing of a livelihood. Indeed, in some instances, marriage would have to be deferred indefinitely, unless the wife remain free to work and help in the establishment of her family. Some couples face problems of profound difficulty in their marital adjustment and it may be deemed vital to defer the birth of children. All such circumstances, when they become a threat to mental health, fall into the categories recognized by Jewish law as ground for the practice of birth control. On the principle that "The heart knows its own bitterness," the individual conscience would, in every instance, be deemed competent to determine the gravity of the pressure and the peril to health which it represents.

The statment continues by taking into consideration modern issues of over-population in certain areas of the Middle and Far East. It expresses concern that over-population may not be the root problem, but that we can best contribute to those areas by helping them achieve more rational methods of production and distribution. Where, however, the peril of over-population is real, and does threaten the life and death of that area, then properly, birth control is indicated; but this is a decision which must not be imposed by others, rather determined by the people themselves.[65]

The vitality of Jewish law is such, the Statement suggests, that it is realistic enough to acknowlege that we sometimes are faced by contradictory obligations and that often conformity with the law may jeopardize life; when such a confrontation occurs, the Biblical statement, "You shall therefore keep My statutes, and My ordinances, which if a man do, he shall live by them," must be invoked. We must "live, and not die by them." In other words, "when the commandment threatens to undermine life, it becomes inoperative, and is to be suspended."

The Statement cautiously appeals not for indiscriminate use of contraceptives, but only for cause or reason, as follows:

Where birth control is to be practiced, it is preferable that the woman use the contraceptive. It is the woman who bears the hardship incidental to childbirth; it is, in other words, her condition primarily which creates the justification for interfering with conception . . .

The law ordaining the duty to bring children into the world, like all law, was a means to an end; its primary end is to serve life. It is one of the Creator's gifts which He bestowed on man, that he can be God's partner in continuing the work of Creation. But man must define the context in which God's gifts can be most fruitfully employed. Man does not fulfill the vocation of parenthood by the mere fact that he brings children into being. Bringing children into the world carries with it a grave responsibility. The vocation of parenthood fulfills its God-endowed mission when it is rendered consistent with the requisites of the life and health of all the constituent members of the family.

Another Conservative rabbi writes:

". . . medieval and modern sages came to the following conclusions: First, all concur that where there is danger to the life of a mother, she may use a diaphragm or an oral anovulent as prescribed by a physician; second, some even permit the male the use of a contraceptive although the sperm is thereby denied natural entry to the female; third, there are reputable scholars who allow *all* women to use contraceptives as they see fit since their use of anovulents does not constitute a breach of natural law; fourth, the great sixteenth century Polish authority, Rabbi Solomon Luria, permits the use of contraceptives where there is a danger of producing immoral or degenerate progeny."[66]

## NOTES

1. Philip N. Ginsbury, *Planning Your Family*, London *Jewish Chronicle*, March 3, 1967.
2. David Feldman, *Birth Control in Jewish Law*, New York University Press, New York, 1968 is the most definitive study of the subject to date. For an excellent article, see Fred Rosner, "Contraception in Jewish Law, *Tradition*, Vol. 2, No. 12, Fall, 1971, pp. 90-114.
3. Gen. 1:28.
4. Mishnah, Yevamoth VI, 6.

5. Yevamoth 63b.

6. Gen. 38:7-10.

7. Shelo titaber v'yikhish yofya.

8. Midrash Rabbah, Gen., Soncino Press, London, 1951, p. 792, note 4.

9. Ibid., p. 793.

10. Gen. 6:1.

11. Midrash Rabbah, op. cit. p. 212.

12. Universal Jewish Encyclopedia, Vol. II, New York, 1940, p. 380.

13. Immanuel Jakobovits, *Journal of a Rabbi*, Living Books, New York, 1966, p. 216.

14. Yevamoth, 12b.

15. Ps. 116:6.

16. Alan Guttmacher, "Traditional Judaism and Birth Control, " *Judaism*, Spring, 1967, p. 162.

17. Immanuel Jakobovits, op. cit., p. 215. See, "Be Fruitful and Multiply," London *Jewish Chronicle*, Frankly Feminine Supplement, Sept. 6, 1968, p. 13.

18. Ibid. Immanuel Jakobovits, p. 215.

18a. Ibid. p. 218

19. Immanuel Jakobovits, op. cit., p. 218.

20. Ibid. p. 486.

21 Moses Tendler, "*The Jewish Attitude Toward Family Planning*," *Jewish Life*, Union of Orthodox Jewish Congregations of America, p. 6.

22. Alan Guttmacher, "Judaism" op. cit. p. 164.

23. Moses Tendler, "Population Control — The Jewish View," *Tradition*, Rabbinical Council of America, New York, Fall, 1966, p. 10.

24. Alan Guttmacher, op. cit., p. 164.

24a. See, *Time*, "Trouble With The I.U.D.," May 25, 1970, p. 73.

25. Alan Guttmacher, ibid.

26. Moses Tendler, op. cit. p. 12. For a sensitive difference between Moses Tendler and David Feldman on chemical spermicides, see *Tradition*, Spring-Summer 1967, p. 205 ff.

27. "Jews and the Pill," *Jewish Life*, Manchester, England, December 1967, p. 8. See also, *Time*, Chicago, December 1967, p. 33.

28. Igrot Moshe, Even ha-Ezer, Vol. IV, No. 17, Noted by Seymour Siegel, *Jews and Divorce*, Jacob Fried, Ed., Ktav, New York, 1968, p. 182. See also David Feldman, ibid., p. 244. See also Immanuel Jakobovits, *Tradition*, Vol. VII, No. 2, Summer, 1965, p. 123.

29. Tosefta, Yevamoth 8:2.

30. Shulhan Arukh, Even ha-Ezer 5:12.

31. Tosefta, Yevamoth 8:2. See, Isaac Klein, Responsa and Halakhic Studies, Ktav, New York, 1975, p. 164.

32. Shabbath 110b. Maimonides, Issurei Bi'ah, XVI:12.

34. "Hospital Compendium, Commission on Synagogue Relations," Federation of Jewish Philanthropies of New York, New York, 1965, p. 11.

35. Yevamoth 65b. *Also*, Tosefta Yevamoth VIII.

36. Immanuel Jakobovits, op. cit. p. 485, note 348.

37. David Feldman, op.cit. p. 238.

38a. Ibid.

38b. Ibid, p. 246-247, note 76.

38c. David Feldman, "Judaism and the Pill," Women's Outlook, Winter, 1969. *National Women's League*, New York, p. 6.

39. Hospital Compendium, op. cit. p. 19, *See also*, Justin Hoffman, "Why Judaism Opposes Birth Control," *National Jewish Monthly*, Washington, D.C., January, 1968, p. 12, *See also*, Immanuel Jakobovits, "Jewish Medical Ethics," Bloch Publishing Company, New York, 1967, p. 66.

> "The only valid indication for contraceptive practices considered in the responsa is a hazard to life (and possibly health) of the mother."

See also: "Jews and the Pill," Jewish Life, Manchester, England, Dec. 1967, p. 8: "From the Chief Rabbi's office in London it was learned that "when in the opinion of medical authorities, conception may prove dangerous to the life of a woman, Jewish law permits certain forms of control to be exercised by the woman only." See also, Medical Ethics, Federation of Jewish Philanthropies of New York, Rabbi M.D. Tendler, Editor, New York, 1975, pp. 19, 34-35.

40. Immanuel Jakobovits, op. cit., pp. 215 and 486.

40a. Gen. 38:10.

41. Moses Tendler, The Jewish Attitude Toward Family Planning, p. 5.

An interesting question was raised by Rabbi Solomon Freehof when a husband refused to have intercourse with his wife because, since she had had a hysterectomy, this would, he thought, be an act of onanism. Rabbi Freehof notes that "while the general purpose of marriage is to have children, nevertheless it is not prohibited for a man to marry a woman who cannot have children." He quotes the Code of Jewish Law, as follows: "It is permitted to have intercourse with a woman who cannot bear children (and it is not considered wasting seed) since the intercourse is conducted in the normal way. As long as the intercourse is normal, and there is no artificial barrier inserted in the womb before intercourse there is no committing of the sin of 'seed spilling." Rabbi Freehof also says that Rabbi Moshe Feinstein, the chief Orthodox authority in America today, has used the same source.

42. Ibid.

43. Ibid. p. 9.

44. Seymour Siegel, in *Jews and Divorce*, ibid. p. 181.

45. Moses Tendler, op. cit., p. 9.

46. Zev Zahavy, "Birth Control is Ungodly," *Jewish Digest*, Houston, Texas, June 1960, p. 53.

47. Immanuel Jakobovits, op. cit., p. 380.

48. Universal Jewish Encyclopedia, op. cit., p. 380.

49. Ben Zion Bokser, "Statement on Birth Control," *Conservative Judaism*, Rabbinical Assembly, Summer, 1961, p. 32-35.

50. Immanuel Jakobovits, op. cit., p. 163.

51. Gilbert Rosenthal, "Generations in Crisis", Bloch Publishing Company, New York, 1969, p. 39. See also Irving J. Rosenbaum, The Holocaust and Halakhah, Ktav, New York, 1975, p. 40-41.

52. Solomon Freehof, "Reform Responsa," Hebrew Union College Press, Cincinnati, 1960, p. 206. In a letter dated August 26, 1966, Dr. Freehof takes a rabbinic

colleague to task by saying; "it is wrong to say that it is a Mitzvah to use birth control devices . . . I believe you are mistaken when you make a general statement that birth control is a Mitzvah. It would be more correct, it seems to me, to say that Judaism under many circumstances permits the use of birth control devices, especially to be used by women."

53. *Yearbook*, Central Conference of American Rabbis, Vol. XXXVII Cape May, New Jersey, 1927, p. 369.

54. Ibid. p. 377.

55. Ibid. p. 379.

56. *Universal Jewish Encyclopedia*, ibid. p. 381.

57. *Yearbook*, C.C.A.R., vol LXVII, 1958. *See also*, Sermon, "Be Fruitful and Fill the Earth," Roland Gittleson, Boston, Mass. Dec. 18, 1959.

58. *Yearbook*, C.C.A.R., Vol. LXX, 1960, Miami Beach, Florida, p. 71. *See also:* Roland B. Gittleson, " 'My Beloved is Mine,' Judaism and Marriage," Union of American Hebrew Congregations, New York, 1969, pp. 184-191, *See also: Yearbook*, LXXIV, 1964, p. 74.

59. Lev. 18:5.

60. Robert Gordis, *Judaism for the Modern Age*, Farrar Straus and Cudahy, New York, 1955, p. 253. idem. See, "Sex and the Jewish Family" Burning Bush Press, 1966. pp. 36-41. Also, The Jewish View, Marriage, Birth Control, Divorce, Jewish Heritage, B'nai Brith Adult Jewish Education, Washington, D.C., Fall, 1967., p. 42.

61. Ibid., Robert Gordis, p. 255.

61a. Isaac Klein, *Conservative Judaism*, R.A., Summer 1959.

62. *Conservative Judaism*, R.A., New York, Summer, 1961, pp. 33 ff.

63. Isa. 45:18.

64. Prov. 14:10.

65. Writing in Conservative Judaism, Rabbi Isaac Klein, notes "If there is room for doubt whether the use of contraceptives is permissible when it concerns planned parenthood, there can be no doubt that is permitted where the absence of its use will bring the evils accompanying overpopulation." Summer, 1959. Quoted also in Seymour Siegel's article, Some Aspects of the Jewish Tradition's View of Sex in *Jews and Divorce*. ibid.

66. Gilbert Rosenthal, "Generations in Crisis," Bloch Publishing Company, New York, 1969, p. 38.

# CELIBACY
## (and Marriage and Sex Relations)

Celibacy, the deliberate renunciation of marriage, is alien to mainstream Judaism. Orthodox, Conservative and Reform are unequivocally opposed to it as completely un-Jewish.[1a]

Although there exists no precise interdiction against celibacy in Jewish sources, the emphasis placed throughout Jewish tradition on marriage, procreation, and the companionship of husband and wife makes it obvious that celibacy is frowned upon . There exists a beautiful parable in which God is described as blessing the bridegroom and adorning the bride. Another Talmudic saying suggests that He condemns a man who has not married by the age of twenty.

This does not mean that there were not a few individuals, or small sects even especially during the turbulent days of the beginning of the Christian era, who were very much attracted to the practice of celibacy, which to them was a means of attaining a higher state of purity.

> Some lived communally in desert retreats, or in close covenanted associations in the towns and cities, practicing austerities and baptisms, even celibacy, eschewing all private possessions, despising wealth and extolling poverty, and in devout prayer awaiting the coming of the messianic age.[1b]

The historians Philo and Josephus have pointed out that the Essene sect especially refrained from sexual intercourse. They avoided marriage, not so much because they were misogynists, as that they desired to be constantly in the state of purity necessary for the receiving of visions and revelations from God. Some scholars also believe that the Essenes took their vows of celibacy late in life, about the age of sixty, after having been married for years.[2]

The classical Christian doctrine, which was crystallized in the New Testament and later, provided the highest endorsement of celibacy. Marriage, at best, was tolerated as a concession to human weakness, or that seems to be the position that emerges from Paul's declaration:

> It is good for a man not to touch a woman. Nevertheless, to avoid fornication, let every man have his own wife, and let every woman have her own husband. Let the husband render unto the wife due benevolence (conjugal duties) and likewise also the wife unto the husband. The wife hath no power of her own body, but the husband; and likewise also the husband hath not power of his own body, but the wife.

> *   *   *

> He that is unmarried careth for the things that belong to the Lord, how he may please the Lord. But he that is married careth for the things that are of the world, how he may please his wife . . .[3]

A leading authority describes this position and its development in Christianity:

> . . . Hence the ideal state is that of celibacy. Since, however, most people cannot attain to this exalted level, marriage is created, basically as a concession to the lower impulses of human nature. Marriage is necessary for the procreation of the race and can be justified in the eyes of God only on this basis and for this purpose.[4]

Celibacy is thus considered as a high ideal and therefore obligatory upon priests, monks and nuns. Recently, Pope Pius XII censured:

> "Who be they priests or laymen, preachers, speakers or writers no longer have a single word of approbation or praise for the virginity devoted to Christ; who for years, despite the Church's

warnings and in contrast with her opinion, give marriage preference in principle over virginity."[5]

On June 23, 1967, Pope Paul VI in the encyclical "Sacerdotalis Celebatus" (Priestly Celibacy) affirmed the doctrine of the church:

> Priestly celibacy has been guarded by the church for centuries as a brilliant jewel, and retains its value undiminished even in our time, when mentality and structures have undergone such profound change . . .

> After what science has now ascertained, it is not just to continue repeating that celibacy is against nature because it runs counter to lawful physical, psychological and affective needs, or to claim that a completely mature human personality demands fulfillment of these needs. Man, created to God's image and likeness, is not just flesh and blood; the sexual instinct is not all that he has; man is also, and pre-eminently, understanding, choice, freedom; and thanks to these powers he is, and must remain, superior to the rest of creation; they give him mastery over his physical, psychological and affective appetites.

> The choice of celibacy does not connote ignorance, or the despisal of the sexual instinct and affectivity. That would certainly do damage to the physical and psychological balance. On the contrary, it demands clear understanding, careful self-control, and a wise sublimation of the psychological life to a higher plane. In this way, celibacy sets the whole man on a higher level and makes an effective contribution to his own perfection . . .[6]

"Protestantism" writes Dr. Robert Gordis, "never officially surrendered the New Testament attitudes, but acquiesced in their attenuation. Celibacy was abandoned as the highest ideal . . .[7]

Judaism from the very beginning regarded celibacy as an unnatural state, conducive only to constant sinful thoughts.

> . . . but the fundamental difference between the two (Judaism and Christianity) must not be overlooked. For the Christian ascetic the instinct itself was evil, and the aim of those who aspired to higher religiousness was to extirpate it, root and branch. To the Jew its aberrations were deadly sin, but marriage and the begetting of children was not only good and lawful, but voluntary celibacy ran

counter to the very oldest commandment of God, increase and multiply . . .[8]

This positive Jewish attitude toward marriage, which is called "Kiddushin" (Holiness), and the extent to which the rabbis analyzed every intimate aspect of marriage reveals a striking opposition to celibacy.

Here are some Biblical quotations indicative of the Jewish position:

1. And God blessed them; and God said unto them: "Be fruitful and multiply," and replenish the earth.[9]
2. And the Lord God said, "It is not good that man should be alone; I will make him a helpmeet for him."[10]
3. Male and female created He them, and blessed them, and called their name mankind (Adam).
4. Whoever sheds man's blood, by man shall his blood be shed; for in the image of God made He man. And you, be fruitful and multiply; swarm the earth, and multiply in it.[12]
5. If he takes another wife for himself, her food, her raiment, and her conjugal rights, shall he not diminish.[13]
6. He created it (the world) not to be a wasteland; He formed it to be inhabited.[14]
7. Whoever finds a wife finds a great good.[15]

The Talmud only elaborates upon these Biblical bases. Complete tractates are devoted to the theme of marriage, including frank discussions on the subjects of celibacy, abstinence, and conjugal obligations.

The Mishna expands upon the brief reference to conjugal rights mentioned in the Bible:

> The times for conjugal duty prescribed in the Torah (Pentateuch), 'If he takes another wife for himself, her food, her raiment, and her conjugal rights (or marital duties) shall he not diminish,'[16] are: For men of independence (men who have no need to pursue an occupation to earn a livlihood), every day; for laborers, twice a week; for ass-drivers (who carry produce from the villages to town and whose occupation requires their absence from their home town during the whole of the week), once a week; for camel-drivers (who travel the whole of the week), once in thirty days; for

sailors (whose sea voyages take them away for many months at a time), once in six months. These are the rulings of R. Eliezer.[17]

The Talmud, elaborating upon this particular Mishna text, inquires: "How often (when) are scholars to perform their marital duties? Rabbi Judah in the name of Samuel replied, 'Every Friday night.' "[18]

Other texts from the Mishnaic period (100 to 225 A.C.E.) note that "eighteen is the right age for marriage"[18a] and also "that man should not abstain from the performance of the duty of the propagation of the race, that is, be celibate, unless he already has children,"[19]

On this very point the Talmud says:

> This implies, if he had children, he may abstain from performing the duty of propagation but not from that of living with a wife (since the Mishna text mentions only the exemption from the former and not from that of the latter). This provides support for a statement R. Nahman said in the name of Samuel who ruled that although a man may have many children he must not remain without a wife, for it is said in the Scriptures "It is not good that a man should be alone."[20]

Talmudic literature is riddled with sayings vehemently opposed to the single life:

1. As a final decision in this matter, the following statement of R. Nahman, in the name of Samuel, was accepted: "A man is forbidden to remain single, even if he has children from a previous marriage."[21]

2. Although a man may have many children he must not remain without a wife, for it is said in the Scriptures, "It is not good that man should be alone."[22]

3. R. Tanhum stated in the name of R. Hanilai: Any man who has no wife, lives without joy, without blessing, and without goodness.[23]

4. R. Joshua ben Levi said: Whosoever knows his wife to be a God-fearing woman and does not duly visit her is called a sinner; for it is said; "And you shall know that your tent is in peace,"[24] (that is, that your wife is in peace with God, chaste or, reading Shalom as shalem, perfect.)[25]

5. A good wife is a precious gift.[26]

6. It was taught: R. Eliezer stated, "He who does not engage in

propagation of the race is as though he sheds blood," for it is said, 'Whoever sheds man's blood, by man shall his blood be shed,'[27] and this is immediately followed by the text, 'And you, be fruitful and multiply.' "[28]

R. Jacob said: "He who does not engage in propagation of the race acts as though he sheds blood and diminishes the Divine Image; since it is said, 'For in the image of God made He man,'[29] and this is immediately followed by 'And you, be fruitful and multiply.' "[30]

Ben Azzai said: "He who does not engage in propagation of the race acts as though he sheds blood and diminishes the Divine Image; since it is said after both 'Whoever sheds man's blood,' and, 'In the image of God made He man,[31] 'Be fruitful and multiply.' "[32]

7. R. Hisda praised R. Hamnuna before R. Huna as a great man. Said he to him, "When he visits you, bring him to me." When he arrived, he saw that he wore no (head) covering (it was the custom for married men to wear a sudarium (head covering). "Why have you no head-dress?" asked he. "Because I am not married," was the reply. Thereupon he (R. Huna) turned his face away from him. "See to it that you do not appear before me (again) before you are married," he said. R. Huna was thus in accordance with his view. For he said, "He who is twenty years of age and is not married spends his days in sin." "In sin?" — can you really think so? — But say, "spends all his days in sinful thought."[33]

There were, certainly, celibates in Jewish history, as for instance, allegedly the prophet Jeremiah:

> The word of the Lord came also to me, saying: You shall not take a wife, neither shall you have sons or daughters in this place.[34]

The great prophet of lamentations seems to have regarded it as futile to have children doomed to die in the impending national catastrophe?

> They shall die of grievous deaths;
> They shall not be lamented, neither shall they be buried;
> They shall be as dung upon the face of the ground;

And they shall be consumed by the sword, and by famine;
And their carcasses shall be meat for the fowls of heaven,
And for the beasts of the earth.[35]

Yet, the story is told that when the prophet Isaiah was speaking with King Hezekiah, the prophet rebuked the king for not marrying. The king replied that he foresaw that his chilren would be wicked. But Isaiah reprimanded him: "What have you to do with the secrets of the Almighty? Do as you have been commanded."[36]

In ancient Israel there were men and women under vow not to drink wine or liquor, and not to cut their hair. However, even the Nazirites did not pledge themselves to the renunciation of a normal sex life. Sexual asceticism was never given the dignity of a religious value in Judaism.

In the whole Taanaitic period (250-500 C.E.) we know of only one man, Ben Azzai, who refused to marry on the pretext of his overwhelming devotion to the study of Torah.

> They said to Ben Azzai: Some preach well and act well, others act well but do not preach well; you, however, preach well but do not act well. Ben Azzai replied: But what shall I do, seeing that my soul is in love with the Torah; the world can be carried on by others.[37]

This text has become the basis of the law that:

> A man is duty bound to take unto himself a wife in order to fulfill the duty of propagation. This precept becomes obligatory on a man when he reaches the age of eighteen; at any rate he should not pass his twentieth year without taking a wife. Only in the event that he is engaged in the study of Torah with great diligence, and when he has apprehension that marriage may interfere with his studies, he may delay marrying, providing he is not passionate.[38]

Temporary chastity was not only permitted but even obligatory. We only have to remember the prohibition of intercourse during a woman's menstrual period and for seven days following the last trace of blood, when she must take a ritual bath. This cycle of separation and reunion is in fact the very foundation of the Jewish marriage cycle. During a national emergency, the rabbis sometimes made an edict suspending marital relations.

Noah and his sons were told not to have sexual intercourse in the Ark at a time when the world was being destroyed:

> As soon as Noah entered the Ark, cohabitation was forbidden to him; hence it is written, "And you shall come into the ark, you and your sons, (Genesis 6:18) . . . apart; and your wife, and your sons' wives — apart.[39]

When Pharoah passed an edict that all male children should be cast into the river, the Jews abstained from sexual relations:

> "And there went a man of the house of Levi."[40] Where did he go? R. Judah b. Zebina said that he went to seek counsel of his daughter. A Tanna (rabbi of the Talmudic era) taught: Amram was the greatest man of his generation. When he saw that the wicked Pharaoh had decreed, "Every son that is born you shall cast into the river,"[41] he said, "In vain do we labor." He arose and divorced his wife (since all the male children to be born would be killed, and the primary object of marriage was the procreation of sons). All the Israelites thereupon arose and divorced their wives. His daughter (Miriam) said to him: "Father, your decree is more severe than Pharaoh's; because Pharaoh decreed only against the males and you decree also against the females. Pharaoh only decreed concerning this world, whereas you have decreed concerning this world and the world to come. (The drowned babes would live again in the Hereafter; but unborn children do not exist). In the case of the wicked Pharaoh there is doubt whether his decree will be fulfilled or not, whereas in your case, though you are righteous, it is certain that your decree will be fulfilled, as it is said, "You shall decree a thing and it will be established unto you." He (Amram) arose and took his wife back and they all arose and took their wives back.[43]

During the three days before the Revelation on Mount Sinai, the Israelites were told to have no contact with their wives:

> And he (Moses) said unto the people: "Be ready against the third day; come not near a woman.[44]

According to the Talmud, even after the Revelation, Moses refrained from marital intercourse because he had to be ready to receive direct revelation from God at all times.

145

> Three things did Moses do of his own understanding, and the
> Holy One, Blessed be He, gave His approval . . . he separated
> himself from his wife entirely after the Revelation.[45]

The High Priest was separated from his wife and family for
seven days preceding the Day of Atonement. On Yom Kippur itself,
on Tisha B'Av (the national Jewish day of mourning) and the seven
days of mourning (Shiva), sexual intercourse is forbidden. The
Talmud declares that in years of famine, husband and wife should
not live together:

> Resh Lakish said: A man may not have marital relations during
> famine, as it is said, "And to Joseph were born two sons *after* the
> year of famine came to an end.[46] [47]

The Code of Jewish Law reflects this sympathy with nature:

> If there is a famine in the land, God forbid, and grain doubles its
> price, although he has plenty of grain in his house, or if there is,
> God forbid, some other distress in the land, one is forbidden to
> have intercourse except on the night of her immersion. They who
> are childless are permitted to cohabit at any time.[48]

Marriage can also be postponed if the economic difficulties
resulting from it would affect the quality of Torah study. This is
deduced from a text which speaks of a man who got married at the
age of thirty or forty, without being criticized for the delay.

On the other hand, a responsum dealing with the related issue
of birth control in particularly tragic circumstances, states that
women in the Nazi ghettos "whose lives were doomed if found pregnant were permitted to resort to birth control, especially since any
child they might conceive would also be doomed and could thus be
regarded as inviable."[49] Marital relations were so important that
they did not cease even under such circumstances.

The conclusion one comes to is that Judaism is very negative
about celibacy and very positive about marriage, affirming that "a
man is not man and a woman is no woman unless married."
Celibates, according to Judaism, were incomplete human beings.
Even the High Priest, officiating in the Holy of Holies of the Temple
on the Day of Atonement, as representative of his people, had to be
a "whole" man, that is, he had to have a wife.

146

Marriage, and not celibacy, is the ideal state. Only marriage provides the opportunity for the expression of every aspect of human nature. Although propagation was one of the prime purposes of marriage, immediately following the Biblical injunction to "increase and multiply" we find the opinion that "it is not good for man to be alone" so that the companionship of husband and wife is just as important as having children. Even if one cannot have children, marriage is still encouraged. In addition, any kind of sexual play is permissible, although the normal form of coitus is most recommended. There is not the slightest suggestion that there is anything sinful about obtaining pleasure from the sexual act.

In 1749, a decree was issued by the Council in Jerusalem to the effect that bachelors of twenty years of age and upward would not be permitted to live in the Holy City. No one who did not have a wife had the right to reside there. A specified period of time, lasting from the 5th day of Iyar to the beginning of the month of Elul, that is, approximately four months, was given to rectify the condition. At the end of this period the Council was authorized to enforce the regulation, and require the eviction of those who did not comply.[50]

The extent to which Judaism goes in its exaltation of marriage and a good sexual relationship is best described in the following statements:

> Judaism . . . not only did not encourage, but distinctly objected to celibacy. Only one or two instances are recorded of Jewish saints who remained single all their lives . . . Maimonides, with that fine tact so characteristic of him, grouped the marriage laws under the general heading of "Kedusha." (Holiness), while Nahmanides wrote a whole treatise called *The Sacred Letter*, dealing with the most intimate moments in the lives of the sexes, and showing how even such functions as were declared by other religions as distinctly animalic can with the saint be elevated into moments of worship and religious exaltation. It is, in fact, a vindication of the flesh from a religious point of view . . . All the more strongly did the Jewish saint insist upon making these relations pure and chaste, stigmatizing even an impure thought as being as bad as an impure action, if not worse. It was only by reason of the purification of these relations and their thorough sanctification, that the whole vocabulary of love could afterward, in moments of rapture and ecstasy, be used by the saints in their prayers and hymns, to symbolize the relation between the human and Divine, and the long-

ing of man for the moment of total absorption in the Deity . . .
The Song of Songs became the great allegory, picturing the connection between God and Israel. The act of revelation is described
as the wedding between heaven and earth. The death of the
righteous, when the soul returns to God, is described as a kiss,
while each individual mystic considered his particular action of
losing himself in the Divine as a new matrimonial act.[51]

Celibacy is condemned in the law for two reasons: first, because of
the neglect of procreation, second, because of immorality in
thought or action to which the unmarried man falls a victim . . .

The second objection to celibacy . . . ignores completely the question of procreation. Any marriage is therefore satisfactory,
regardless whether the wife is capable of bearing children or not.
On this basis, celibacy is condemned in any man no matter what
his age and no matter how large the family he has already
raised . . .[53]

That marriage is a basic mitzvah in Judaism is affirmed by all the
Codes of Jewish law. The context of the citation by the codes is
primarily one of procreation, since such is the core of the legal
imperative. The human benefits of companionship and fulfillment
while not properly the object of legislation are exalted in Jewish
tradition and even incorporated into the legal language of the
Codes. With procreation as the thrust, but for all the reasons
taken together, marriage per se is a requirement of the law and
even its deferral must be justified.[54]

. . . if strict logic were to be pursued, abstinence from sexual relations or postponed marriage or celibacy could also be considered
"murder." Just as the Talmud declares that he who destroys his
seed is "as if he shed blood" we are also told that "he who does not
engage in procreation is as if "he shed blood," though no act of
destruction took place. The latter is passive, says Chief Rabbi
Isaac Herzog in a volume of Responsa published in 1967, while
the former contaminates the soul.[55]

An extraordinary document dating from the Middle Ages
comes close to holding an almost sacramental view of sexuality.
Rabbi Moses ben Nahman (Nahmanides) states:

. . . intercourse is a holy and pure thing when it is done in an ap-

148

propriate way, at an appropriate time, and with an appropriate intention. Let no man think that in proper intercourse there is anything blameworthy or perverse, Heaven forfend, for intercourse is called 'knowing' . . . and if it were not a matter of great holiness it would not have been called that. The matter is certainly not as Maimonides thought, as described in the *Guide of the Perplexed, where he praises Aristotle for saying that the sense of touch is a shame to men. Heaven defend us from such errors. The matter is certainly not as the Greek has said, for there is in this discussion a touch of heresy . . . But we, the children of the masters of the holy Torah, believe that God created all things according to the wisdom of his will . . . and if our sexual organs are a disgrace how could it happen that God created a thing which was blemished, shameful or faulty?*[56]

## NOTES

1a. See Celibacy, *Encyclopedia Judaica*, Yearbook 1974, Jerusalem.

1b. Abba Hillel Silver, *Where Judaism Differed*, Jewish Publication Society of America, Philadelphia, 1957.

2. 'Celibacy,' *Universal Jewish Encyclopedia*, Vol. 3, New York, 1941, page 73.

3. 1 Corinthians, 7.

4. Robert Gordis, *Sex and the Family in the Jewish Tradition*, Burning Bush Press, New York, 1967, p. 16.

5. *New York Times*, September, 1952.

6. Ibid., June 24, 1967.

7. Robert Gordis, *Judaism for the Modern Age*, Farrar, Straus and Cudahy, 1955, New York, p. 248.

8. George Foot Moore, *Judaism*, Vol. II, Harvard University, Cambridge, Mass., p. 270., Also. p. 119.

9. Gen. 1:28.

10. Ibid. 2:18.

11. Ibid. 5:2.

12. Ibid. 9:6, 7.

13. Exod. 23:10.

14. Isaiah 25:18.

15. Prov. 22:10.

16. Exod. 21:10.

17. Ketuvoth 5:6; Code of Jewish Law, CL:7; Even ha-Ezer 1.

18. Yevamoth 62b.

18a. Ethics of the Fathers, 5:14.

19. Yevamoth VI, 19.

20. Gen. 2:18.

21. Yevamoth 61b.

22. Ibid. 61b; Gen. 2:18.

23. Yevamoth 82b.

24. Job 5:24.

25. Yevamoth 62b.

26. Yevamoth 63b.

27. Gen. 9:6.

28. Ibid 9:7.

29. Ibid 9:6.

30. Ibid 9:7.

31. Ibid 9:6.

32. Ibid 9:7.

33. Kiddushin 29b.

34. Jer. 16:2.

35. Ibid 16:4.

36. Berakhoth 19a.

37. Yevamoth 63b.

38. Code of Jewish Law, CXLV, 1.

39. Gen. Rabba to verse 6:18 of Genesis.

40. Exod. 2:1.

41. Ibid 2:22.

42. Job 22:28.

43. Sotah 12a.

44. Exod. 19:15.

45. Shabbath 87a.

46. Gen. 41:50.

47. Ta'anith 11a.

48. Code of Jewish Law, CL:12.

49. Immanuel Jakobovits, *Journal of a Rabbi*, Living Books, Inc., New York, 1966, p. 163.

50. J. D. Eisenstein, *Ozar Dinim Uminhagim*, (Treasury of Laws and Customs), Hebrew Publishing Company, New York, 1938, p. 382.

51. Solomon Schechter, *Studies in Judaism*, Second Series, Jewish Publication Society of America, Philadelphia, 1938, p. 175.

52. Gen. 1:2.

53. Louis Epstein, *Sex Laws and Customs in Judaism*, American Academy of Jewish Research, 1948, New York.

54. David M. Feldman, *Birth Control in Jewish Law*, New York University Press, New York, 1969, pp. 27, 123.

55. Eugene Borowitz, *Choosing a Sex Ethic*, Schocken Books, 1969, New York, p. 164. See also, Seymour Siegel, *Jews and Divorce*, Ktav Publishing House, New York, 1969, p. 173; Robert Gordis, *Sex and Family in Jewish Tradition*, Burning Bush Press, New York, p. 35; Henry E. Kagan, 'A Jewish View of Sex and the Family,' in 'Currents and Trends' in *Contemporary Jewish Thought*, Binyamin Efron, Ed., Ktav Publishing House, New York, p. 225.

56. For a fascinating study of this great personality, See Seymour J. Cohen, *The Holy Letter:* A Study of Sexual Morality, Ktav Publishing House Inc., New York, 1976.

# CRYOBIOLOGY
## (Freezing of Human Bodies)

Cryobiology is a term describing the medical procedure of freezing the body of a dying or recently dead man so that he can be thawed out and revived when a cure has been found for the disease which is affecting him. Three cryonic societies are in existence, in California, Michigan and New York. The Life Extension Society published a newsletter, "Freeze-Wait-Reanimate."[1]

While scientists are not completely satisfied with their methods of revival they are putting a great deal of intensive research into improvements in this area. Some patients have already been frozen. *Life* magazine carried an editorial entitled "The Cold Way to New Life," which describes the process under which a 73-year-old psychology professor was frozen under the auspices of the Cryonic Society of California.[2] A twenty-four-year-old Jewish student requested that he be frozen as soon as he was medically pronounced to be dead. His wish was carried out, making his body the first on the East Coast to be placed in what is called "cryonic suspension."[3] Officials of the society speak of the freezing process as "life extension." A participating doctor called the process "cryonic interment."

A cursory examination of the subject raises many problems of a sociological and theological nature. Beyond these, there is the whole question of the time-gap — the world may have changed almost beyond recognition since the patient's last moment of consciousness.

The Talmudic account of Honi the Circle Drawer describes a comparable kind of incident:

Honi sat down to have a meal and sleep overcame him. As he slept a rocky formation enclosed upon him which hid him from sight and he continued to sleep for seventy years. When he awoke he saw a man gathering the fruit of the carob tree and he asked him, Are you the man who planted the tree? The man replied: I am his grandson. Thereupon he exclaimed: It is clear that I slept for seventy years. He then caught sight of his ass who had given birth to several generations of mules; and he returned home. He there inquired, Is the son of Honi the Circle Drawer still alive? The people answered him, his son is no more, but his grandson is still alive. Thereupon he said to them; I am Honi the Circle Drawer, but no one would believe him. He then went to the Bet Hamidrash and there he overheard the scholars say, The law is as clear to us as in the days of Honi the Circle Drawer, for whenever he came to the Bet Hamidrash he would settle for the scholars any difficulty that they had. Whereupon he called out, "I am he;" but the scholars would not believe him nor did they give him the honor due him. This hurt him greatly and he prayed (for death) and he died. Raba said: Hence the saying: Either companionship or death.[4]

Other questions have to do with the most suitable candidate for this kind of second chance, how long life should be in such circumstances, and when, if ever, death should be taken as final. What will happen to our sense of the internal rhythm of human life, if there is no definite moment of death?

What does Judaism have to say about freezing the body? Is there a time qualification involved which stipulates that a body can only be frozen before, at, or after death? What religious and Halakhic laws are involved? Although the subject is new, the questions have already been crystallized and Jewish sources are in process of being sifted for guidance.

## A REFORM VIEW

One of the first statements on this subject is to be found in a book by Dr. Solomon Freehof.[5] The author was asked:

Is it permissible by Jewish law and Jewish legal tradition to take the body of a person dying of a disease at present incurable and freeze it for a long time, even years, and then to revive him when a cure for his sickness will have been discovered? . . . Has a person the right to consent to such a procedure with regard to himself?

What is the status of his wife and children? Are they in mourning as if the person were dead? When shall he be revived? Who will determine, etc.?

The proposal is to freeze such bodies in cases only of people already dying or virtually dead of an incurable disease. So it amounts to the delaying of the death of a dying person. This is clearly prohibited by Jewish law. While one may not do anything at all to hasten the death of a dying person, one may also not do anything at all to prevent this dying. Such a person has a right to die.

He concludes:

In other words, the answer would be that if there were a trustworthy remedy already available for the disease but the remedy involved freezing, it would be permitted. But if there is only speculation that some day a remedy might be discovered and on the basis of that speculation the process of dying is prevented, that is contrary to the spirit of Jewish Law.

## AN ORTHODOX VIEW

A more definitive study, entitled "Refrigeration, Resuscitation and Resurrection,"[6] crystallizes the issue in greater detail.

Is it permitted to freeze a person who has just died, or would it constitute *halanat ha-met*, holding back a corpse from burial? Is there any possibility that freezing a terminal patient just *before* his death, which might increase the chances of successful resuscitation, could be allowed? For that matter, with all the new techniques for keeping a patient clinically alive (heart-lung machines and the like), are we allowed to let a terminal patient die to begin with? What would be the halakhic status of a frozen patient, not only with regard to the laws of burial and mourning, but with respect to such basic problems as marriage and inheritance? Can his wife remarry? Does his estate pass to his heirs? Finally, is not the very concept of life prolongation by refrigeration and resuscitation a denial of our belief in *tehiat hametim*, the resurrection of the dead?

The writer, Dr. Rabbi Azriel Rosenfeld, begins with the basic issues:

The problem of the permissibility of freezing cannot even be raised until . . . (the) . . . question has been resolved: Are we ever allowed to let a terminal patient die a natural death, or is it our duty to keep him alive by artificial means as long as this is physically possible, at which point, presumably, his body would be so far gone as to make freezing pointless? Are we perhaps halakhically required to keep a dying person connected to a heart-lung machine indefinitely, or at least as long as the machine can keep some semblance of life in his body by maintaining circulation and respiration?

After dealing with various sources in the codes and responsa, the author summarizes:

It is mandatory to prolong life as long as the patient is conscious, or as long as there is any chance of his recovery. But if his case is hopeless, and he can no longer be restored to consciousness, it is permitted — and perhaps even required — to remove any obstacles to his natural death. And once he is dead, it is certainly not mandatory to resuscitate him as long as there is no hope of his regaining consciousness or recovering. We can now legitimately consider the Halakhic status of refrigeration.

A second section, "Status of the Patient," discusses the question of legal death.

Since he has presumably died before being frozen, and in any event is certainly dead by ordinary definition — once he has been frozen, it would seem as though this question, too, must be answered affirmatively. At the same time, it seems clear that when the patient is later thawed out and revived, he is legally alive. But as already pointed out, the concept of a person being alive again after having been legally dead has very disturbing implications, particularly with respect to the laws of marriage and inheritance. The complex consequences of legal "life after death" could be avoided if it were possible to rule that the frozen patient is legally alive. Are there any precedents relevant to this question?

A number of parallel incidents are cited from the Talmud and Codes, and the author concludes:

In any event, all the cases considered . . . deal with a dead person who is revived miraculously at the time of death, when there were

154

no grounds for suspecting that he might come to life again. In the case of the frozen patient, on the other hand, assuming that techniques for successful resuscitation have been perfected, there is every reason to believe that he will eventually be revived. It seems clear that under such circumstances . . . the patient's wife would not be allowed to remarry. In fact, the frozen patient would very likely not be considered legally dead in any respect; otherwise great legal complications would arise whenever a person dies for a few moments and is resuscitated, as happens very often in accidents, or during surgery. Since questions of this type do not seem to have been raised, it is safe to conclude that as long as restoration to life by natural means remains possible, a person cannot be Halakhically regarded as dead.

Finally, the central problem is touched upon:

When a patient has died, or when his condition has been pronounced as hopeless, is it permitted to freeze him in anticipation that a cure for his condition may some day be found?

There appear to be good grounds for answering this question in the affirmative . . .

Talmudic sources are again quoted in support of the affirmative position, leading to the statement:

This suggests that in a hopeless case it might even be permitted to turn the patient over to others who would freeze him before he has actually died. If he is not frozen, death is certain, but if he is frozen, there is a possibility that he may be revived and cured.

In a brief final section entitled "Refrigeration and the Resurrection," the author makes short shrift of the question whether resuscitation of the frozen body does not deny the resurrection of the dead in the end of days, by maintaining that a resurrection will indeed occur and also that we have to "bear witness to our faith that there will come a day when 'death is swallowed up forever, and the Lord God has wiped away all tears.' "

An Orthodox weekly regards the whole issue as hypothetical, "for to date (it) has not been successful because man has not as yet unlocked the secret of life. However, Judaism believes in a hereafter, where the soul of every person departs when he dies. We are not permitted to save the body and we have to bury it immediately."[7]

The writer proceeds to put forward a series of Talmudic sources dealing with resurrection and the hereafter as the concepts have evolved from Scriptures. *The Book of Beliefs and Opinions* by Saadya Gaon, Maimonides' first volume of *Mishneh Torah* and the last chapter of the Talmudic tractate Sanhedrin devote special attention to this subject matter.

In the chapter, "When Life Ends," in *Medical Ethics*, body-freezing is included with cremation and above-ground burial crypts as a violation of the Jewish law of burial.[8]

## A CONSERVATIVE VIEW

Writing on the subject of Euthanasia, a Conservative Rabbi notes:

> Recent advances in medical science provide a halakhically acceptable and plausible alternative to Euthanasia, i.e., refrigeration. This alternative offers a chance to preserve life indefinitely through suspended animation. When there is a dilemma posed by certain death and a possibility of revival, we should choose the latter. If the situation is such that death is imminently certain but if the patient is frozen, there is a possibility that he may be revived, we are not prohibited from choosing the latter course of action. This does not mean, however, that we are obliged to employ medical technology to prolong life indefinitely and artificially.[9]

### NOTES

1. See Joseph Fletcher, "Our Shameful Waste of Human Tissue" *The Religious Situation*, Donald R. Cutler, Ed., Beacon Press, Boston, 1969, p. 247. "Its founder, Robert Ettinger, professes to use cryogenics as a way to freeze the bodies of its members after birth by liquid nitrogen, and then to resurrect them by artificial resuscitation when a cure has been found for whatever fatal malady struck them down. (Capsules to hold the bodies cost $400, plus $150 annually to maintain them.) One woman says, "With bad luck, I'll simply stay dead. With good luck, I may live again. It's worth trying." A half-dozen or more of those who have signed up have now been frozen in this long-range lay-away plan in the Society's facilities in Phoenix and New York. It makes an interesting gamble, with heavy odds on two counts: 1) finding the cure, and 2) reanimating the corpse. How the odds are set is undisclosed . . . Their gamble is, of course, a new version of Pascal's Wager. 'If I profess faith in God and eternal life and there is none, I lose nothing; if I profess this faith and it is grounded in fact, I gain everything; therefore, I believe.

See also, Isaac Asimov, *See You in the Hereafter*, Penthouse, p. 175-82. In a letter to the author, D.M. Wharton, Editor of Technical Economics Associates, publishers of Cryogenic Information Report, says that "The industry as a whole, does not seem to consider freezing of bodies in death, as a scientific branch of cryobiology. He asks, "Have you considered what the problem of the coming over-population might have in store for it, should it be increased by the return of the deceased?"

2. *Life*, New York and Chicago, January 27, 1967.

3. *New York Times*, August, 1968. See also, *The Miami Herald*, March 9, 1972, p. 9, which records a card carrying the wording: "The bearer of this card is a cyronic suspension donor under the anatomical gift act . . . If bearer dead, immediately cool head with ice, ice water or cold water. Do not embalm."

4. Taanit 23b. See also, George St. George, 1991, *Look*, New York, July 14, 1970, p. 55 ff., describing book "Notes From the Future."

5. Solomon Freehof, *Current Reform Practice*, Hebrew Union College Press, New York, 1969, p. 236.

6. Azriel Rosenfeld, *Tradition*, R.C.A., Vol. 9, No. 3, Fall 1967, p. 82ff.

7. *The Jewish Press*, New York, January 5, 1968, p. 4.

8. *Medical Ethics*, Federation of Jewish Philanthropies of New York, edited by Rabbi M. D. Tendler, New York, 1975, p. 20.

9. Byron L. Sherwin, *To Be Or . . . A Jewish View of Euthanasia*, United Synagogue Review, Spring, 1972, p. 5.

# DRUGS
## (Including Smoking and Alcohol)

D rug addiction is a widespread social problem in the United States and in the world at large. No community can afford not to give serious thought to means of combating this epidemic. Nor is the drug craze limited to youth. Older people and children in Junior and Elementary schools have become drug pushers as well as drug users. Uri Avneri, a member of the Israeli Knesset, made it his boast that he had tried all possible kinds of drugs from hashish to LSD.

Whatever the rationale for its use, the need for escape from reality, revolt against the establishment, the desire to expand the consciousness and sensitivity of the mind, or the quest for a mystical and religious experience in which barriers of time and space melt into oblivion,[1] what their proponents have not taken into account is their physical and mental effects in long-term. Only now are intensive studies on these being thoroughly documented.

While marijuana, the unrefined form of hashish deriving from the cannibis plant, has been found by some not to be physically addictive, according to almost all opinions, its use often results in some psychological addiction and dependency.[2] Some are convinced that the future will reveal the same kind of physical impairment and element of risk as is involved in cigarette smoking.

> . . . At that time (a few decades ago) cigarettes were supposed to enhance digestion, restore energy, expand mental capacity, comfort nerves . . . At present no one knows whether smoking pot can cause cancer. What is certain is that the burning of many types of leaves produce carcinogens, and it has been said that marijuana

158

users in India often complain of coughs and bronchitis, symptoms which may precede cancer. Marijuana simply has not been in common use in the United States long enough to produce the deaths from which statistics are calculated.[3]

Other more highly addictive drugs, such as heroin and LSD, have been proven scientifically to be destructive of the chromosones. They have produced defective births, disturbed biological and mental equilibrium, generated disorientation and depression, blurred the addict's reality sense, and led to heinous crimes. Newspapers will testify to the perpetration of ritual murders, conducted under the influence of drugs.

On this pressing contemporary issue we can look to Judaism for guidance. Where drugs are detrimental to life, Judaism is unequivocally opposed to their use. In fact, there is comparatively little reference to drug abuse in responsa literature.[4] In today's society, however, the historic Jewish invulnerability to drug addiction has been completely overturned.

> Heroin use appears to be gaining among Jewish youth, to the horror of older Jews, who have the reputation of shunning intoxicants ... Alcohol which makes people aggressive, is not for Jews ... but drugs which heighten introspective, artistic and defensive feelings are attractive to Jews.[5]

> Drug use among Jewish youth is on the increase. It is a Jewish concern.[6]

> While no census on drug abuse or addiction within the Jewish community has ever been taken, informed sources ... close to the drug problem show that of the city's 60,000 to 100,000 'visible addicts,' age 12-21, about 12,000 are Jewish. It is believed that in 1965, the maximum figure among Jews was 2,500. The extent of drug abuse or addiction among Jews older than 21 is not known ...

> Citing the scope of the drug problem in the Jewish community, an authoritative source at the Jewish Federation noted that in one Brooklyn high school alone, where the enrollment is over 75 per cent Jewish there is evidence that 80 percent of the student body's Jewish component has experimented with drugs ...

> What is clear ... is that drug abuse, which had not been regarded

159

as a problem relevant to Jews, must now be placed in its proper perspective. Drug use has penetrated all levels of the Jewish community; even ultra-Orthodox Jews have reportedly experimented with drugs. A number of Day School Principals have reported incidents of drug use among their teen-age students . . .[7]

While Jewish authorities have been strongly opposed to drunkenness, they have not viewed drugs as a Halakhic issue, the rabbis preferring to recommend the positive picture of a totally fulfilled and integrated human-being, who is concerned for his physical, as for his mental well-being, than to make any prohibitive pronouncements. Jewish scholars throughout the ages, however, have not hesitated to legislate concerning hygiene, or inveigh against any act which is detrimental to either mental or physical health.

"Be very careful and look after yourself scrupulously" or another translation; "Look after yourself and take care of your life" is probably the most obvious Biblical source for the rabbinic preoccupation with health.[8]

### From the Bible:

1. Do not stand idly by the blood of your brother.[9]
2. Love your neighbor as yourself.[10]
3. You shall not place a stumbling block before the blind.[11]
4. If a man kills any human being, he shall be put to death.[12]
5. When you build a new house, you shall make a parapet for your roof so that you do not bring blood guilt on your family.[13]
6. Cursed be the person who misdirects a blind person.[14]

### From the Talmud:

If one wounds his fellow, he is guilty on five counts: for damage, for pain, for healing, for loss of time, and for insult (degradation, indignity, or loss of self-respect).[15]

Regulations concerning dangers to life are more stringent than ritual prohibitions.[16]

### From the Codes:

. . . Similarly, regarding any obstacle which is dangerous to life, there is a positive commandment to remove it, to beware of it, and to be particularly cautious in this matter, for Scripture says: "Look after yourself and take care of your life."[17]

160

Many things were forbidden by the Sages because they involve a danger to life. If one disregards any of these and says, "If I want to put myself in danger, what concern is it to others . . ." or, "I am not particular about such things . . ." disciplinary flogging is inflicted on him.[18]

The following are the acts prohibited: One may not put his mouth to a flowing pipe of water and drink from it, or drink at night from rivers or ponds, lest he swallow a leech, etc.[19] Similarly, if one leads astray another who is blind to any matter by giving him bad advice, or if one encourages a transgressor who is blind and cannot see the true path because of his heart's desire, he transgresses a negative commandment, for Scripture says: "Before a blind man you must not put a stumbling block."[20] Which means that if one comes to you for advice, he should be given advice appropriate to the situation.[21]

And so, one must be particularly careful about all actions involving danger, for (infringing a prohibition involving) danger to life is a worse transgression than (infringing) ritual prohibitions, and one must be more concerned about the possibility of incurring a danger to life than about the possibility of transgressing a ritual prohibition . . . And all this is because of the command to watch over one's life . . .[22]

One should beware of all things that are dangerous because regulations concerning health and life are more important than ritual laws, and the possibility of danger is to be apprehended even more than the risk of infringing a precept.[23]

These selected passages reflect Judaism's deep concern for physical and mental well-being, and the demand that extreme care be exercised to prevent any act which might prove an impairment to health. Whatever is detrimental to health, is a clear violation of Jewish law.

From all this, the attitude of Judaism to the use and sale of drugs, can easily be inferred. However, there are also more straightforward pronouncements dealing with this subject. For example, the Talmud notes: Rab said to his son Hiyya, "Do not take drugs." And the commentator Rabbi Samuel ben Meir takes this to refer specifically to addictive drugs: "Do not drink drugs (samim) because they demand periodic doses and your heart will crave them.

You will waste much money thereby. Even for medical cure do not drink them, and if possible, obtain another mode of healing."

Two related areas to which this Talmudic test can be said to apply are alcohol and cigarette smoking.

While Judaism does not forbid the drinking of wine, but in fact encourages its use in the celebration of a Sabbath or a festival, alcoholic dependency is regarded with horror. "A drunken person is forbidden to say the prayers. One who recites the prayers while drunk is like one who serves idols."[23a] "An intoxicated man may not decide a legal question."[24] "An intoxicated man must not pray and if he did pray, his prayer is an abomination."[25] Priests are forbidden to perform the sacred service while drunk. "Drink no wine or other intoxicant, you and your sons, when you enter the Tent of Meeting."[25a] The reasons are clear; the mind is very much affected by alcohol, making communion with God, which requires extreme lucidity, absolutely impossible.

Where alcohol falls into the category of self-destruction and danger to health, it comes under the same prohibition as drugs.

Cigarette smoking is another case in point. A recent article entitled "Smoking and the Halakhah" analyzes the issues involved:[26]

> Since the facts (hazard to health) are hardly in dispute, one would have expected Halakhic authorities to take a clear and decisive stand on the issue. Judaism has always been a faith embracing all facets of our daily activities, and where Pikuah Nefesh (saving of life) is involved, all other considerations are usually set aside . . . Anything hazardous to life and limb or detrimental to health is strictly forbidden.

The author quotes Maimonides:

> "Likewise, it is a positive commandment to remove any stumbling block involving danger to life, to take heed and to be extremely careful with it, as it says, 'Be very careful and take care of yourself scrupulously.'[27] And if one does not remove any stumbling block liable to cause danger, one has thereby failed to carry out a positive precept as well as having transgressed the negative commandment, 'You shall not bring blood-guilt . . .' "[28]

After a careful analysis of smoking, based upon the Jewish concept of saving of life, the author reaches the conclusion:

... The medical and statistical evidence demonstrates that smoking is hazardous to health and can lead to fatal diseases. The idea that smoking is liable to shorten a person's life is virtually undisputed.

It follows, therefore, that the numerous halakhic rules prohibiting dangerous activities should be extended to include smoking. This extension should be enacted by the leading rabbinic authorities of our times, preferably acting jointly. A general rabbinic injunction against smoking has every chance of being gradually accepted, at least in strictly Orthodox circles. Thus, many Jewish lives would be saved, and the health of our people would substantially improve. Finally, not the least fringe benefit would be a demonstration of the relevance of Judaism — and especially halakhic Judaism to our times.[30]

Another rabbi agrees:

I fail to see how any rabbi, modernist or traditional, who accepts the principle of vahai bahem ("and you shall live by them") can fail to declare to his congregation that cigarette smoking is flatly forbidden and is even, in traditional terms, a far more serious aveira (transgression) than eating treifa (prohibited meats) and being m'halel Shabbat (violating the Shabbat); that life is the salient feature of Jewish law, and that a Jew who considers himself religious may not smoke cigarettes whose dangers are many times better established than that of marijuana. . .[31a]

A recent treatment of this subject, however, puts forward an opposing opinion, to the effect that smoking is not prohibited according to Halakhah. In *Tradition*, Rabbi J. David Bleich writes:

A pronouncement by the Sephardic Chief Rabbi of Tel Aviv, Rabbi David Halevy, declaring cigarette smoking to be a violation of Jewish Law has received much publicity in the press . . . Rabbi Halevy is reported to have ruled that the risk posed by cigarette smoking renders this act a violation of Deuteronomy 4:15 which bids man to preserve his health and that offering a cigarette to a friend is tantamount to 'placing a stumbling block before the blind.'

In the opinion of this writer (Rabbi Bleich), it is not possible to sustain the argument that smoking, in addition to being foolhardy and dangerous, involves an infraction of Halakhah as well. Halakhic structures against placing oneself in danger are not applicable to the case at hand for two reasons. The first argument is stated by Rabbi Moses Feinstein . . . smoking falls within the category of permissible activity. There is little doubt that although the road is fraught with danger, it is — at least for the present — a path well trodden by the multitude . . . The second argument relates to the distinction between an immediate danger and a potential or future danger. Immediate danger must be eschewed under all circumstances; future danger may be assumed if, in the majority of cases no harm will occur . . . No danger is present at the time the act is performed. The health hazards posed by smoking lie in the future. To be sure, certain physiological changes occur immediately upon inhalation of cigarette smoke, but such changes assume clinical significance only when they develop into symptoms of smoking-related illnesses. Since even in light of presently available evidence it appears that the majority of smokers do not compromise their health and do not face premature death as a result of cigarette smoking, there is . . . no halakhic reason to ban this activity."[31b]

Two major articles have been written on the question of the use of the psychedelic drugs. One is a response to the question as to whether psychedelic drugs may be used as a spur to religious insight.[32]

In answer to this, Dr. Freehof concludes that "the essence of the Jewish position in the search for God is through the calm intellect and not through the superheated emotions."[33]

Associating drugs with the use of abuse of alcohol, the author concludes: "It is clear, therefore, that any sort of befuddling of the clear mind was considered a hindrance to a true and sincere religious life."[34]

Furthermore, on the question of health, Dr. Freehof sums up:[35]

According to the spirit of Judaism, the path to religious knowledge is the clear mind, not the confused emotions. Any sort of drunkenness or bemusing of the senses is an impediment to true worship, and any willful endangering of legal tradition.

A second article entitled *LSD: A Jewish View*, evaluates in greater detail "the validity of (the drug's) religious claims, from the Weltanshauung of Halakhah and Jewish thought."[36]

Dr. Menahem Brayer stresses Judaism's concept of the *real* world as distinguished from the "world of the trip."

> For Judaism the real is the world of creation in all of its diversity . . . and man's role in it is to act as a partner in hallowing all of its aspects. If the state of the world is depressing, 'neither are you free to set yourself apart from it.' If social institutions such as marriage and family have disintegrated, the Jewish answer is not their abandonment. The salvation of man is dependent on his capability to raise up *his* world, not on his ability to raise himself out of it . . . Some claim that the drug experience gives the user character traits that will be useful upon his return to normal consciousness. The fact that one has increased sensitivity while under drug influence would not justify their use unless this sensitivity extended into the olam ha'asiya (real world).[37]

The prime objections the author puts forward to the use of drugs are:
1. Self injury: hahovel be'atzmo.
2. Injury to others: hahovel b'rabbim.
3. Placing a stumbling block before the blind by enticing others to use drugs.
4. Injuring the group: hezeika derabbim.

Maimonidies is quoted as reiterating "the deep concern of the Torah for the mental welfare of the Israelites, whether they be sinful or righteous."

> In many of his medical works, he stresses "the importance of mental health, and the improvement of behavior which is the core of the mind and its faculties," stating repeatedly, "how dangerous it is to indulge in medicine, tranquilizers, sedatives, or stimulants and becoming habituated to them."[38]

Taking psychedelic drugs, with all the possible psychotic repercussions, can be considered a transgression of the positive commandment in the Torah, v'nishmartem m'od nafshoseykhem (to take protective measures for the safeguard of health), and committing an act of haballah b'atzmo (willful self-damage).[39a]

A leading scholar and rabbinic authority, Rabbi Aaron Soloveichik writes:[39b]

. . . The use of drugs is conducive toward the total deterioration and emasculation of the human personality, depriving it of every vestige of freedom. This fact makes the use of drugs an extremely impure and immodest act. Use of drugs is forbidden by the Law of the Torah inasmuch as it involves the violation of three positive commandments and numerous negative commandments. The first violation relates to the positive commandment, 'Ye shall be holy.' As Nachmanides points out, this commandment implies that one is obligated to lead a life that conforms to the concept of purity. Secondly, the use of drugs involves a violation of the positive commandment of "Thou shalt follow in His ways." According to Maimonides, this means that a person is obligated to become a *baal midot*, to strive for the perfection of his character. Thirdly, the use of drugs involves the violation of the positive commandment of "Let your camp be holy." According to the *Sefer Mitzvos Katan*, this stipulates that a person must be modest in his behavior. The use of drugs also involves the violation of the negative commandment, "You should not follow after your own heart and eyes." Accordingly, a person should not allow himself to be swayed by his appetites to such an extent that the formulation of a habit infringes upon his freedom. Moreover, since the use of drugs is to impair one's health, it involves a violation of the negative commandment of 'inflicting harm upon oneself' as well as the negative commandment of 'Look after yourself and take care of yourself.'

The use of drugs, far from removing the tensions of life in the long run, deprives a person of his freedom and dignity and gradually results in the disintegration of the human personality.

Dr. Leo Landman, in his definitive study, *Judaism and Drugs*, reproduces an open letter issued by the National Conference of Synagogue Youth in Vancouver pledging to avoid the use of marijuana on Halakhic grounds.[40]

An Open Letter to the Jewish Community from the National Conference of Synagogue Youth, N.C.S.Y (Youth arm of Congregation Shaare Tzedek)

Dear Parents, Brothers, Sisters and Friends:

We the undersigned, like most other teenagers, have faced the serious issue of drugs and drug use. As members of an Orthodox

Youth Group, we feel that our decision must reckon with the traditions of Judaism and with the specific demands of Halakhah. Because of the controversial nature of the problems, especially the question of marijuana, we have this past week consulted with some of the greatest Halakhic authorities of our time. They are: Rabbi A. Soloveitchik, Dean, Hebrew Theological College; Rabbi M. Feinstein, Dean, Yeshiva Tiferet Yerushalayim, Chairman, Council of Torah Authorities; and Rabbi Dr. Immanuel Jakobovits, Chief Rabbi of the British Commonwealth.

Their unanimous decision was that the use of marijuana constitutes a violation of basic Jewish Law. We have studied the text of their decision and understand their condemnation based on the following principles:

A. Being involved with marijuana is a violation of the sacredness of human potentiality. A man created in the image of God must constantly walk in the ways of his Creator; just as the God of the universe is alive, active and creative so must be the world of Man. Marijuana leads a person to withdrawal, passivity, laziness; concentration becomes difficult for the study of the Torah and the fulfillment of mitzvoth burdensome. Such a person divests himself of his unique calling to be a real man in the image of God and in nakedness stalks the earth in search of the tree of sensuality to avoid and escape this world of reality. Marijuana, its culture and its climate, is so far removed from the Torah's call to HOLINESS.

B. One who is a user of marijuana violates Numbers 15:39. ("And it shall be unto you for a fringe, that you may look upon it, and remember all the commandments of the Lord, and do them; and that you go not about after your own heart and your own eyes after which you used to go astray"), and leads to addiction to sensuousness. He places himself in a position where destruction of his free will and degradation of his inner personality is imminent. Such a person slowly loses his options and his choices and the mechanism of his decision-making powers.

Judaism teaches that the only difference between man and animal is that man can think, argue, foresee, conclude, and go back on his former decisions; marijuana helps diminish that distinction and makes man more closely related to the ape.

167

C. It is also a violation of Deuteronomy 22:8 which stresses the obligation on man to zealously protect his body from anything that may be harmful and injurous. The fact that it is not now harmful to a person does not preclude the chance that it may one day be. A man who does not put up a fence around his roof, is in violation of the biblical mandate irrespective of whether someone has fallen off his roof or not. A biblical verse so concerned about loss of limb would be much more concerned about possible loss of mind and soul as well.

We, therefore, publicly commit ourselves to the Halakhic view that drugs are a deviation from the basic tasks of a purposeful Jewish life.

## NOTES

1. See Walter N. Pahnke and William A. Richards, Implications of LSD and experimental Mysticism, *Journal of Religion and Health*, Volume 5, Number 3, July 1966.

2. See 'Drugs,' Jerusalem Post, March 13, 1967, Jerusalem, Israel, page 14.

3. Dr. Alton Ochsner, quoted in 'The Drug Scene,' by Steven M. Spencer, *Readers Digest*, New York, January, 1968.

4. This does not mean that the rabbis of the Talmud were oblivious to marijuana or cannibis sativa, otherwise known as Indian hemp, a hardy botanic cousin to the fig, the hop and the nettle, which produces marijuana. Both cannibis and marijuana, the latter by its Talmudic name, k'sanin or kisnin or ksanin, are mentioned. Professor Marcus Jastrow defines kisanin as nibblings, desert, quoting nibblings as roasted ears. Kanbos or kanbis, he defines as hemp planted in a vineyard.

Mention of cannabis is noted in the Mishnah:

If his field were sown with hemp (or kanbos, whose seed often lies on the ground three years before germinating) or serpentaria, he must not sow over the top of them, because they produce only after three years.

*Mishnayoth, Seder Zeraim, Kilaim,*
Translated by Philip Blackman, Judaica Press, 1965, p. 188.

Hemp, (kanbos) says R. Tarfon, is not forbidden junction, but the Sages say, it is forbidden.

Ibid., V, 8, p. 210

Abaye stated: Nurse told me that roasted ears (Kisanin) are beneficial to the heart (others say to the digestive system) and they banish morbid thoughts.

Eruvin 29b.

What (sign is there at the wedding of) a widow? R. Joseph taught: A widow has no roasted ears (kisanin) or corn distributed at her wedding.

Ketuvoth 17b.

And the absence of the ears of corn (kisanin) is the sign that she is a widow.

Rashi, ibid.

See also, Talmud Yerushalmi, referring to a loaf derived from kisanin and suggesting that its distribution following a meal is laden with blessings.

Berakhoth, VI:5.

Balaam's advice to Balak in suggesting that the availability of kisanin coupled with an encouragement of prostitution would make the Israelites vulnerable to the Moabites.

Sanhedrein, X:2.

See also, Dr. Y. Lowenbach, "What the Sages Say About Marijuana," *Jewish Day Journal*, New York, New York, September 29, 1969.

The most comprehensive study of this subject is Leo Landman's *Judaism and Drugs*, Commission of Synagogue Relations, Federation of Jewish Philanthropies, New York, 1973.

5. Dr. Leon Wurmser, quoted in "Teen-Age Use of Heroin Rising But Data are Few," by Robert Reinhold, *New York Times*, February 16, 1970.
See also, *The Jewish Famiy, A Compendium*, Norman Liner, editor, Commission on Synagogue Relations, New York Philanthropies, New York, 1972, Chapter on Drugs, p. 123.

6. Robert A. Raab, "Jewish Youth and Drugs," *The Jewish Spectator*, New York, Oct., 1969, p. 20. See also, "Drug Problems Among Jewish Students," *The Jewish Day-Journal*, May 13, 1969.

7. Report, "Jewish Federation Proposes Six Point Program To Fight Drug Abuse," Federation of Jewish Philanthropies of New York, Jan. 1970. See also, "Drugs Are Not the Problem," "Drugs Are Still Not the Problem," "Drug Abuse," B'nai B'rith Youth Organization, Washington, D.C.

8. Deut. 4:9, also Deut. 4:15.

9. Lev. 19:16.

10. Lev. 19:18.

11. Lev. 19:14.

12. Lev. 24:17.

The sages of Israel, deriving ethical guidance concerning all aspects of human conduct and behavior from the commandments, say: "To put one's neighbor publicly to shame is like shedding blood" (Bava Metziah 58b), for "A man should throw himself into a fiery furnace rather than put his neighbor publicly to shame" (ibid., 59a). According to the Mishnah, "Whosoever destroys a single soul, Scripture regards him as though he had destroyed a whole world." (Sanh. 37a).

13. Deut. 22:8.

14. Deut. 27:18.

15. Mishna, Baba Kamma, VIII, 1.

16. Hullin 10a.

17. Deut. 4:9. "Code of Maimonides," *The Book of Torts*, Translated by

Hyman Klein, Yale Judaica Series, New Haven, Conn., Vol. IX, p. 227. 1954. Section, Murder and Preservaton of Life, XI.

18. Ibid., p. 227-228.

19. Ibid., pp. 228.

20. Lev. 19:14.

21. Ibid., p. 232, XII; 14.

22. Shulhan Arukh, *Code of Jewish Law* (Abridged). Translated by Hyman Goldin, Hebrew Publishing Company, Vol. I, 1927, XXXIII, p. 109.

23a. Berakhot 31b.

24. Eruvin 64a.

25. Ibid.

25a. Lev. 10:8.

26. Moses Aberbach, "Smoking and the Halakhah," *Tradition*, RCA, New York, Vol. 10, No. 3., Spring 1969.

27. Ibid. pp. 49, 51 and quoting Deut. 4:9.

28. Deut. 22:8.

29. Ibid. Moses Aberbach, note 14.

30. Ibid. note 24, page 58.

31a. Richard L. Israel, "The New Morality and the Rabbis," *Conservative Judaism*, R.A., New York, Vol. 24, No. 1, Fall, 1969.

31b. *Tradition*, R.C.A., Vol 16, No. 4, Summer 1977, New York, page 121.

32. Dr. Solomon Freehof, *Current Reform Responsa*, Hebrew Union College Press, Cincinnati and New York, 1969, p. 247. Dr. Freehof was kind enough to send the author a mimeographed copy of the responsa before publication.

33. Ibid., page 248.

34. Ibid., page 249.

35. Ibid., page 250.

36. Menachem M. Brayer, "LSD; A Jewish View," *Tradition*, RCA, New York, Vol. 10, No. 1, Summer 1968, p. 32.

37. One might well include the negative commandment of Maimonides, not to give misleading advice. "By this prohibition we are forbidden to give misleading advice. Thus, if one asks your advice on a matter which he does not fully understand, you are forbidden to mislead or deceive him: you must give him what you consider the right guidance. The prohibition is contained in His words, Nor shall you place a stumbling block before the blind" (Lev. 19:14 ) on which the Sifra says: "If one is 'blind' in a certain matter, and asks you for advice, do not give him advice which is not suitable for him." Maimonides: *The Commandments*, Volume Two, Soncino Press, London and New York, 1967, p. 277. Translated by Charles R. Chavel.

38. Ibid., page 36.

39a. Paraphrase of Ibid., page 37.

39b. Aaron Soloveichik, "Torah Tzniut Versus New Morality and Drugs," *Tradition*, Vol. 13, No. 2, Fall 1972, R.C.A. New York, p. 55.

40. Leo Landman, *Judaism and Drugs*, ibid., p. 29-30.

# EUTHANASIA

Euthanasia, literally meaning a good, pleasant or happy death, was a term coined by Sir Thomas More[1] (1478-1535) to describe the painless and merciful killing of incurables. Discussion about the actual practice of euthanasia, however, dates back many millenia.

In principle, Plato and Aristotle endorsed its use, and it was common in Ancient Greece, and especially in Sparta. Closer to our times, Sir Thomas More advocated it on a voluntary basis. Sweden has legalized passive euthanasia, drawing a distinction between killing with bad and good intentions and Joseph Fletcher has urged the legalization of euthanasia on grounds that "suffering is purposeless, demoralizing and degrading, that the human personality is of greater worth than life per se and that the phrase, 'blessed are the merciful for they shall obtain mercy'[2] is as important as 'you shall not murder.' "[3]

Confrontation with this issue[3a] immediately provokes moral, religious and legal reverberations, striking at basic human and social values. The subject calls into question the inviolability and sacredness of life and the right of a man himself, his close relatives or a physician to determine when life should end. The emotional problem arises as to the value of a life carried on in pain or in a state of unconsciousness. Though rarely overtly expressed, financial considerations are also important, when an obvious incurable is kept alive by drugs or other artificial means. Yet who will step forward to accept the responsibility of action?

The problem has been well stated by E.E. Fibley: 'When a tortured man asks: "For God's sake, doctor, let me die, just put me to sleep," we have yet to find the answer as to whether compliance is for God's sake, the patient's sake, our own, or possibly, all three.' Even if the moral issue of euthanasia could be circumvented, other questions of logistics would immediately arise: Who is to initiate euthanasia proceedings? The patient? The family? The physician? Who is to make the final decision? The physician? A group of physicians? The courts? Who is to carry out the decision if it is affirmative? The physician? Others?3[b]

An additional question concerns the right to die. One's right to live is unquestioned, but does one also have the right to die? Is that right violated when a person is kept alive unnecessarily under excruciating or degrading circumstance?

Religious groups believe that life and death are Divine gifts, and that man should not usurp the will of God. Life ends when God decrees. Though one may not understand unnecessary suffering and may want to terminate it, to do so is not given to man.

This is the position of Judaism which has as its underlying premise the affirmation that God, and not man is the final arbiter in life. Otherwise, if mercy killings were permitted in one instance, they soon would be in others also:

> A recent editorial stated: If euthanasia is granted to the first class, can it long be denied to the second . . . Each step is so short, the slope so slippery; our values in this age, so uncertain and unstable . . .3[c]

The fundamental principle is that life is absolutely holy, not relatively so, and that its sacredness is inviolable.

All denominations in Judaism agree upon this point. The Catholic position is stated as follows:

> The teaching of the Church is unequivocal that God is the supreme master of life and death and that no human being is allowed to usurp His dominion so as to deliberately put an end to life, either his own or anyone else's without authorization . . . and the only authorization the Church recognizes are a nation engaged in war, execution of criminals by a government, killing in self-defense . . . The Church has never allowed and never will allow the killing of individuals on grounds of private expediency; for instance . . . even the putting to an end prolonged suffering or hopeless sickness.

Relative to passive euthanasia, the Church distinguishes between "ordinary" and "extraordinary" measures, and Pope Pius XII issued an encyclical not requiring physicians to use extraordinary measures for the preservation of life in circumstances where death might be desirable. Thus, passive euthanasia is sanctioned.[3d]

The Protestant attitude varies and a clear-cut posture has not emerged.

Euthanasia has been discussed in the Bible, the Talmud, the codes and the commentaries for many centuries. Here are some selections which serve as the bases of rabbinic decisions:

## I. From the Bible:

1. Whoever sheds the blood of man, by man shall his blood be shed, for in His image did God make man.[4]

2. When a man schemes against another and kills him treacherously, you shall take him from My very altar to be put to death.[5]

3. You shall not commit murder.[6]

4. Now the Philistines fought against Israel and the men of Israel fled from before the Philistines and fell down slain in Mount Gilboa. And the Philistines pursued hard upon Saul and upon his men. And the battle went hard against Saul and upon his men. And the battle went hard against Saul and the archers overtook him and he was greatly afraid by reason of the archers. Then said Saul to his armor-bearer: "Draw your sword and thrust me through with it, lest these uncircumcised come and thrust me through and make a mock of me." But his armor-bearer would not! for he was greatly afraid. Therefore, Saul took his sword and fell upon it. And when the armor-bearer saw that Saul was dead, he likewise fell on his sword and died with him. So Saul died and his three sons and his armor-bearer and all his men that day.[7] And David said to the young men who told him: 'How do you know that Saul and Jonathan his son are dead?' And the young man that told him said: 'As I happened by chance upon Mount Gilboa, Saul leaned upon his spear; and lo, the chariots and the horsemen pressed hard upon him. And when he looked behind him, he saw me, and called to me. And I answered, Here am I. And he said to me: Who are you? And I answered: I am an Amalekite. He said to me: Stand, I pray you, beside me for the agony has taken hold of me; because my life is just yet in me. So I

stood beside him, and slew him, because I was sure that he would not live after that he was fallen.[8][9]

5. Naked did I come out of my mother's womb and naked shall I return. The Lord gave and the Lord has taken away. Blessed be the name of the Lord.[10]

6. When Job's wife, herself prostrate at the sign of her husband's affliction cries out, "Do you still hold fast to your integrity? Blaspheme God and die." Job indignantly replies: "You speak as one of the impious women. What? Shall we receive good at the hand of God and shall we not receive evil?"[11]

7. The spirit of God has made me and the breath of the Almighty gives me life.[12]

8. Behold, all souls are Mine.[13]

## II. From the Talmud:

1. A dying man is considered the same as a living man in every respect. He may obligate to levirate marriage, and he may release from levirate marriage. He may confer the right to eat of the heave offering and he may disqualify from eating of the heave offering. He may inherit property and he may bequeath property. If a limb is severed from his body, it is regarded as a limb severed from a living person, if flesh, as flesh from a living person . . . All this applies until the moment he dies . . . His jaws may not be bound, nor his orifices stopped, and no metal vessel or other cooling object may be placed upon his belly until the moment he dies . . . He may not be stirred, nor may he be washed, and he should not be laid on salt or sand, until the moment he dies . . . His eyes may not be closed. Whosoever touches him or stirs him sheds blood. Rabbi Meir used to compare a dying man to a flickering lamp; the moment one touches it he puts it out. So, too, whosoever closes the eyes of a dying man is accounted as though he has snuffed out his life . . . .[14]

2. Therefore, (for this reason) was man created alone, to teach you that whosoever destroys a single soul, Scripture imputes guilt to him as though he had destroyed a complete world.[15]

3. One may not close (the eyes of a corpse) on the Sabbath, nor on week-days when he is about to die, and he who closes the eyes of a dying person when the soul is still departing (such an act promoting death) is a murderer. (Literally, he sheds blood because he hastens death).[16] Our Rabbis taught: He who closes the eyes of a dying man at the point of death is a murderer. It may be compared to a

flickering lamp that is going out. If a man places a finger upon it, it is immediately extinguished.[17]

4. On the day when Rabbi Judah the Prince died, the Rabbis decreed a public fast and offered prayers for heavenly mercy. They, furthermore, announced that whoever said that Rabbi Judah was dead would be pierced with a sword. Rabbi Judah's handmaid (a famous character known for her sagacity and learning) ascended the roof and prayed: "The immortals (angels) desire Judah (to join them) and the mortals (men) desire Rabbi Judah (to remain with them); may it be the will of God that the mortal overpower the immortals." (i.e., that he not die). When, however, she saw how often he resorted to the privy, painfully taking off his tephillin, (phylacteries) and putting them on again, she prayed: "May it be the will (of the Almighty) that the immortals may overpower the mortals (i.e., that he die.)" As the Rabbis incessantly continued their prayers for (heavenly) mercy, she took up a jar and threw it down from the roof on the ground. (For a moment) they ceased praying and the soul of Rabbi Judah departed to its eternal rest.[18]

5. They (the Romans) brought up Rabbi Hanina ben Teradion and asked him, "Why have you occupied yourself with the Torah?" (This was forbidden by Hadrian under penalty of death). He replied, "Thus the Lord my God commanded me." At once they sentenced him to be burnt, his wife to be slain, and his daughter to be consigned to a brothel . . .[19]

\* \* \*

On their return, (the great men had gone to the funeral of Rabbi Jose ben Kisma) they found Rabbi Hanina ben Teradion sitting and occupying himself with the Torah, publicly gathering assemblies and keeping a scroll of the Torah in his bosom. The Romans took hold of him, wrapped him in the Scroll of the Law, placed bundles of branches round him and set him on fire. They then brought tufts of wool, which they had soaked in water, and placed them over this heart, so that he should not expire quickly. His daughter exclaimed: "Father, that I should see you in this state." He replied, "If it were I alone being burnt it would have been a hard thing to bear; but now I am burning together with the Scroll of Law. He who will have regard for the plight of the Torah will also have regard for my plight." His disciples called out, "Rabbi, what do you see?" He answered them: "The parchments are being burnt but the

175

letters are soaring on high. (Scrolls of the Torah may be destroyed but the spirit is immortal and indestructible). "Open your mouth," his disciples called, "So that the fire enters you (and put an end to your agony)." He replied, "Let Him who gave me my soul take it away, but no one should injure himself." The executioner then said to him, "Rabbi, if I raise the flame and take away the tufts of wool from over your heart, will you cause me to enter into the life to come?" "Yes," he replied. "Then, swear to me," he urged. He swore to him. He then raised the flame and removed the tufts of wool from over his heart and his soul departed speedily. The executioner then jumped and threw himself into the fire. And a Bath Kol (Divine Voice) was heard to exclaim: "Rabbi Hanina ben Teradion and the executioner have been assigned to the world to come." When Rabbi Judah heard it he wept and said, "One may acquire eternal life in a single hour, another after many years."

### III. Codes and Commentaries

1. It seems to me that there are times when it is necessary to pray that he die, as for example, if the sick person suffers greatly and it is (in any case) impossible for him to continue living much longer.[20]

2. Whoever kills a healthy person and whoever kills a sick person who is dying, though his death is imminent, all are guilty of murder.[21]

3. One who is dying is for all intents and purposes considered to be alive. Hence, nothing must be done to hasten death . . .[22]
Whoever touches him is as though he shes blood and it is to be compared to a flickering light, the mere touch extinguishes it.[23]
. . . it is forbidden to hasten death. However, if there is an impediment preventing the soul's departure, for example, a knocking noise produced by a wood-chopper chopping wood, or there is salt on his tongue, and these hinder the departure of the soul, it is permissible to remove them because there is no active, positive act here except the removal of the impediment to death.[24]

4. One who is dying is to be considered as a living being in all matters and it is forbidden to touch him (for fear of accelerating the end) for anyone who touches him is like one who sheds blood. With what is this comparable? With the lamp's flickering flame which becomes extinguished as soon as a person touches it. If he be a long time in a dying condition, and it causes great distress to himself and

his relatives, it is nevertheless forbidden to hasten his end, for instance, to remove from under his head the pillows, because people believe that a certain kind of feathers prevents death, or to place the keys from the synagogue under his head; all this is forbidden. Still if there is a cause that prevents the exit of the soul, such as the noise of knocking, it is permitted to remove that cause, inasmuch as that is not a direct deed which hastens the end, but the removal of an obstacle whereby no one touches the dying person.[25]

These sources are the basis for any discussion of the Jewish attitude to euthanasia.

## THE ORTHODOX POSITION

It is clear . . . that even when the patient is already known to be on his deathbed and close to the end, any form of active euthanasia is strictly forbidden . . . At the same time, Jewish law sanctions, and perhaps even demands, the withdrawal of any factor . . . whether extraneous to the patient himself or not . . . which may artificially delay his demise in the final phase . . .[26] Jakobovits is quick to point out that all the Jewish sources refer to an individual in whom death is expected to be imminent, three days or less in Rabbinic sources. Thus passive euthanasia in a patient who may yet live for weeks or for months may not necessarily be condoned."[27]

"That Jewish teachers were not out of sympathy with every effort to deliver incurables from their agony is shown by the sanction to seek death as a release from suffering by resorting to prayer or to occult devices.[28]

"Euthanasia proper, that is, an attempt to relieve suffering by actively and deliberately hastening death is of course condemned as sheer murder by all authorities . . . Far more complex and controversial is the problem of indirect euthanasia when the patient's death is merely the result of either some medication given only to relieve pain or of the withdrawal of treatment."[29]

On the latter question, authorities have differed, some allowing action on the basis of the Talmudic account of Rabbi Hanina ben Teradion, while others have strenuously opposed any relaxation of energies to extend life "however artificial or ultimately hopeless."

"Furthermore, in the case of an incurably ill person in severe pain, agony or distress, the removal of an impediment which hinders his soul's departure, although permitted by Jewish law, as described by Rama, may not be analogous to the withholding of medical therapy that is perhaps sustaining the patient's life unnaturally. The impediments spoken of in the Code of Jewish Law, whether far removed from the patient as exemplified by the noise of wood chopping, or in physical contact with him such as the case of salt on the patient's tongue, do not constitute any part of the therapeutic armamentarium employed in the medical management of this patient. And for this reason, these impediments may be removed. However, the discontinuation of instruments and machinery which is specifically utilized in the treatment of incurably-ill patients might only be permissible if one is certain that in doing so one is shortening the act of dying and not interrupting life. Yet who can make the fine distinction between prolonging life and prolonging the act of dying? The former comes within the physician's reference, the latter does not."[30]

A recent article in the London *Jewish Chronicle* noted:

> "In Jewish teaching all life is equally valuable and everything possible must be done to save life, however slight the hope for success. It is not for humans to assess the respective merits of other human beings. It would therefore be considered wrong to set an age limit on patients to be helped. Nothing, according to Halakhah, must be done to bring life to an end, nor must any person be deprived of natural needs, such as food or blood, i.e., by transfusion. But if humanely speaking there is no further hope of survival a doctor may not be required to resort to artificial means such as drugs or electrical stimulation of the heart. But the authorities of the Orthodox rabbinate have not yet come to any final or agreed answers to some of the problems raised by the latest advances in medical science.[31]

## THE REFORM POSITION

In 1946 the Commission on Justice and Peace recommended a study be prepared on the attitude of the Reform tradition toward euthanasia.[32] Two years later the Commission on Justice and Peace advised that a special committee of the Conference be appointed to study the question. This body concluded that the "Jewish ideal of the sanctity of human life and the supreme value of the individual soul would suffer incalculable harm if, contrary to moral law, men were at liberty to determine the conditions under which they might put an end to their own lives and the lives of other men."[32a]

At the same Conference the question was raised as to whether life should be prolonged beyond the point at which nothing more than biological function could be looked for. The problem of euthanasia and this kind of prolongation of a merely biological existence was summarized by Dr. Solomon B. Freehof, who stated that 'the act of killing a patient, for whatever motive, is absolutely forbidden.'[32b] Then, after a thorough discussion of the question of prolonging life Dr. Freehof went on to say that he concluded 'from the *spirit* of Jewish law that while you may not do anything to hasten death, you may, under special circumstances of suffering and hopelessness, allow death to come.'[32c]

"Modern medical techniques for the prolongation of life make the protection of 'the right to die' much more significant than when it was enunciated in the thirteenth century."[32d]

Therefore, while Reform Rabbis disapproved of euthanasia, they acknowledged a person's right to die.[33]

An interesting insight is offered by Solomon Freehof in response to a question as to whether cryobiology, is permissible. He answers:

> The proposal is to freeze such bodies in cases only of people already dying or virtually dying of an incurable disease. So it amounts to the delaying of the death of a dying person. This is clearly prohibited by Jewish law. While one may not do anything at all to hasten the death of a dying person, one may also not do anything to prevent his dying. Such a person has a right to die.[34a]

## THE CONSERVATIVE POSITION

Conservative Judaism has taken no official position on this issue, but is obviously in general agreement with the Orthodox stance, perhaps moderated by a more liberal perspective towards indirect or passive forms of euthanasia. In an article entitled "To Be Or . . . A Jewish View of Euthanasia, a Conservative rabbi stated that "recent advances in medical science provide a halakhically acceptable possible alternative to euthanasia, i.e., refrigeration." He goes on to conclude that:

> Though prolonging life is always obligatory, artificially prolonging the life of a terminal patient is optional.[34b]

In a symposium on death under the auspices of the Rabbinical

Assembly's Committee on Bio-Ethics, two papers, "The Definition of Death" and "Updating the Criteria of Death" were presented. The two rabbis, Seymour Siegel and Daniel Goldfarb, agreed that Jewish religious law does not require that "vegetative comatose patients be maintained when all traditional signs of death would be present without these means." They agreed that there be no artificial interference with the course of a patient's terminal illness and that the patient should not be maintained longer than "sound medical judgment indicates that artificial means could achieve a positive medical result." Rabbi Siegel noted, "And where death is present, it is not necessary to sustain breathing and heart activity by mechanical means."[34c]

Rabbi Siegel made the following recommendations to the Convention of the Rabbinical Asembly; they were referred to the Committee on Jewish Law and Standards:

> The Rabbinical Assembly, in convention assembled, recognizing that recent developments in medical science and technology have created situations in which the traditional criteria for the determination of death — the loss of spontaneous respiratory and cardiac functions — are inapplicable; and as a result, uncertainty and confusion exist for doctors, hospitals, families of patients being maintained by machines, and clergy and other counselors trying to offer comfort and guidance; and that consequently serious problems arise in treatment of situations involving (i) victims of criminal attack (ii) the potential donation of organs for transplant purposes, and (iii) irreversibly comatose patients in a vegetative state; hereby resolves that:
> 1) The determination of death on the basis of a measurement of the cessation of spontaneous brain function, in situations where responsible medical opinion indicated its propriety, would be consistent with Jewish law, and that
> 2) a bill proposing a definition of death, such as H. Bill 7860-A, which includes brain functions as a criterion in appropriate cases, is strongly endorsed;
> 3) the use of artificial means after death has been declared, for the preservation of organs for transplant purposes, is permissible;
> 4) a "hopeless" person is not to be considered a dead person;
> 5) whether a person whose condition is considered "hopeless" by physicians exercising their best judgment according to current medical practices (should be subject to euthanasia) is a question

independent of and unrelated to the question of when death occurs, and that

6) the removal of life support devices from patients whose condition is considered "hopeless" as described above is entirely consistent with Jewish law, and thus treatment decision to this effect made in good conscience by competent physicians can be supported by rabbis in contact with the patient or the family.[34d]


## RELATED SUBJECTS

### A. The Karen Ann Quinlan Case

The Karen Ann Quinlan case has sharpened many of the issues discussed here.

Karen Ann Quinlan had suffered irreversible brain damage and was in a coma. Her foster parents filed a petition in court asking for authorization to remove the respirator so that their daughter might die with grace and dignity.

Three rabbis, one from each of the three major groupings within Judaism, were asked for comment.

Rabbi Norman Lamm, President of Yeshiva University, said that "parents simply are not a party to the case from the point of view of Jewish law and that to bestow upon them the legal right to determine the life or death of their daughter would be a reversion to ancient Roman times when parents had absolute authority over the life and death of their progeny. He declared that the general principle of the Halakhah is that "we are not required to utilize heroic measures to prolong the life of the hopelessly sick patients, but we are forbidden to terminate the use of such measures once they have begun . . . If we are asked whether or not to use such extraordinary measures to prolong biologically the life of a patient who has suffered irreversible brain damage, then there are grounds, depending on the individual case, for responding negatively. But . . . I cannot see how Jewish law can sanction pulling the plug which is tantamount to severing a vital organ of the patient, which is forbidden."[34e]

Rabbi Seymour Siegel, Chairman of the Committee on Jewish Law and Standards of the Rabbinical Assembly, speaking on his own behalf rather than as an official of the Conservative Movement said that "the basic question is whether the woman is to be considered dead or still alive, though in a coma. In traditional Judaism, he said, criteria for determing death have been the cessation of respiratory functions and the cessation of heart beat. These criteria represented the best scientific knowledge of the day and once those functions stopped, the person was judged to be dead. He added that in the judgment of Orthodox decisions, these criteria should not be changed since they have been enshrined in the traditional texts. But in the judgment of more liberal decisors, . . . the criteria for death should reflect the best scientific knowledge of the time, not dogmatic principles. At the present time, he said, there is near consensus in the scientific community that brain death does indeed indicate the cessation of human life and that, therefore, the basis for decision in this vital area has been established. On the assumption that Miss Quinlan is not dead by current medical standards, the next question, he said, is the issue of euthanasia . . . Removing the respirator would be a situation of passive euthanasia, which, he said would be permitted if medical opinion is that the woman is dead. Since active euthanasia is forbidden, the respirator may not be removed if the person is held to be alive . . .''

Rabbi Joseph Perman, Chairman of the Subcommittee on Bio-Ethics of the Central Conference of American Rabbis, "agreed that traditional Jewish law does not speak of brain death because this was beyond the limits of medical knowledge at the time it was written. In any event, he added, we do not need to go beyond the law; we need to get behind it in order to understand the ethical sensitivity and human compassion that has determined all Jewish bio-ethical decisions . . . The question he said, was whether artificially to prolong the condition or not to prolong it. We ought not do it. He said it could not be ethically justifiable to extend a vegetative state for weeks, let alone months and that no patient should have to suffer such indignity, regardless of state of consciousness.''[34/]

## B. The Natural Death Act of California

On September 30, 1976, Governor Jerry Brown signed into California law, the so-called ''Natural Death Act,'' making California the first state to legalize what has become known as a ''living will.'' The act says that an adult, by signing a witnessed document, can direct his physician to withhold or withdraw life-sustaining procedures in the event of a terminal condition, which means, when death is imminent. The provisions *require* a physician to act in this way if the document was executed at least fourteen days before the patient was diagnosed as having a terminal condition.

Other states are considering similiar statutes.

A number of Jewish views reflecting the groupings within Judaism were recorded in *Sh'ma*, the particular issue created by Elliot Horowitz.

Two Orthodox rabbis, Rabbi Moshe D. Tendler and Rabbi J. David Bleich take positions that the Natural Death Act is not in keeping with Jewish Law. Rabbi Seymour Siegel, a Conservative Rabbi, and Rabbi Hillel Cohn, a Reform Rabbi, take opposite positions, Rabbi Siegel writing from the perspective of Halakhah.

Rabbi Bleich, in his article on *Legal Immorality Not Personal Freedom*, asserts that personal freedom is not the real issue:

> " . . . in point of fact, the California statute does not at all strike a blow for human freedom; it serves but to legislate recognition of disparity in the value of human life. The legislature is saying that some life is more sacred than others. The remaining life-span of the terminal patient is not of much value, therefore, it may be foreshortened with impunity. This is a value judgement which can — and should be disputed. But to identify this dubious judgment as a realization of human freedom is a sham and should be recognized as such . . . Judaism knows too well the dangers inherent in quality of life determination. Human life, in all its guises, is sacred and inviolate."

Rabbi Tendler in his article *Torah Ethics Prohibit Natural Death*, notes:

> . . . How terminal must a patient be before he becomes really terminal? When is it (life) "unnecessary" or "not beneficial" to the patient . . . If we are committed to the fundamental concept of the infinite worth of human life, then a piece of infinity is infinity . . . "Dying with dignity" is an ill-conceived slogan; nothing more. Death with dignity is the end result of a dignified life style. In itself, death is a truly undignified life style. In itself, death is a truly undignified behavior. If those attending the dying patient behave in sensitive dignified fashion, no indignity other than that of death itself is involved . . .
> The decision to withdraw life-support mechanisms can only be made by equating terminal illness with death; the imminent with

the actual. What dangers lurk in such an assumption! Can active euthanasia be far behind! . . .

The living will has . . . little ethical validity in the absence of intractable pain or when the patient is in coma . . . Living Will legislation may bring active euthanasia a step closer to social acceptance, just as abortion legislation has made passive euthanasia legislation more palatable.

Rabbi Seymour Siegel in his article *Jewish Law Permits Natural Death*, writes:

> . . . It is clear that where death is imminent and where the procedure cannot bring a cure or even a significant amelioration of pain, that what is best for the individual (especially if he expresses his opinion through a will) is to allow him to die naturally . . .
> . . . We have the duty to prolong life, not to prolong death. The ethical approach, it would seem to me, is to determine what is best for the sufferer — not merely to use all methods that might exist. The patient, under the California statute, has the opportunity to express his own preference as to what is best for him. Therefore, it has a very good outcome and should be supported . . .
> . . . There are well-known passages in the traditional literature which permit a person who is on his deathbed to be allowed to die "naturally" . . . What the Living Will makes possible is the giving of the privilege to the patient himself to stop those things "that delay the soul's leaving the body."
> The developments of medical technology have caused problems which our ancestors could hardly have foreseen. We must not forget, in our loyalty to tradition, the welfare of the suffering patient who, when the Giver of Life has proclaimed the end of his earthly existence, should be allowed to die in spite of our machines.

Rabbi Hillel Cohn, in his article *Natural Death — Humane, Just and Jewish*, writes:

> . . . I begin with the acceptance of the premise that the right to die is as fundamental as many other rights. Freedom in the most basic sense includes the right to self-determination . . .
> The Natural Death Act enables the Jew, I feel, to perform a religious act of the highest quality. It enables the Jew to consider his or her life and death and to make some responsible determina-

tion as to what he or she wishes done in the event he or she is suffering from an incurable injury, disease, or illness . . .

How much better it would be if we were all better able to make such determinations without the need for enabling legislation. Our society does not yet assume our ability to make crucial decisions. In the absence of such an assumption it is good for the liberal Jew to be able to perform yet another deeply religious act by opting for natural death . . .[34g]

## C. The Siamese Twins Case

One of the most dramatic events in recent years, relative to Euthanasia, occurred October, 1977, at Children's Hospital in Philadelphia, and was beautifully described by Donald C. Drake in the Philadelphia Inquirer.[34h] Siamese twins had recently been born to a young Orthodox couple. The twins were joined at the chest. When brought to Children's Hospital, it was quickly noted that only one heartbeat was audible. Further examinations showed that one baby, (called Baby Girl B), had a four-chambered heart, and the other baby, (called Baby Girl A), a two-chambered heart; only a very narrow wall separated them. Thus, one and one half hearts existed for two people — not enough to sustain both lives. There was a possibility that if the twins were severed, the twin with the four-chambered heart might live. But the act was a positive one and, therefore, the questions of Euthanasia, the infinite worth of human life, and whether one life is more important than another. Is it moral to kill Baby Girl A so that Baby Girl B might live?

The issue was brought eventually to Rabbi Moshe Feinstein and his son-in-law, Rabbi Moses Tendler. They discussed the issues for a number of days. (In addition to the problem raised by the Jewish couple, the nurses, many of them Catholic, also questioned their own heritage.)

To reach a decision, the rabbis pondered many aspects. Rabbi Tendler repeatedly asked the Chief of Surgery, Dr. C. Everett Koop, many questions. For example, "are the twins one baby or two babies? If the twins were only one baby with two heads, then it would be ethical to remove one baby as an unnecessary appendage. If they were two babies, with distinct nervous systems, then more scholarly discussions would be required." The doctor would only recommend that "the twins should be separated" because the hearts could fail at any moment.

Further questions were asked. "Could the six-chambered heart be given to Baby Girl A instead of Baby B?" Or could the baby with the two-chambered heart accept the entire heart. While the doctor could not understand the question, he responded in the negative. "The circulatory system," he said, "was so constructed, that the transfer could be made only to Baby B." The rabbi asked whether he was sure "that Baby Girl B would also die, even with the surgery." The doctor responded "that Baby Girl B would die regardless of what was done, but that was not a certainty."

Rabbi Tendler projected this thesis: "Two men jump out of a burning airplane. The parachute of a first man opens and he falls slowly and safely to earth. The parachute of a second man does not open. As he plunges past his friend he manages to grab onto his foot and hold on. But, the parachute is too small for both. They are both plunging to their death." Rabbi Tendler concludes "that it is morally justified for the first man to kick his friend away because they would both die if he didn't, and it was the second man who is *designated for death*, since it was his parachute that didn't open."

One of Rabbi Tendler's sons, Dr. Yaakov Tendler, a rabbi and physician, reacts: "Take the case of the baby who is being born, something goes wrong, just the baby's head comes out of the vagina. It is stuck and cannot be pulled out. The choice would be either kill the baby and dismember it to get it out of the mother's body or let them battle it out to see who wins. Biblical ethics demands that you take the 'hands-off policy.' You have two human beings in conflict with each other. Neither is guilty of a crime. You have no right to select the life of one over the life of another. It is only in the unique situation in which the child is in the uterine world, totally dependent on the mother for sustenance, that the mother's life takes precedence over the fetus. In the case of the twins you have a situation where both heads come into the world, each one making an independent claim to life. You have no right to forfeit one for the other."

Another scholar present adds: "But then there is the case of the caravan, surrounded by bandits. If the bandits demand the caravan surrender a hostage for execution or everyone be killed, it would be wrong to sacrifice someone. But, on the other hand, if the bandits name a particular member of the caravan, it would be morally justified to give up this person because he has been *designated for death*. And then it would be foolish to give up the lives of all along

186

with the life of the one designated for death. So it is with the twin who has been designated for death."

Another adds: "But wait, has one of the twins been designated for death?" They call the doctor and they ask the question, "Could Baby A survive if the heart was given to her? Is Baby B also designated for certain death or is there a possibility — remote though it might be — that Baby B could survive with surgery."

*   *   *

It is interesting to note that the lawyers, requested by the doctors to secure legal protection from a charge of premeditated murder, used an analogy similar to the parachute jumpers. "The mountain climber who falls from his perch is saved from instant death by a rope attached to a partner who has a more secure hold. But the hold is not so secure that he can keep both himself and his friend from plunging to their deaths. Because under such circumstances both would die, the climber with the more secure hold would be justified in cutting the rope."

The rabbis agreed to the surgery, aware of the results. They stipulated that the body of Baby Girl A be returned home for burial before sundown of the day of surgery, in keeping with Jewish tradition.

## D. Selected Examples of Applying Jewish Law

Where a woman in intense, unbearable pain, asks her husband to pray for her death, an authority, quoting Rabbenu Nissim, ruled that it was permissible to do so even *before* the patient began her death agony. *Afterwards*, however, when the soul was, as it were, leaving the body, prayer was forbidden since it was held that even such a slight move as a cry might help to recall it and hence keep death from coming.

Quoting Rabbenu Nissim, above, an authority notes that there are times when it is necessary (the Hebrew word used is "tzarich", *required*) to pray for a merciful release for those in great pain but, while prayer might be permissible, a positive act of euthanasia would be strictly forbidden.[36]

The same authority quotes the Talmudic saying that sometimes the advent of death was an act of mercy.[37]

"According to one rabbinic view . . . even medicines must not be used to delay the departure of the soul." The same authoirty asks, but does not answer the question as to whether it is lawful to withdraw insulin injections from a diabetic who had developed inoperable cancer and was in great pain. He cites a case: "In 1923, a rabbi expressed the view that one must not withdraw food from an incurable to expedite his death, even if (that) would relieve his agony, 'for a doubtful contingency, viz., the doctor's verdict that the disease will be fatal cannot disestablish a certainty, viz., the patient's death, if the food is withdrawn . . . But this judgement does not necessarily determine the decision in cases where the withdrawal of a medicament would lead to an easier death."[38]

Where a person is hopelessly sick and suffering intense pain and a small amount of food is being given to him whereas if the food is withheld he would die immediately, the question posed is whether it is legally permitted to "starve" him to relieve him of his suffering? The ruling is negative since the case is in the category of hastening death.[39]

In the case of a dying patient where the issue is whether medicine should be specially prepared for him, and the pharmacist (physician) is doubtful whether such medicine would be helpful, but is certain that the patient will die if no medicine is administered, the ruling permits experimentation. While there is the possibility that death might be speeded up, this is considered to be a passive result. However, the pharmacist must be a specialist in his field, and know what he is doing.[40]

Rabbi Jacob Reisher was asked whether, according to Jewish law, a physician might administer to a patient a drug which might either cure him or hasten his death. In his response, the author emphasizes "the great responsibility of such a decision. The prolongation of the life of the dying man is, according to Jewish law, equal to saving the life of a healthy one, and we are obliged even to violate the Sabbath in order to extend his life to the last possible moment. Taking into consideration that there is hope for a complete recovery, the drug may be administered to the patient despite the risk involved. However, it is necessary to proceed with great caution after consultation with the most competent physicians in the city." The author also required the consent of the head of the local rabbinical court.[41]

In a case where an arm or leg is so infected that, if the limb is not amputated, the patient will certainly die, but if it is, there is a remote possibility that he might recover, although, on the other hand, he might also die while the operation is taking place, the operation is permissible.[42]

In a case where if no drugs are administered to a patient he will die, but if he receives them there is a remote possibility that he might recover, the drugs should be administered.[43]

The above indicate that in any decision affecting euthanasia, each case must be determined according to individual circumstance.

## NOTES

1. Immanuel Jakobovits notes that Lecky first used the term in 1869. *Jewish Medical Ethics*, Bloch Publishing Company, New York, 1959, p. 124.

2. Matt. 5:7.

3. Exod. 20:13, Deut. 5:17.

3a. Fred Rosner, *Jewish Attitude Toward Euthanasia*, New York State Journal of Medicine, Vol. 67, p. 2503. Also published in Media Judaica, Vol. 2, No. 1, Chicago, Jan.-March, 1972. A pro-euthanasia article entitled "Euthanasia: The Good Death" by Mary Mannes appeared in *VIVA*, September 1972, excerpted from the book *Last Rights*, N.Y. See also, Elaine Freeman, the "God Committee" *Time Magazine*, May 21, 1972, in which parents refused permission for the surgery which would have enabled a mongoloid child to survive.

See, "Establishing Criteria of Death," J. David Bleich, *Tradition*, Rabbinical Council of America, Vol. 13, No. 3, Winter 1973, p. 18, in which the author questions the concept of "right to die with dignity." "Certainly one has a right to dignity both in life and in death. But is death, properly speaking, a right? . . . Man does not possess absolute title to his life or to his body . . . man lacks the right to assess the quality of any human life and to determine that it is beneficial for that life to be terminated; all human life is of inestimable value. If the comatose may be caused to "die with dignity" what of the mentally deranged and the feeble-minded, incapable of "meaningful" human activity? . . . See also, Keeping Posted, *Bio-Ethics, Applying Moral Insights to Medicine and Science*, Union of American Hebrew Congregations, Vol 21, No. 2, Nov. 1976. See also, David Novak, *Euthanasia in Jewish Law*, Beth T'filoh Congregation, Balitmore, Md.

3b. Ibid. p. 2501.

3c. Ibid. p. 2502.

3d. The Catholic and Protestant positions are explained in an excellent paper by Fred Rosner, "Jewish Attitude Toward Euthanasia," *Media Judaica*, Vol. 2, No. 1, Chicago, Jan.-Mar., 1972, p. 25.

4. Gen. 9:6.

5. Exod. 21:14.

6. Exod. 20:13, Deut. 5:17.

7. I Sam. 31:1-6.

8. II Sam. 1:5-10.

9. Gersonides in his commentary notes: "Why did David sentence to death the

young man who did the killing not only with Saul's consent, but even at his request?" He answers: "The command of a king cannot overrule the commandment of God's prohibiting murder under all circumstances." Simon Federbush, *The Problem of Euthanasia in Jewish Tradition*, Judaism, Vol. 1, 1952, New York, p. 66.

10. Job 1:21.

11. Ibid. 2:9.

12. Ibid. 33:4.

13. Ezek. 18:4.

14. Semahoth, Mishna I, 1-2.

15. Sanhedrin 37a (Gemara); Mishna IV, 5.

16. Shabbath, Mishna XXIII, 5.

17. Shabbath, 151b.

18. Ketuvoth 104a.

19. Avodah Zara 17b-18a.

20. Rabbi Nissim Gerondi commenting on Nedarim 40a. Quoted by Solomon Freehof, *A Treasury of Responsa*, Jewish Publication Society, Philadelphia, 1962, p. 222. Also by Y. Greenwald, *Aveluth Kol Bo* (Laws of Mourning), p. 20; Also, Immanuel Jakobovits, *Jewish Medical Ethics, p. 306, note 47.*

21. Maimonides, Hilkhot Rozeah, 2:6.

22. Yoreh Deah, Code of Jewish Law, 339, 1.

23. See ibid. Shakh, Commentary.

24. Text of R. Moses Isserles (Rama), Ibid.

25. Condensed Code of Jeiwsh Law, Solomon Ganzfried, Tr. by Hyman Goldin, Vol. IV, pp. 89-194.

26. Immanuel Jakobovits, *Jewish Medical Ethics*, p. 123, 124. See, Rabbi Alfred Cohen, An Analysis on Whether, 'Pulling the Plug' is Ever Permissible Under Jewish Law, Young Israel Viewpoint, Nov. 1976, New York.

27. Fred Rosner, op. cit., p. 2505.

28. Immanuel Jakobovits, op. cit. p. 124.

29. Immanuel Jakobovits, *Journal of a Rabbi*, Living Books, New York, 1966, p. 165.

30. Fred Rosner, op. cit. p. 2505. See, David Bleich, *Karen Ann Quinlan: A Torah Perspective* (a portion of this article appeared in Sh'ma), New York, December 12, 1976, p. 20.

31. London Jewish Chronicle, London, England, "Ask the Rabbi" column, September, 1967.

32. CCAR Yearbook, Vol. LVI, 1946, p. 104.

32a. Ibid. Vol. LX, 1950, p. 107-120.

32b. Solomon Freehof, *Reform Responsa*, Hebrew Union College Press, Cincinnati, 1960, p. 118. See also, Solomon Freehof, *Modern Reform Responsa*, HUC Press, Cincinnati, 1971 in which the author discusses the subjects allowing a terminal patient to die, choosing which patient to save, and determination and postponement of death.

32c. Ibid. p. 122.

32d. Sefer Hsidim 723; 234.

33. CCAR Yearbook, Vol. LXXIV, Atlantic City, N.J., 1964, pp. 71-72.

34a. Solomon Freehof, *Current Reform Responsa*, HUC Press, Cincinnati, 1969, p. 239. The subject of freezing bodies is also discussed by Azriel Rosenfeld, *Tradition*, Vol. 9, No. 3, Fall, 1967. See also, William B. Silverman, "Remember Us Unto Death," *CCAR Journal*, Vol. 21, No. 2. Spring 1974.

34b. Byron L. Sherwin, United Synagogue Review, Spring, 1972, p. 3. See also, Bernard Raskas, "*When a Life is No Life — The Right to Die*," Sh'ma, New York, Dec. 12. 1975.

34c. Conservative Judaism, Rabbinical Assembly, Vol. 30, No. 2, Spring 1974. See also, Seymour Siegel, "*The Ethical Dilemmas of Modern Medicine: A Jewish Approach*," United Synagogue Review, Fall, 1976, p. 4.

34d. Proceedings, Rabbinical Assembly, New York, 1976, p. 317.

34e. See, J. David Bleich, "Karen Ann Quinlan: A Torah Perspective," Sh'ma, A Second Look, 1978, p. 12.

34f. From, The Jewish Week and The American Examiner, Philip Hochstein, Editor, New York.

34g. Sh'ma, Eugene B. Borowitz, editor, April 15, 1977, New York.

34h. This account is based on a fascinating article, *The Twins Decision: One Must Die So One Can Live; Parent Doctors, Rabbis in Dilemma*, by Donald C. Drake, Inquirer Medical Writer, which appeared in The Philadelphia Inquirer, October 16, 1977. Quotations by permission of the Philadelphia Inquirer.

35. Solomon Freehof, *Reform Responsa*, ibid. pp. 117-122; Also, *A Treasury of Responsa*, pp. 220-223.

36. Y. Greenwald, *Aveluth Kol Bo*, p. 20, Sec. 9. Also, Solomon Freehof, *A Treasury of Responsa*, p. 222.

37. Baba Meziah 84.

38. Immanuel Jakobovits, *Jewish Medical Ethics*, p. 306 notes 42, 54.

39. Y. Greenwald, op. cit., p. 21. sec. 10.

40. Ibid. sec. 12.

41. Simon Federbush, *Judaism*, Vol. 1, 1952, p. 64. See also, H.J. Zimmels, *Magicians, Theologians and Doctors*, Feldheim, New York, 1952, p. 25.

42. Greenwald, op. cit., 21, note 16.

43. Ibid. Note 16.

# HOMOSEXUALITY

In 1955, the American Law Institute recommended the reform of criminal laws by making private sexual acts between consenting adults a moral, rather than a legal issue.

> No harm to the secular interests of the community is involved in a typical sexual practice in private between consenting adult partners. This area of private morals is the distinctive concern of spiritual authorities.

In the summer of 1966, following years of debate especially after the publication of the Wolfenden Report, the United Kingdom changed the laws against homosexuality; what consenting adults do in private is now left as a matter of individual conscience rather than of law, although public solicitation and sexual acts between minors remain within the domain of criminal law and demand stiff penalties.

In August of 1967, the American Civil Liberties Union affirmed its policy on homosexuality by saying:

> The right of privacy should extend to all private sexual conduct and should not be a matter for invoking the penal statutes.

Again;

> The state has a legitmate interest in controlling, by criminal sanctions, public solicitation for sexual acts, and particularly, sexual practices where a minor is concerned.

The Supreme Court of the United States has been asked to hear a challenge to the New York vagrancy law in which it is at present a criminal offense for men to wear women's clothing in public.[1a]

Columbia University has granted permission for the organization of the first student homosexual group in America, the Student Homophile League.

A recent article notes that there are four million homosexuals in the United States.[1b] There are 12 gay synagogues joined by a National Union of Gay Synagogues.

What has Judaism to say about homosexuality? Does the Bible deal with the issue? Would a reform of the law, allowing the individual conscience to be the arbiter of its own morality be acceptable to Judaism?

"Whatever may have been the case in the past, homosexuality is today a Jewish issue. More and more, the Jewish homosexual is coming out of the closet' and refuses to conceal either his homosexual identity or his attachment to Judaism. Therefore, the problem of homosexuality must be confronted by Jewish religious and communal agencies . . .

"There are already 12 gay synagogues in the world . . . the 1979 convention (of a new international conference) will be held in Israel . . ."[1c]

A recent issue of the Jewish Post and Opinion contains two pages on various aspects of the subject reflecting differing viewpoints: Gay Rabbi Tells Interviewer He's One of Several Dozen; Condemn Homosexuals, Urges Orthodox Rabbi; Conservatism Urged to Accept Homosexuals — Reject Practice; Homosexuals As Rabbis Should be Accepted.[1d]

While there may be extenuating circumstances diminishing the gravity of the law with regard to abortion, contraception, and premarital sex, Judaism is crystal clear on homosexuality. *Mishkav zakhar*, literally "lying with a male" is regarded as both unnatural and immoral. On this standpoint Judaism goes further than Christianity:

> Public opinion in many lands had been unduly hard upon homosexuality, for of itself, as a pathological state, it deserves psychological treatment, not moral blame; but when it issues in overt act, it is regarded unnatural vice.[2]

The Bible provides both a legal and an allegorical or folkloristic perspective on homosexuality.

The legal view is derived from two precise injunctions in the Pentateuch:

1. Under the heading *Forbidden Immoral Practices:*

> Do not lie with a male as one lies with a woman, it is an abhorrence.[3]

2. Under the chapter heading *Laws Bearing On Immorality*, two chapters later, the Bible records:

> If a man lies with a male as one lies with a woman, the two of them have done an abhorrent thing; they shall be put to death — their bloodguilt is upon them.[4]

3. Under the heading *Immorality:*

> Neither shall there be a sodomite of the sons of Israel.[5]

Connected with the practice of homosexuality is that of transvestism, the wearing of clothes of the opposite sex by "people who are either actively attracted to members of their own sex or willing to lend themselves to homosexual practices."[6]

> A woman must not put on man's apparel, nor shall a man wear woman's clothing; for whoever does these things is abhorrent to the Lord your God.[6a]

A commentator explains that "an interchange of attire between man and woman would promote immodesty, and consequently immorality."[7]

> It seems more than probable that the very strong emphasis the Biblical law puts on the prohibition of this practice has something to do with the custom of homosexuals of wearing the garb of the opposite sex.[8]
>
> The prohibition of wearing the clothing of the opposite sex may point to a libidinous ritual in Canaan . . . to a form of homosexuality.[9]
>
> Among the many regulations about dress included in the Jewish code of sex morality is the biblical injunction: 'A woman must not

put on a man's apparel, nor shall a man wear woman's clothing, for whoever does these things is abhorrent to the Lord your God.' (Deuteronomy 22:5). The obvious meaning is a prohibition against the practice of homosexuality in any form, with which is generally associated wearing the garments of the opposite sex. Perhaps the biblical author knew of the psychosis of males desiring and imagining themselves to be females, and of females delighting in imagining themselves males, and creating the illusion by donning the garments of the opposite sex; except that he treated it not as pathology but as moral depravity. The likelihood, however, is that the abandonment of the heathens to corruption and unnatural lust, such as sodomy and the like, created a class of depraved males and females who actually played the part of the opposite sex sexually, and the biblical author condemned the practice and warned his people against it.[10]

A few Biblical narratives both in the Pentateuch and in the Prophets treat of the practice of homosexuality.

The first recalls the Biblical cities, Sodom and Gomorrah, which were eventually destroyed. Sodomy, a term borrowed from the name of that city, covers both homosexuality and also sexual relations with animals.

The story tells of Abraham's nephew, Lot, who had gone to Sodom, where evil practices were common. God decrees that the two cities be destroyed and He sends three messengers, one of whose task it is to bring about the destruction of the city after he has saved Lot and his family. The men arrive in Sodom where they are accorded hospitality by Lot.

> They had not yet lain down, when the townspeople, the men of Sodom, young and old — all the people to the last man — gathered about the house. And they shouted to Lot and said to him, "Where are the men who came to you tonight? Bring them out, that we may be intimate with (know) them." So Lot went out to them to the entrance, shut the door behind him, and said "I beg you, my friends, do not commit such a wrong. Look, I have two daughters who have not known a man. Let me bring them out to you, and you may do to them as you please; but do not do anything to these men, since they have come under the shelter of my roof."[11]

The phrase "that we may know (be intimate with) them," many commentators explain to refer to unnatural intercourse. The

Midrash also explains; "for sexual purposes" (i.e., pederasty, 'know' being understood as in Genesis: "And the man knew Eve his wife and she conceived."[12]

Other sages, however, suggest that the purpose of this overt act of aggression was "to keep the strangers away, as they were anxious to keep all the wealth of the place for themselves. Although they were wicked in other ways, their doom was their punishment for this selfishness and their refusal to help the poor."[13]

A later commentator analyzes the phrase *"do not do this thing"* by commenting, for it is wickedness before the Holy One, blessed be He, as it says, 'How can I do this wickedness and sin against God?' (Gen. 39:9) [and there, also, the reference is to immorality — to adultery.] The Almighty enjoined the children of Noah (all men) likewise, 'A man shall cleave to his *wife,* and they shall be one flesh' (Gen. 2:24) *but not to a male* with whom he cannot become one flesh."[14]

An almost identical experience is recounted in the Book of Judges describing their outrage at Gibeah. A Levite of Mount Ephraim had taken a concubine from Bethlehem of Judah. She deserted him and returned home. After a time, the man paid her a visit, was openly welcomed by her father, and persuaded her to return with him. On the return journey, overtaken by darkness, they decided to spend the night at Gibeah, a Benjamine city, where a kindly man invited them into his house. The citizens surrounded the house and insisted that the stranger be handed over to them. The law of hospitality demanded that his guest be protected, and the host offered the crowd his own daughter as well as the concubine.

> As they were making their hearts merry, the men of the city, certain base fellows beset the house round about, beating at the door; and they spoke to the master of the house, the old man, saying: "Bring forth the man who came into your house, *that we may know him.*"[15]

The commentator expatiates upon the last phrase: "The citizens were addicted to unnatural vice."

There are other allusions to homosexuality in the Bible. Some suggest that the flood inundated the world in the time of Noah because of this practice. A Midrash puts forward the idea that Potiphar, captain of Pharoah's guard, purchased Joseph "for the purpose of sodomy, whereupon the Holy One, blessed be He, emasculated him."[16]

## In Talmudic Literature

The Talmud discusses homosexuality in terms of the injunctions of the Bible, and also in relation to other impinging issues. The following are selections dealing with the subject:

1. The Mishna, elaborating on the Bible text states:

> These are they who are to be stoned . . . he that has sexual intercourse with a male . . .[17]

The Gemara imposes the death penalty on both the solicitor and the consenting partner.[18] The inclusion of the passive partner is derived from another passage in the Bible:

> There shall be no sodomite of the sons of Israel.[19]

The condemnation is reinforced by a passage in the prophets:

> And there were also sodomites in the land; and they did according to the abominations of the nations which the Lord had cast out before the children of Israel.[20]

2. Another Mishna records a difference of opinion, as follows:

> R. Judah said: An unmarried man must not tend cattle, nor may two unmarried men sleep together under the same cover. But the sages permit it.[21]

Elaborating on the text, the rabbis say:

> It was taught: They (the Sages) said to R. Judah: Israel is not to be suspected of either pederasty or bestiality.[22]

3: Another Mishna text discusses, not homosexuality as such, but a related issue, so as to determine the legal status of such acts. Under consideration are hermaphrodites (androgynous, man-woman, one who exhibits traces of both male and female organs) and cryptorchitics (indeterminates).

Rabbi Judah says: A hermaphrodite may marry (a wife) but may not be married (by a man). (He has the status of a male rather than that of a female, and his cohabitation with a male would be an act of sodomy.) Rabbi Eliezer (whose opinion is accepted in law) stated: (For copulation) with an hermaphrodite the penalty of stoning is incurred as (if he were) a male.[23]

It may seem that no difference exists between the two views. The Talmud discusses whether the hermaphrodite is to be regarded as a male in terms of the penalty of sodomy and concludes that the only difference between the two authorities is that Rabbi Judah held that the penalty of stoning is incurred by copulation through either of the two organs (even if it were effected through the female organ) and Rabbi Eliezer was of the opinion (that it was incurred through the male organ only) as if he were a male.[23a]

To sum up, another Rabbi, R. Jose, stated: "The hermaphrodite is a creature sui generis, and the Sages did not determine whether he is a male or a female."

In respect to the hermaphrodite, Jewish law agrees with that of Rabbi Jose.

### In Later Literature and Codes

Continuing the earlier lead, the commentators after the Talmudic era made these objections to the practice of homosexuality into law.

Maimonides' Code lists among eighteen capital crimes that of:

he who has intercourse with a male.[23b]

Maimonides also notes that even if this act occurred "during a single spell of unawareness," it is sinful and that he who commits and he who suffers the act fall into a single class."[24]

This prohibition passed into Maimonides' Code as follows:

A male who has intercourse with a male, or who brings a male upon him, since there is sexual contact; if both are adults, they are subject to the punishment of stoning, as it is said, "You shall not lie with a male." The law applies to both parties, active and passive. If the male had intercourse with a minor, that is, nine years and a day old, the adult male is to be punished by stoning, and the minor is not guilty. If the male was nine years and younger, both are not guilty. It is proper, however, for the Court in its discretion, in contradistinction to the Biblically ordained penalty, to provide punishment for disobedience.[25]

A later code-commentator states the following in the text of his compendium:

> Israel (Jews) are not suspected of lying with a male or of bestiality. Therefore, there is no prohibition in the association of men (as in the case of man and woman alone). Yet, it is to be considered praiseworthy if one does. In our generations, however, with the increase of immorality, one should keep his distance even from a male.[25a]

The commentator, discussing the phrase, *"In our generation with the increase of immorality,"* notes that the separation is not mandatory by law, rather advisory, as an expression of greater piety. When two men sleep together, especially two bachelors, they should be careful to keep their distance.[26]

Female homosexuality is not prohibited in the Bible itself and there is only one condemnatory reference to the subject in the entire Talmud.[27]

> ... Rabbi Huna said: Women who practice lewdness with one another are disqualified from marrying a priest. And even according to Rabbi Eleazar, who stated that an unmarried man who cohabited with an unmarried woman with no matrimonial intention renders her thereby a harlot, this disqualification ensues only in the case of a man, but when it is that of a woman (indulging in lewdness with another) the action is regarded as mere obscenity.[28]

> "The law, however, does not treat the practice (female homosexuality) so severly, but accounts it an unseemly, immoral act, which Maimonides advises should be disciplined by flagellation. He declares that women known to be addicted to this vice should be excluded from the company of decent women. It is reported that Samuel's father, a saintly Babylonian teacher of the third century, did not permit his daughters to sleep together, probably for this reason. (The Talmud imputes Samuel's father with the wish that his daughters should not become habituated to the feel of another female body in bed.) The final Halakhah, however, condemning

the act and imposing disciplinary penalties, did not recognize the restriction of Samuel's father or any other restriction against private association between woman and woman."[29a]

"Jewish law treated the female homosexual more leniently than the male. It considered lesbianism as *issur*, an ordinary religious violation rather than *arayot*, a specifically sexual infraction, regarded more severely than *issur*. R. Huna held that lesbianism is the equivalent of harlotry and disqualified the woman from marrying a priest. The *Halakhah* is, however, more lenient, and decides that while the act is prohibited, the lesbian is not punished and is permitted to marry a priest. However, the transgression does warrant disciplinary flagellation. The less punitive attitude of the *Halakhah* to the female homosexual than to the male does not reflect any intrinsic judgment on one as opposed to the other, but is rather the result of a Halakhic technicality; there is no explicit Biblical proscription of lesbianism, and the act does not entail genital intercourse."[29b]

Contrast this unreserved condemnation of homosexuality, and the equally persistent injunction against the waste of human seed, masturbation in any form, and unnatural sexual commerce, with the extolling of sex and marriage as an essentially sacred institution, and the Jewish view towards this issue become clear. Homosexuality is unnatural, atypical, and illegal in religious law, and its practice cannot be condoned even in private quarters by consenting adults.

There seems to be no doubt that the homosexual way of life does not fulfill the religious demand for true community among sexual partners.[30]

There is no suggestion here that homosexuality cannot or ought not to be treated therapeutically, or that rabbis are not sympathetic to the problem:

All the resources of the medical profession as well as the counseling of religious teachers should be directed to the curing of the illness.[31]

A recent volume entitled Jewish Values and Social Crisis[32] notes:

200

An inevitable corollary of the sexual revolution is the questioning of the right of society to intrude upon the private behavior of consenting adults. The harsh treatment of homosexuals has recently emerged as a primary test of the morality and propriety of the law. In many parts of the world, reformers have pleaded for a more humane and modern approach to the problem of homosexuality . . . Most psychologists regard homosexuality as a profound emotional disturbance, resulting from deep psychological distortion in early childhood . . .

There is no doubt where traditional Judaism stood on this issue . . . But it is doubtful that most modern Jews, including rabbis, will be content to accept so harsh an approach to so vexing a problem.

The author quotes from a rabbi who regards the Bible's insistence on regulating even the private details of a man's life as contrary to the modern outlook.[33]

On the other hand, he also pays respect to the opinion of an Orthodox Rabbi, Norman Lamm, who:

condemned the statement of ninety Episcopal priests from New York that homosexual acts, like all sexual behavior, cannot be classified as right or wrong as such. He took strong exception to their statement that a homosexual relationship between two consenting adults should be judged by the same criteria as a heterosexual marriage — that is, whether it is intended to foster a permanent relationship of love.[34]

## ORTHODOX VIEWS

Writing in an Orthodox monthly, Rabbi Lamm says:

While I do not believe that homosexuality between two consenting adults should be treated as a criminal offense, to declare homosexual acts as "morally neutral" and at times "a good thing" is scandalous . . .

What bothers me in reading the reports in the press on the recent Episcopal conference as well as earlier papers by Swedish and British churches, is the readiness to condone and even approve, although not encourage, homosexuality on the basis of "genuine love, fulfillment and happiness."

. . . the exaggerated importance Christians have traditionally accorded to the term "love" and the hedonistic ethic of the contemporary Western World, have joined together to kick away whatever is left of social and religious restraint in a progressively amoral society. To aver that a homosexual relationship should be judged by the same criteria as a heterosexual one — "whether it is intended to foster a permanent relationship of love" is to abandon the last claim to representing the Judaeo-Christian tradition.

. . . Are we not justified, to use a *reductio ad absurdum*, in using the same reasoning to sanction an adulterous relationship? Love, fulfillment, and happiness can be attained in incestuous contacts, too — and certainly in polygamous relationships. Is there nothing left at all that is "sinful" "unnatural" or "immoral" if it is practiced between "two consenting adults

. . . Judaism began its career as the standard bearer of morality in a world which mocked it. Apparently, it is destined to carry on in the twentieth century in the same isolation — and I pray — with the same sense of dedication.[35]

Having asserted the Orthodox position, Rabbi Lamm wrote:

". . . society . . . must offer its medical and psychological assistance to those whose homosexuality is an expression of pathology, who recognize it as such, and are willing to such help. We must be no less generous to the homosexual than to the drug addict, to whom the government extends various forms of therapy upon request."

"Second, jail sentences must be abolished for all homosexuals, save those who are guilty of violence, seduction of the young, or public solicitation.

Third, the laws must remain on the books, but by mutual consent of judiciary and police, be unenforced . . . by affirming a halakhic prohibition, yet no punishment is mandated. It is a category that bridges the gap between morality and law. In a society where homosexuality is so rampant, and where incarceration is so counterproductive, this hortatory approach may well be a way of formalizing society's revulsion, while avoiding the pitfalls in our accepted penology.[36]

Medical Ethics, a compendium of Jewish moral, ethical and religious principles, pursues similar recommendations:

"Since the Jewish moral code categorically forbids homosexual relations, it is inconceivable for any agency that is concerned with the preservation or promotion of Jewish values to condone, sanction, let alone advocate or foster homosexual relations. The establishment of "gay synagogues" or of any institutions designed to place the mantle of acceptability or respectability upon homosexuality, represents not merely sacrilege but an act of Jewish spiritual self-destruction.

. . . homosexuals should be given every possible opportunity to take their place within the Jewish community in conforming with the Rabbinic adage — "A Jew remains a Jew — no matter how serious his sin."[37]

## REFORM VIEWS

Without official action, the Reform movement has not discouraged the establishment of gay synagogues. However, in a responsum written by Rabbi Solomon Freehof to a query made by Rabbi Alexander M. Schindler as to whether the organization of gay synagogues is "in accordance with the spirit of Jewish tradition to encourage the establishment of a congregation of homosexuals," a negative position is submitted. Following an evaluation of the Biblical and also the ethical objection to homosexuality, but yet insisting that homosexuals cannot by Jewish law be excluded from synagogue participation, Rabbi Freehof concludes:

> "Homosexuality is deemed in Jewish tradition to be a sin, not only in law but in Jewish life practice. Nevertheless it would be in direct contravention to Jewish law to keep sinners out of the congregation. To isolate them into a separate congregation and thus increase their mutual availability is certainly wrong. It is hardly worth mentioning that to officiate at a so-called "marriage" of two homosexuals and to describe their mode of life as Kiddushin (i.e. sacred in Judaism) is a contravention of all that is respected in Jewish life."[38]

At its most recent conference in San Francisco, November 1977, the Union of American Hebrew Congregations, adopted the following resolution under the caption Human Rights of Homosexuals:

> WHEREAS the UAHC has consistently supported civil rights and civil liberties for all persons, and

WHEREAS the Constitution guarantees civil rights to all individuals.

BE IT THEREFORE RESOLVED that homosexual persons are entitled to equal protection under the law. We oppose discrimination against homosexuals in areas of opportunity, including employment and housing. We call upon our society to see that such protection is provided in actuality.

BE IT FURTHER RESOLVED THAT we affirm our belief that private sexual acts between consenting adults are not the proper province of government and law enforcement agencies.

BE IT FURTHER RESOLVED THAT we urge congregations to conduct appropriate educational programming for youth and adults so as to provide greater understanding of the relation of Jewish values to the range of human sexuality.

Writing in *The Sentinel*, a columnist describes Beth Chayim Chadashim (House of New Life), the first homosexual congregation to be established on the West Coast, in Los Angeles. When approached, the director of the Southwest Council of UAHC had said that they were offering the facilities of their office for the formation of a gay synagogue, as they had done in the past and would continue to do in the future to any group of Jews who demonstrated to their satisfaction that they were sincerely interested in the creation of a synagogue. There are sixty members in the group. Some of its major decisions include the insistence that its rabbi must be a homosexual on grounds that no matter how sincere the straight Jews who offer help may be, the problems of the gay community can only be understood by one of themselves. Membership in the group was to be open, though they seek to maintain control of the congregation because the homosexual community is best served from within its ranks. The co-president of the synagogue is quoted as saying that the congregation was "bringing beauty, understanding, creativity, productivity, a sense of responsibility and, above all, Judaism, to people who have been left out of the mainstream of our culture and a sense of pride, a sense of belonging, to those of God's children forced to have a duality."[39]

A weekly advertisement, appearing together with religious announcements of synagogues in the New York Times, also notes Sabbath Evening services at the gay synagogue in New York.

An article in the *San Francisco Examiner*, October 14, 1977, describes Congregation Sha'ar Zahav (Temple of the Golden Gate). The Director of the Union of American Hebrew Congregations (Reform) is quoted as finding no difficulty accepting a gay synagogue. He points out that there have been houses of worship that have attracted specialized segments of the community: "In the United States we try to organize synagogues that are all-embracing, but a specialized group may organize. In Hollywood, for example, there is a synagogue for members of the performing arts.

"Services are an eclectic mix of traditions ranging from prayers in English and Hebrew to Chassidic-type dancing and singing and a social hour at the conclusion . . .

"The prayerbook's cover emblem is rich in symbolism for gays and Jews. One triangle that forms the Star of David is pink, commemorating the badge gays wore in concentration camps. The other triangle is blue. Their point of convergence is lavender, a traditionally gay color, and in the center of the star is the Greek letter, lambda, another gay symbol."[40]

## CONSERVATIVE VIEWS

The position of Conservative Judaism, while undefined, would probably retain the traditional perspective. To a query in May 1976 on the question "as to whether a gay synagogue could be accepted into membership by the United Synagogue, the Rabbinical Assembly Law Committee, under the chairmanship of Rabbi Seymour Siegel, wrote, "No separate homosexual synagogues should be established."

A Conservative rabbi, however, reflecting his own view and preparing a doctorate on the subject has written:

> Separate gay synagogues have been formed precisely because the homosexual has not felt comfortable in existing religious institutions. It is the opinion of this writer that as long as this condition prevails, these synagogues perform a vital religious function. We need not alienate any Jew or group of Jews who wish to gather for study and prayer, sexual preferences notwithstanding. On the other hand, how wonderful it would be if the Conservative Movement, with its interest in improving the quality of the world, should become a pioneer in welcoming all the lonely and isolated

of our people, thus making separate synagogues unnecessary. We must serve those who feel displaced by society precisely because the synagogue provides the chance of creating a sense of belonging to a group which can lead to stablility, empathy and trust. In opening the doors of Jewish communal life to those who have not accepted procreation as a way of life, the synagogue might be surprised to find a large number of congregants struggling with homosexual impulses.

The homosexual as a human being should be accepted without his homosexuality being sanctioned or condemned. Accepting is not tantamount to condoning or encouraging. In receiving homosexuals openly, we need not sacrifice our traditional standards and the Jewish ideal of heterosexuality.

Homosexual men and women need support because of the indignities and injustices they suffer, but to whom can they go? With our help, they can enter our House of God where they can find understanding, sympathetic rabbinic guidance, and spiritual and emotional support from the congregation of Israel.[41]

A similar appeal is made in a recent article in *Judaism* by a Conservative rabbi, also reflecting his personal opinion.

"The most truly Jewish stance would be one that takes with equal seriousness the authority of traditional standards and the significance of modern knowledge . . . such a stance would maintain the traditional view of heterosexuality as the God-intended norm and yet would incorporate the contemporary recognition of homosexuality as, clinically speaking, a sexual deviance, malfunctioning, or abnormality — usually unavoidable and often irremediable."

The author, on the question of gay synagogues, says:

"Since the present reality is that such a welcome is not asured and is perhaps even unlikely, the formation of gay congregations is legitimate. Gay congregations, however, must not . . . restrict its own membership or leadership to homosexuals."

Further:

"We would advocate that the only roles from which homosexuals should be excluded are those of adoptive or foster parents and of religious leader — since these two roles of parent and rabbi are, by definition, meant to serve as models of what a Jewish woman or man should be."

On the solemnizing of marriages between two homosexuals, Rabbi Matt notes:

"it is hardly conceivable that a homosexual departure from the Torah's heterosexual norm would ever be accepted by Halakhically faithful Jews, or ever be recognized as *k'dat Moshe v'Yisrael* (in accordance with the law of Moses and Israel.).[42]

In an article on "Homosexuality and the Halakhah," in an issue of *Sh'ma*, fully half of which was devoted to homosexuality, David Feldman concludes:

I see homosexuality, in the accepted sense of the term, as a sin, violative of the letter and spirit of the Halakhah and of the Jewish instinct and experience — regardless of the findings of psychology or the demands of sexual liberationists. I think that pastoral compassion should, of course, be bestowed on transgressors, and that in this case our human concern ought to go even further. If, for example, prison conditions are as scandalously conducive to forced or indifferent homosexual compliance . . . then reform of those conditions — such as by permitting conjugal visitation or otherwise — should become our activist concern. But above all, I think we ought unabashedly to affirm our moral stance. We need not be ashamed of holding fast to standards in an age of nihilism. We do, after all, more highly regard holiness than freedom as a personal value.
So much of the Jewish sexual code has as its purpose — to the extent that we can speak of the law's purpose — the preservation of the marriage bond and the family unit. As committed Jews, our responsibility in an age of family dissolution is all the more urgent and positive.

A second article entitled *"To Be a Jew and a Homosexual,"* is written by a practicing homosexual who pleads "for those gays who are Jews, a place in the People of Israel."

He urges for this recongition in the following words: "The Lambda is the symbol of the Gay Militants. On June 25th this year, at the end of June each year, we gays march. The sign in the air is not for sodomy or homosexuality. It is for liberty, for pride, for·

justice; not for homo-sex, the one-sex society, the men-all-together; but for men-and-women equal. And wearing this same sign, though hidden, many Jewish people, women and men, through our history, lived and died. They dressed, laughed, were (some of them) orthodox, some atheist. But they made their way through life like the heterosexuals. If the Holocaust took them they were not singled out and kept from the slaughter as being less Jewish. In the Yishuv they fought like their heterosexual brothers and sisters. Here in America they live as honestly as they can, and as well or badly as anyone.

I do not find them immoral.

I ask for those gays who are Jews, a place in the People of Israel.


## NOTES

1a. Webster Schott, "A Four Million Minority Asks for Equal Rights," *New York Times Magazine*, New York, November 12, 1967.

1b. See *"Homo-sex: Luring the Life,"* Fanburi Bowers, *Saturday Review*, Feb. 12, 1972, A list of books on homosexuality is included.

1c. Barry Dov Schwartz, *"Homosexuality, A Jewish Perspective"* United Synagogue Review, United Synagogue of America, 1975, New York, p. 4.

1d. National Jewish Post and Opinion, Indianapolis, Indiana, Feb. 10, 1978, p. 3.

2. *The Interpreters Bible*, Abington Press, Vol. 2, New York, 1953, p. 103.

3. Lev. 18:22.

4. Lev. 20:13.

5. Deut. 23:18, The new translation of the Jewish Publication Society reads: "Nor shall any Israelite man be a cult prostitute (i.e., a male prostitute).

6. Ralph Patai, *Sex and Family in the Bible*, Doubleday, New York, 1959, p. 173.
See also, Robert M. Greenblatt, *Search the Scriptures*, Chapter 13, A Woman's Garment, J.B. Lippincott Company, Philadelphia, 1963, pp. 74-79.

6a. Deut. 22:5.

7. J.H. Hertz, Ed. *The Pentateuch and Haftorah*, Soncino Press, London, 1963, p. 853.

8. Ralph Patai, op. cit., p. 173.

9. *Universal Jewish Encyclopedia*, Vol. 9, New York 1943, p. 484.

10. Louis M. Epstein, *Sex Laws and Customs in Judaism*, American Academy of Jewish Rsearch, 1948, p. 64.

11. Gen. 19:4-8.

12. *Midrash*, Gen., Rabbi H. Freedman and Maurice Simon, Soncino Press, London, 1951, Ch. L; Sec. 5, p. 437.

13. See, *The Soncino Chumash*, Dr. A. Cohen, Ed., Soncino Press, 1947, p. 94.

14. *Encyclopedia of Biblical Interpretation*, Menahem M. Kasher, Vol. III, American Biblical Encyclopedia Society, New York, 1957, p. 60.

15. Solomon Freehof, Current Reform Responsa, pp. 236-238. Judges 19:22.

16. Midrash, Gen. Rabba, ibid, p. 802.

17. Mishna, Sanhedrin, VII, 4.

18. Sanhedrin 54a.

19. Deut. 23:18.

20. I Kings 14:24.

21. Mishnayoth, Kiddushin IV:14, Philip Blackman, Ed., Vol. III, Judaica Press, New York, 1965, p. 481.

22. Kiddushin 82a. See, Solomon Freehof, *Current Reform Responsa*, Hebrew Union College Press, New York, 1969, pp. 236-238.

23. Yevamoth 81a, 82b. See also, Symposium on Medical Dilemmas and the Practice of Milah, N.Y. Board of Rabbis and Brith Milah Board, New York, June 1978, p. 26.

23a. Ibid.

23b. Maimonides, *Code of Maimonides, Book of Judges*, Tr. by A.M. Hershman, Yale Judaica Series, Vol. III, New Haven, 1949, p. 44.

24. Code of Maimonides Book of Offerings, Tr. by Herbert Danby, Yale Judaica Series, Vol. IV, Ch. 4:1, New Haven, Ct., 1950, p. 109.

25. Code of Maimonides, Book of Holiness, Treatise 81:14. See also, Maimonides, The Commandments, Vol. II, Tr. by Charles Chavel, Soncino Press, London Press, London, 1967, p. 315.

25a. Even HaEzer, Laws of Marriage, Hilkhot Ishuth 24.

26. Solomon Freehof, Current Reform Responsa, Ibid., pp. 236-238.

27. See, David Feldman, *Birth Control in Jewish Law*, New York University Press, New York, 1968, p. 125. See also, Enid Nemy, *The Woman Homosexual*, New York Times, New York, Nov. 17, 1969, p. 62.

28. Yevamoth 76a.

29a. Louis Epstein, *Sex Laws and Customs in Judaism*, ibid. p. 138.

29b. Norman Lamm, op. cit., note 35.

30. Seymour Siegel, "Jewish Traditions View of Sex," quoted in *Jews and Divorce*, Jacob Fried, Editor, Ktav Publishing House, New York, 1968, p. 180. See also series of articles, "Jews, Judaism and Homosexuality" in the *National Post and Opinion*, Aug. 27-Sept. 25, 1971, Indianapolis, Indiana.

31. Ibid. See also *Time*, New York, October 31, pp. 56-57. The American Psychiatric Association, altering a position held for almost a century decided at its Board of Trustees meeting, Dec. 15, 1973, that homosexuality is not a mental disease. It is categorized as "a sexual orientation disturbance." This is defined as a category "for individuals whose sexual interests are directed primarily towards people of the same sex, and who are either disturbed by, in conflict with, or wish to change their sexual orientation". This diagnostic category, the board of Trustees said, is distinguished from homosexuality, which by itself does not necessarily constitute a psychiatric disorder.

32. Albert Vorspan, *Jewish Values and Social Crisis*, Union of American Hebrew Congregations, New York, 1969, p. 217.

33. Everett Gendler, *National Jewish Post and Opinion*, New York, Jan. 12, 1968.

34. Albert Vorspan, ibid., p. 219, See also Richard Foster, *The Homosexuals*, December 14, 1969, p. 41.

35. Norman Lamm, *The New Dispensation on Homosexuality*, Jewish Life, New York, January 1968, pp. 11-16.

36. For an excellent, comprehensive and analytic study by Rabbi Lamm, entitled "*Judaism and the Modern Attitude to Homosexuality*," see Encyclopedia Judaica, Yearbook 1974, Jerusalem.

37. *Medical Ethics*, Rabbi Moses D. Tendler, Editor, Federation of Jewish Philanthropies, New York, 1975, page 4. See also, Rabbi Sholom Klass, *Homosexuals and the Jewish Religion*, Jewish Press, New York, November 25, 1977.

38. Ibid, *CCAR Journal*, note 36a.

39. Ben Gallob, *The Sentinel*, "First Homosexual Says Its Rabbi Must Also be Gay," Chicago, 1973. See also *CCAR Journal*, Summer 1973, containing a number of articles detailing and evaluating the establishment of gay synagogues.

40. Band of Brothers: The City's Gay Synagogue, *San Francisco Examiner*, October 14, 1977.

41. Barry Dov Schwartz, Homosexuality — A Jewish Perspective, *United Synagogue Review*, United Synagogue of America, New York, 1975, p. 3.

42. Ibid, note 1c, Hershel Matt, *Sin, Crime, Sickness or Alternative Life-Style? A Jewish Approach to Homosexuality*, Judaism, Vol. 27, No. 1, American Jewish Congress, New York, p. 13ff.

43. David Feldman, *Homosexuality and the Halakhah*, Sh'ma, May 19, 1972, New York, p. 99ff.

# ORGAN TRANSPLANTS

This century has seen a medical revolution in organ transplants. In 1905 the first cornea graft took place, and transplants of kidneys, the liver and single and double heart valves have taken place. Attempts to transplant the lungs have not yet succeeded.[1] In December, 1967, the first human heart transplant operation was performed in Capetown, South Africa.[1a] Although the patient subsequently died, scientists and physicians continue their advance in heart transplant surgery, while jurists and religious leaders, are trying to "place" this progress within some scheme of human values.

The whole area of organ transplants, with its religious, moral and legal ramifications, has proved to be more problematic than the first corneal operation would have led people to suspect.[1b] The issue of human dissection, mutilation and self-mutilation, the rights of the living as they balance against rights of the dead, come to the fore, as do the related issues of autopsy and post-mortem. The definition of death and the meaning of life loom large in philosophical, theological, and ethical discussions of this question, as does the controversial topic of euthanasia. Since the new heart must be transferred as close to the moment of death as possible, it is crucial to determine when death occurs.[2] Does it take place when the heart stops beating, when the electroencephalogram is horizontal indicating no pulsation, when the heart actually stops pumping, or with the cessation of breathing? Should we try to anticipate the moment of death as much as possible in order to make use of an undamaged organ? Is there room for error, in which case the hearts of living human beings might be extracted prematurely? What of the concept of the heart as the center of emotion, feeling, and the intellect? Will the brain be next on the transplant program? A news story from Russia reports that the head of one dog has been attached to another, and that the second dog is playfully biting at the ear of the first. When the brain transplant does occur, who will the new person be, and how will his memory be affected?[3]

What does Judaism specifically have to say about transplants?[4a] Are there any sources to be tapped for the evaluation of a Jewish position? May a person will various organs, such as eyes, kidneys, and sex organs, for scientific research?[4b] Does the offering of one kidney or one lung, by a perfectly healthy donor constitute a form of self-mutilation or even suicide? Does a man have the moral right to give his body, or part of it during his life, thereby threatening his own existence or shortening its length?

Jewish sources do provide some basis for an understanding of this whole issue. These have mainly to do with the value given to life and the treatment of death.

Judaism maintains unequivocally that the life of a human being is of infinite value, and any reduction of that life, in any way, by human hands, constitutes homicide, no matter the condition, age, or circumstance. So absolute is this principle that even a moment's lessening of life is deemed murder. The Talmud cites a hypothetical instance. If someone shoots and kills a person while the latter is falling from a height to certain death, he is nevertheless guilty of murder.

The value of human life is so absolute that, for its sake, Judaism suspends every law, of whatever kind, excepting the primary crimes of incest, idolatry and murder.

> Rabbi Simeon ben Gamiliel said: "For a day-old infant the Sabbath is desecrated; for David, King of Israel, dead, the Sabbath must not be profaned. For a day-old infant, the Sabbath is desecrated; the Torah ordered, 'Desecrate one Sabbath on his account so that he may keep many Sabbaths.' For David, King of Israel, dead, the Sabbath must not be desecrated; Once a man dies, he is free from all obligations."[5]

Another major source which stresses the insistence on the saving of life is the following:

> Mishna: A case of risk of loss of life, or of any illness that engenders the risk of loss of life supersedes the Sabbath law.[6]
> Gemara: How do we know that in the case of danger to human

life, the laws of the Sabbath are suspended. Rabbi Ishmael answered, "From *the passage*, If a thief is found breaking in, in which case, in spite of all the other considerations, it is lawful to kill him."[7]

Rabbi Simeon ben Menassia said: "(From *this* passage) 'And the children of Israel shall keep the Sabbath,'[8] The Torah said: Profane for his sake one Sabbath, so that he may keep many Sabbaths."

Rabbi Judah said in the name of Samuel: "If I had been there, I should have told them something better than what they said: '(From *this* passage) 'He shall live by them.'[9] but he shall not die because of them."

Raba said: "The exposition of them all could be refuted, except that of Samuel, which cannot be refuted."

Ravina, or Rabbi Nahman ben Isaac, said: "Better is one corn of pepper than a whole basket full of pumpkins," that is, a commentary on Samuel's irrefutable simple interpretation, as against the more involved and less perfect interpretations of the other rabbis.[10]

As if to strengthen the principle of the value of life the Talmud states:

Rabbi Johanan said in the name of Rabbi Simeon ben Jehozadak: "By a majority vote, it was resolved in the upper chambers of the house of Nithza in Lydda that every other law of the Torah, if a man is commanded: 'Transgress and suffer not death' he may transgress and not suffer death, excepting idolatry, incest and murder."[11a]

Related to this emphasis on the high value placed upon life is the necessity, if organ transplants are to be carried out, to ascertain as nearly as possible the exact moment of death.[11b] While a sixteenth century scholar has asserted that "we are no longer competent to establish the moment of death with sufficient precision," the Talmud does touch upon this issue indirectly in relation to the permissibility of violating Sabbath laws of rest where the saving of life is in question.

Mishna: If debris fall on someone, and it is doubtful whether or not he is there, or whether he is alive or dead . . . one should open (even on the Sabbath) the heap of debris for his sake . . . If one finds him alive, one should remove the debris, and if he be dead, one should leave him there (until the Sabbath day is over).[11c]

Gemara: How far does one search (if a person buried under the debris gives no sign of life at the point at which debris has been removed from him?) Until (one reaches) his nose. Some say: Up to his heart . . .

Rabbi Papa said: The dispute arises only as to from below upwards (if a person under the debris has his feet up and his head down. According to one view, one must examine the core, i.e., the heart; according to the other, even though the heart seems to have suspended action, the definitive diagnosis depends on the action or failure of the function of the nose) but if from above downwards, one had searched up to the nose, one need not search any further, as it is said: "In whose nostrils was the breath of life."[12, 12a]

In the Talmud and later authorities, breathing seems to have been taken as the criterion for the existence of life, and its cessation to have marked the moment of death.[13a]

(It ought to be noted that in Judaism, the moment of death is of significance only in relation to the question of ritual defilement).

People are presumed to be alive unless positive information is known to the contrary. "Hezkath Hayyim" is the Hebrew term for this presumption.

The insistence on immediate and dignified burial is one of the absolute rights of the body in death. This law applies to the *whole* body, without the removal of any of its parts.[13b] The source of this regulation is the Bible:

> If a man is guilty of capital offense and is put to death, and you impale him on a stake, you must not let his corpse remain on the stake overnight, but must bury him the same day. For an impaled body is an affront to God; you shall not defile the land that the Lord your God is giving you to possess.[14]

The Mishna extended this injunction to include all people:

> And not only this one (a criminal) did they (the sages) say it (that the corpse must not be left hanging over night) but whosoever lets his dead lie overnight transgresses a negative command. But if he kept him over night for the sake of his[15] honor, to procure for him a coffin or a shroud, he does not transgress thereby.[16]

The Talmud expands upon this Mishna:

Rabbi Johanan said on the authority of R. Simeon ben Yohai: "Whence is it inferred that whoever keeps his dead (unburied overnight transgresses thereby a negative command?) From the verse: You must bury him: (the infinitive indicates that the command concerns *all* dead, not only those executed by the court) whence we learn that he who keeps his dead (unburied) overnight transgresses a prohibitory command."[17]

The Talmud continues to deal with a related issue which serves as the basis of later responsa about organ transplants:

The scholars propounded: Is burial (intended to avert) disgrace (decomposition and putrefaction make the dead loathsome; burial may be intended to spare them and their relatives that disgrace) or a means of atonement (for sins committed during the life-time and the process of decay in the earth is a means of expiation). What is the practical difference? If a man said, "I do not wish myself to be buried." If you say that the purpose of burial is to prevent disgrace, then it does not depend entirely upon him (because his relatives are humiliated along with him) but if it is for atonement, then, in effect, he has declared, "I do not desire atonement," (and so, even if he is buried, he does not attain forgiveness.)[18]

The Talmud elaborates:

Come and hear: If he (the relative) kept him (the dead) overnight for the sake of his honor to procure for him a coffin or a shroud, he does not transgress thereby.[19] (Mishna)
Now surely that (for the sake of his honor) means for the honor of the *dead* (hence it follows that anything done in connection with the dead is for the honor of the dead.) No! for the honor of the *living*. And for the sake of the honor of the *living*, the dead is to be kept overnight? Yes. When did the Merciful One say, "his body shall not remain all night upon the tree" — only in a case similar to the hanged, where it (the keeping of the corpse) involves disgrace, (that is, the longer the body remains exposed, the greater the disgrace; and even in the case of an ordinary person, if the funeral is delayed without cause; but simply out of neglect, it is likewise accounted a disgrace to the dead; therefore, it is forbidden). But here, where there is no disgrace) the delay not being due to neglect but to the needs of the living) it doesn't apply.

215

The defilement or uncleanness resulting from a Kohen's coming into contact with the dead, has ramifications that could affect organ transplants. In Temple times, the Kohen, performed the sacrificial ritual, assisted by the Levite. Though the Temple no longer exists, traditional Judaism has retained a number of the duties and restrictions related to the priesthood, one of these being the limits set on contact with the dead. The Bible specifies:

> . . . speak to the priests, the sons of Aaron, and say to them: None shall defile himself for any (dead) person among his kin, except for the relatives that are closest to him; his mother, his father, his son, his daughter, and his brother; also for a virgin sister, close to him because she has not married, for her he may defile himself . . .[20]

> Commentary: Contact with the dead defiles and temporarily renders a priest unfit to perform his duties. This law only held good when the dead person was "among his people"; that is, if there were others who were not priests able and willing to attend to the burial. In the case of the unattended dead body of a friendless man, everyone, even a High Priest had to busy himself with the last rites.

The principle that one may not derive material benefit from either the actual body or the appurtenances of the dead, also has bearing on the issue of organ transplant. The Rabbis derive their attitude from the Biblical account of the death of Miriam, Moses' sister: ". . . and Miriam died there, and was buried *there*."[21] The Talmud points to the seemingly unnecessary repetition of the word *there*, and comments:

> It has been stated: If one wove a shroud for a dead person: Abaye rules, It is forbidden (to be used for any other purpose): and Rava says, It is permitted. Abaye rules, It is (forbidden; (he holds) Designation is a material act (that is, mere designation for the dead, subjects it to the same law as though it has been employed for the purpose). What is Abaye's reason? He deduces (identity of law) from the use of (the Hebrew word) *shahm*, (there), both here (with reference to the dead) and in connection with the broken-necked heifer, (an issue discussed in the following chapter of the Bible). In connection with the dead: "And Miriam died *there* and was buried *there* (shahm);"[22] with reference to the heifer, "and

shall break the heifer's neck *there.*"[23] Just as the broken-necked heifer becomes forbidden through designation (even the mere bringing it down to the valley renders it forbidden for any other purpose) so this, too, (shroud woven for the dead) becomes prohibited through designation . . .[24]

Any disfigurement of the dead is forbidden by Jewish law as an act of desecration. One of the leading authorities of the 18th century, Rabbi Ezekiel Landau, derives this principle from the Talmud:

The Talmud forbids heirs to open the grave of a person to establish whether he was a minor or had reached his majority by the appearance of pubic hair; the reasons given are that this would constitute a desecration of the dead and that, moreover, the signs to be ascertained may have changed after death.[25]

The related issues of autopsy and dissection also may have bearings upon the transplant question. Although opinions are not clear-cut, the general position now held in the Orthodox world is that autopsies to ascertain the cause of death are forbidden unless the civil authorities order otherwise. In the same way, dissection is regarded as a desecration of the human body.

The establishment of the State of Israel made autopsies an urgent issue. The Israeli government and Chief Rabbinate came to an agreement that post-mortem examinations would only be sanctioned when:

a) it was legally required;

b) in the opinion of three physicians, the cause of death could not otherwise be ascertained;

c) it might help save the lives of others suffering from an illness similar to that from which the patient had died;

d) in cases of certain hereditary diseases, doing so might safeguard surviving relatives.[27]

The question of whether, according to Jewish law, one may bequeath one's body for science and medical studies also can have bearings upon the transplant issue. Despite fierce opposition, the office of the Israeli Chief Rabbinate has issued a statement that it does not object to the use of bodies of persons who gave their consent, in writing, of their own free will, during their lifetime, for anatomical dissections as required for medical studies, provided the dissected parts are carefully preserved so as to be eventually buried with due respect according to Jewish law.[28]

This point of view appears to have been shared, at the beginning of the century, by the Chief Rabbi of England, Hermann Adler, who stated publicly, in the course of a memorial address:

> His (Fredric David Mocatta) selflessness is proved by a remarkable instruction he gave to his physician. He directed that, in the event of his dying of an obscure disease, after death examination should be made, the cost to borne by his estate, for the advance of medical science and for the benefit of those who might suffer hereafter from a similar ailment.[29]

## IN GENERAL

A recent responsum[30] entitled *On the Matter of Transplanting an Organ from the Dead to the Living* divides the issue into three parts. The writer says modestly, although his conclusions are based on Halakhic principles, they should not be applied before greater authorities have been resorted to for advice. He deals with three areas:

> A. The Prohibition Against Desecration of the Dead.
> There is a general opposition to disfigurement, mutilation or dissection of the dead, especially since the middle of the 18th century when Rabbi Jacob Emden issued the prohibition against using the body for scientific study. There is a general consensus, however, that such an injunction applies only where there is no immediate use to be derived from the practice. But where tampering with the dead can afford direct, tangible relief to the living, the prohibition is waived.
> Also, burial may be delayed, where the dead is honored, rather than humiliated by the postponement, as, for example, when a coffin or shroud has to be procured or time has to be allowed for the arrival of relatives.
> There is no relation, the writer asserts, between dissection for medical purposes prohibited by Rabbi Jacob Emden and the practice of organ transplants. Emden's prohibition was rooted in the fact that no immediate tangible need was present, only the interest of scientific research in the abstract. However, where immediate benefit might be derived, the case could even be argued that transplants are permissible without having to resort to the over-

riding principle that the necessity of saving life supersedes all other prohibitions.

B. The Duty of Immediate Burial.

The writer argues that the Biblical injunction that the whole body be buried immediately is not necessarily infringed upon by organ transplants.[31]

He explains that the Talmud gives two reasons for the practice of burial. On the one hand burial covers up from sight the decomposition of the body, and therefore prevents disgrace to the dead, and on the other, burial may have been considered an atonement for sin.[32] If the former was the case, it has already been shown that where there is clear, immediate, tangible need, dissection is permitted, and certainly, in the case of organ transplants, this would be true. If, however, burial is practiced as an atonement for sin, no difficulty would arise where organ transplants are concerned. In this case the burial may be delayed, since this is permitted when the honor of the dead is involved. The only question raised, is whether atonement of the dead is also postponed with the delay in burial. The writer asserts that the postponed burial does not affect the atonement of the dead. In the case of an organ transplant to a living person, the particular organ in question will one day be buried, and the time factor is completely irrelevant here.

C. The Prohibition Against Deriving Material Benefit from the Dead.

Although Jewish law forbids material benefit to be derived from the dead, it makes no such prohibitions where the living are concerned. So, an organ transplant from a dead person, which still fulfills a living function, adopts the characteristic of life, is alive, hence not dead, and therefore not prohibited.

The writer of this responsum concludes, that a dead person (or organ) returned to life, does not have the laws of the dead apply to him or it. Hence, the prohibition of material benefit is not relevant. It is therefore permissible to transplant an organ from a dead person to a living person.

## CORNEAL TRANSPLANTS

Responsa literature has concentrated its attention first upon corneal transplants. Treatment of this comparatively minor area can serve, however, as a basis of the larger issues involved. Since the first corneal operation was performed in 1905, many rabbinic scholars have delved into Jewish sources, seeking religious sanction. Each of the three major denominations within Judaism has discussed the question and, although their reasoning may have been different, the conclusions to which they came are very similar.

## THE ORTHODOX POSITION

Here are selections reflecting the *almost* unanimous Orthodox point of view:

> ... most authorities have endorsed the now classic argument by the Chief Rabbi of Israel.[34] (Issar Judah Unterman), that any tissue from the dead grafted to a living patient, by being literally restored to life, loses it forbidden character as a part removed from the dead and may therefore be utilized. Only one scholar rejects this reasoning although he still allows the operation on the ground that saving a person from complete blindness, which may make him more easily liable to fatal accidents, is tantamount to saving his life. This argument is also mentioned by others. Hence, and because of further considerations on the rights of the dead, it has been suggested that, in making the necessary provisions during his lifetime, the donor should stipulate that his eye be used for a person suffering from, or threatened with, blindness of both eyes, and that the disused part of the eye, after the cornea has been removed, be disposed of by burial only. One rabbi also urges informing the donor that the gift of his eyes, however meritorious, may compromise his atonement after death by reason of the deliberate mutilation of his body.[35]
>
> It is forbidden not only to violate the integrity of the dead body, but also to derive any material benefit from any part removed from it. An exception to this rule, is the donation and subsequent utilization of the eye for keratoplastic operations (provided the unused part of the eye is eventually buried), because the cornea, after being grafted to a living body, itself becomes alive again, and thus loses its forbidden character by ceasing to be dead tissue. In addition, the restoration of sight to the blind is equivalent to saving them from death.[36]
>
> Jewish law raises no objection to the donation and subsequent utilization of eyes for corneal transplants, provided the disused part of the eye is eventually buried. This is permitted because the

cornea is, through the graft, literally restored to life, thereby losing the forbidden status it had as tissue removed from the dead, and because the gift of sight to the blind is regarded as tantamount to the saving of life. Hence, it should be stipulated that the eye be preferably used for grafting on a patient suffering from, or threatened by, blindness in both eyes.[37]

All Orthodox rabbis do not agree with this position. The writer of an article in a rabbinic journal dissents from the above view on all counts.[38]

## THE REFORM POSITION

At its annual convention at Estes Park, Colorado, in 1953, the Committee on Responsa of the Central Conference of American Rabbis, resolved:

> We must . . . conclude that the authorized removal of the eyes of a deceased person in order to restore sight to the blind, is not an act of mutilation, which is forbidden, but an act of healing and restoration, which in Jewish law takes precedence over almost all other religious injunctions.[39]

Three years later, the question was discussed in a responsum and considered with respect to some of the deeper implications involved. The conclusion reached stated:

> . . . we are justified in deciding that even though the entire eye is taken out and kept under refrigeration, the cornea may be used to restore the sight of the blind.[40]

In 1964, the Commission on Judaism and Medicine reaffirmed the two statements.

The responsum prepared by Rabbi Solomon Freehof, outlined the questions raised:

> Physicians in recent years have developed a technique of transplanting the cornea from the eyes of people recently dead, onto the eyes of the blind, and thus, in many cases, restoring their sight. Is this procedure permitted in traditional law?[41]

The author expatiates upon the question of whether, and under what circumstances, an invalid may make use of normally forbidden

objects, and also deals with the issue of defilement, and the requirement of immediate, dignified and complete burial.

> An invalid who is not in grave danger, may make use in healing of
> all forbidden things which are forbidden by *rabbinic* law, but not
> of such as are forbidden by the stricter law of the Pentateuch
> itself. Whereas, an invalid who is in imminent danger, may make
> use for his healing, even of such objects which are forbidden by
> the strictest Biblical law. A man who is blind in one eye would be
> considered as an invalid, not in immediate danger, but, one who is
> blind in both eyes, would be considered as one who is in imminent
> danger. Therefore, there is no question that a person totally blind
> or in imminent danger of becoming totally blind, may make use of
> *anything* that may bring him healing, in this case, vision.

The writer concludes as follows:

> Because the general spirit of the law is to allow the dangerously
> sick to use anything otherwise prohibited, and since there is
> justification in the law for not even being required to bury that
> which is "less than an olive," and since it is doubtful whether the
> eye is one of the "limbs" which must be buried, and since at all
> events we have become accustomed to permit autopsies in which
> even the limbs of the body are not buried for a while, we are
> justified in deciding that even though the entire eye is taken out
> and kept under refrigeration, the cornea may be used to restore the
> sight of the blind.

## THE CONSERVATIVE POSITION

In 1953, the Committee on Jewish Law and Standards of the
Rabbinical Assembly adopted as its official view a responsum by
Rabbi Theodore Friedman. His analysis and presentation was an ex-
pansion of a query addressed to him originally by the Eye Right
Organization, sponsors of the Eye Bank, as to the permissibility of a
Jew's gifting his eyes to science in his will, or of a sightless Jew's
taking advantage of modern methods of cornea grafting. The
answer given in the case of both donor and recipient was that
transplant was not in violation of Jewish law.

There are various approaches to the issues involved. It is open
to discussion whether the prohibition of the use of a corpse is

*biblical* (hence more strict) or *rabbinic* (hence more liberal), the majority tending to the former position.

> For our purposes, we may accept this latter opinion and yet find our conclusion unaffected by it. It should be readily granted that blindness should be deemed a case of "saving of life," or at the very least, an impairment that can be characterized as a dangerous situation.

This attitude toward the blind is underscored by the Aggadic notion to be found in the Talmud that a sightless person is as unfortunate as if he were dead. Furthermore, the Talmud suggests that on a capital charge, being blinded was considered a penalty tantamount to execution. Since the cure of blindness is placed in the category of the saving of life, although the use of the corpse is a biblical prohibition, in this case it gives way to the higher life-saving principle involved.

Rabbi Friedman's position is that one may will his eyes to science after death. Many of the Talmudic prohibitions against mutilation and dissection are not related to cases where there "is question of achieving any significant enhancement of human life thereby." Contrarywise, he offers a case in which the Talmud might be prepared to permit an autopsy (or mutilation) of a corpse, if it might possibly lead to the saving of life. At all events, the prohibition against disfiguring the body is, at most, expressive of a Talmudic attitude, and can not be technically categorized as a rabbinic prohibition.

In light of contemporary popular opinion, a gift to science would redound to the honor, and not to the discredit, of the deceased.

A question asked of the Rabbinical Assembly Committee in 1961 as to whether eyes may be willed to an eye bank, elicited a positive response.[42] We should not hesitate to declare, in accordance with the letter and the spirit of the Halakhah, that "the saving of life is greater than honoring the dead."

## HEART TRANSPLANTS

When the world's first heart transplant was performed, the Jewish Telegraphic Agency released the following statement from Johannesburg:

Rabbinical authorities here and in Britain have hailed the first successful transplant of a human heart, the operation performed on Louis Washkansky of Cape Town, as an act that conforms to the over-riding consideration of Jewish law, the saving of a human life.

Rabbinical opinion of the medical feat in the light of Jewish law was sought by the South African *Jewish Times* whose editor cabled Dr. Immanuel Jakobovits, Chief Rabbi of the British Commonwealth, and spoke to Chief Rabbi Bernard Casper, of Johannesburg, Chief Rabbi Israel Abrahams, of Cape Town, and Rabbi Arthur Super, Chief Minister of the Reform congregation of Johannesburg.

Dr. Jakobovits, regarded as a world authority on Jewish medical ethics, declared in a cable to the paper that "Judaism cannot but enthusiastically applaud the medical triumph in service of human life."

Rabbi Casper said that while the Halakhic position remains to be studied and defined in light of the new operation, the over-riding consideration of Jewish law is the saving of life and "it would be hard to find a clearer and more direct application of this principle than in the case of the heart transplant."

Rabbi Abrahams said that the operation falls within the category of "acts that might normally be regarded as transgressions of Jewish law, in order to save life."

Rabbi Super said that "as far as Reform Judaism is concerned, we are very much in favor of human transplant and autopsies and in fact anything which is likely to result in human life being saved, however remote the chances."

## ORTHODOX POSITIONS

One of the first statements dealing with heart transplants appeared in an Orthodox Anglo-Jewish weekly[43] in response to a reader's question as to whether a Jew is permitted to undergo a heart transplant operation. The editor at first presents the case against autopsy and dissection as held by some Jewish authorities, and states:

. . . many rabbis would permit removing a heart if it had been bequeathed before the person died, because it would go immediately to a person who would benefit by this operation.

On the question whether one may subject oneself to an operation when the outcome is uncertain, the respondent quotes a Talmudic case where, although the results of the operation are open to doubt, it is certain that, without an operation, the patient will die. In this case, the operation should be performed, however questionable the results. The Talmud explicitly sanctions such surgery when it is certain that, without it, the patient will eventually die.[44]

. . . the administration of doubtful remedies in a desperate gamble to save life, is, in fact, encouraged, and several authorities expressly permit giving a patient a possibly effective drug even at grave risk of hastening his death if it proves fatal . . .[45]

In another article, the same authority says:

Jewish law specifically permits the administration of doubtful or experimental cures, if safer methods are unknown, or not available. In fact, the authorities encourage giving a terminal patient a possibly effective drug even at the grave risk of hastening his death, should it prove fatal, if the alternative to this risk is the patient's certain death from his affliction later. In that case, the chances of the drug either bringing about his recovery, or else accelerating his death, need not even be fifty-fifty; any prospect that it may prove helpful is sufficient to warrant its use, provided the majority of the specialists consulted are in favor of its employment. The same considerations would, of course, apply to doubtful surgical operations in a desperate gamble to save a patient.[46]

A definitive article entitled "Lev Hadash (A New Heart)" appeared soon after the first heart transplant, in the leading Israeli monthly magazine Panim El Panim, which described the new surgical procedure photographically and in precise detail. A subheading read: "Rabbis: From the point of view of Halakhah there is no deterrent for heart transplants. The only prohibition is to withdraw the heart while the donor lives, though physicians have given up hope. Chief Rabbi Issar Yehudah Unterman says: 'It is a great privilege, zekhuth, for him whose heart saves another's life.' "

The article concludes with the caption "The Halakhah Permits." Rabbi Unterman is quoted as having said, "Heart transplants are permissible according to Jewish law." He cautions, however, that we must be certain that the donor is totally dead (which requires testimony on the part of two physicians, and that the operation takes place immediately, that is, that the recipient is at hand, that two physicians testify that no more cutting than absolutely necessary will be done, and that the family consents. He advises that the consent should be solicited by rabbis who are in favor of the transplant and can explain its importance and that there is no issue involved of disgrace to the dead; on the contrary, it is a great privilege for them and for the dead that through the use of one of his organs the life of another man should be saved. The principle that "he who saves one life is considered as having saved an entire world," is enunciated in this connection.

The Sephardic Chief Rabbi of Israel, Yitzhak Nissim, has said that transplants are acceptable "in the case of danger to life and as long as clinical death is insured."

> A published responsum dealing specifically with heart transplants is that of the Chief Rabbi of Israel, Rabbi Issar Yehudah Unterman . . . He begins by stating that consent from the family of the donor must be obtained. Otherwise, the doctors and the recipient would transgress the Scriptural Commandment, "You shall not steal" . . .
>
> Then reviewing the Halakhic definition of death, (he) states that under ordinary circumstances, death occurs when respiration ceases. However, sudden, unexplained death in young, otherwise healthy individuals should be followed by resuscitative measures. A hopelessly ill person with less than three days of life left, need not be resuscitated when respiration ceases . . .
>
> A novel pronouncement by Chief Rabbi Unterman is that heart transplants may not be Halakhically sanctioned until such time as the chances for survival from the surgery are greater than the risk to the recipient . . .
>
> Rabbi Unterman explains . . . that the recipient of a new heart is in a different situation from all other desperately ill (but not necessarily dying) people. After his diseased heart is implanted, the recipient has lost his *Hezkath Hayyim* (hold on life, or presump-

226

tion of still being alive). Once he loses his *Hezkath Hayyim*, the heart transplant recipient is no longer permitted to risk his life if the chances for success are not greater than the chances of failure. A person apparently dying of cancer, on the other hand, never loses his *Hezkath Hayyim* and, therefore, may subject himself to any risk, however great, if there is a small chance of cure . . .

Rabbi Unterman concludes, in the case of a human heart transplant receipient, removing the patient's old heart removes from him his hold on life, and thus, the removal of the recipient's heart can be sanctioned only if the risk of death resulting from the surgery is estimated to be smaller than the prospect of lasting success. On the other hand, one must violate the Sabbath to rescue someone from under a collapsed building even if the person may already be dead, because he retains his *Hezkath Hayyim* until proven otherwise. Similarly, a patient dying of an incurable illness may subject himself to a potentially lethal medication or operation on the small chance that cure might be achieved, because this patient never lost his *Hezkath Hayyim*.[48]

Following the first spate of positive responses to heart transplant surgery, many more responsa on the subject were published in rabbinic journals all over the world.[49]

Questions were raised dealing with the precise moment of death, and the manner in which death is determined. Doctors and theologians differed. Statements made by doctors that some degree of life must exist in the heart for it to be worth transplanting disturbed many people. Fear was expressed that in the desire to save another life, not enough effort would be made to save the life of the donor.

A reaction against such surgery took place in March-April, 1969 when the editor of *Hapardes*, a leading rabbinic journal, delivered a scathing denunciation of Sephardic Chief Rabbi Yitzhak Nissim for having given his "blessing" to heart transplants "which is against the Halakhah . . . permitting the murder of two people," and "in sharp opposition to Chief Rabbi Issar Unterman. The editor views this act as irretrievably divisive between the world of Torah (Orthodox) Judaism and the Chief Rabbinate in Israel.[50]

The same issue contains an unusually stark statement by Rabbi Moshe Feinstein, President of Agudat Harabanim, the Union of Orthodox Rabbis of America, asserting that, where heart transplants were concerned:

"I do not wish to engage in proofs, evaluations or pilpulism because I insist that the more discussion the greater the danger that leniency will seep into our thinking; there is a threat that it will be claimed that the rabbis are divided on the issue and hence we might perhaps be more lenient. Therefore, I say clearly, decisively, as a responsum (Teshuvah) to be executed as Law, that heart transplantation is the unequivocal murder of two human beings; literally killing the one from whose body the heart is taken, since he is still living — not only according to Jewish law, but even according to physicians, many of whom admit to the truth that he is still alive — but because of their evil are not concerned with his life since he is going to die in a short time anyway, and also murdering the recipient who might well live for a long time — we know that many live for extended periods with heart ailments. By taking his heart from him and transplanting it with another's, he is being killed; some [recipients] have only lived for a few moments and none have remained alive. It is indeed surprising that governmental authorities have permitted physicians to commit two murders. They, the physicians, should be punished as murderers. Even if the patient consents to the transplant operation, his consent is invalid. One is not permitted to kill even onself."

It is only by using such extreme and forceful language, Rabbi Feinstein concludes, that all debate about this subject will be at an end.

Despite his responsum, however, even for the Orthodox world, this matter did not end there. In the June 1969 issue of *Or Hamizrah*, Rabbi Yehudah Gershuni reopened the question.[51] He did not come to any decision nor did he violently oppose Rabbi Feinstein's pronouncement. All he attempted was a straightforward treatment of the issues, offering various sources which could lead to a different ruling than that affirmed by Rabbi Feinstein. He deals with the question as to whether, when death occurs, the heart of a person who is "terefa" (who cannot live) may be removed and placed into the body of one who, with the help of the transplant may survive. He also considers whether, where the recipient is concerned, it is permissible to remove his own heart prior to the insertion of the new one. The author in no way commits himself, but concludes with the traditional statement, "this requires deeper reflection."[52]

A leading physician and rabbinic scholar has written:

A personal interview with Rabbi Feinstein by this writer (Dr. Fred Rosner) as well as careful reading of his lengthy unpublished responsum on this subject discloses the following clarification of his position. If the donor is absolutely and positively dead by all medical and Jewish legal criteria, then no murder of the donor would be involved and the removal of his heart or other organ to save another human life would be permitted.

Concerning the recipient, when medical science will have progressed to the point where cardiac transplantation becomes an accepted therapeutic procedure with reasonably good chances for success, then the operation upon the recipient would no longer be considered murder. Additional animal experimentation, continues Rabbi Feinstein, is essential to overcome major obstacles . . . such as organ rejection, tissue compatability typing, and immunosuppresive therapy, before heart transplantation in man can be condoned. In the present state of medical knowledge, however, where chances for success are miniscule and the recipient's life is probably shortened rather than lengthened by this procedure, heart transplantation must still be considered murder of the recipient.[53]

The author of the article concludes:

The majority of Rabbinic opinion expressed to date in regard to heart transplants is of a permissive nature provided the donor was definitely deceased at the time his heart was removed.[54a]

## CONSERVATIVE POSITION

In a paper entitled *Judaism and Heart Transplantations*, Rabbi Jack Segal of the Rabbinical Assembly Committee on Law and Standards, analyzes the various positions on death, the moment of death and euthanasia, as reflected and recorded in Talmudic and Responsa sources. He asserts that:

It would seem that the spirit of Conservative Judaism could subscribe to the four principles proclaimed by a committee of thirteen top-ranking Harvard professors which was reported in the Journal of the American Medical Association and summarized in the August 19, 1968 issue of *Newsweek* magazine.

The professors stated that irreversible coma, or *death*, should be considered to have occurred if:

1. There is total lack of response to external stimuli, including extreme pain.

2. There is absence of all spontaneous movements, notably breathing (if he is on a respirator, it may be turned off for three minutes in order to establish that he is incapable of breathing by himself).

3. There is no sign of reflexes.

4. There is no sign of brain activity when measured by the electroencephalogram.

In addition to these four requirements it would be best to have at least *two* physicians make the decision that death has occurred. It is also advisable that if there is any prospect of a transplant, those physicians who would declare the individual dead, should *not* be members of the transplant team.

Rabbi Siegal reaches the conclusion:

Judaism is not a stagnant religion. It must keep pace with the advances of science and evaluate each new advance in the spirit of our tradition. The decision as to the permissiblity or non-permissibility of performing heart transplants is a difficult one. However, it would seem that Judaism would permit it in order to perpetuate the life of an individual. Each life is important to Judaism. We do not have a right to squander it.

Two Conservative rabbis, Seymour Seigel and Daniel Goldfarb, hold the following position on the question of "moment of death."[54b]

Rabbi Goldfarb:

"I believe that the determination of death on the basis of a measurement of the cessation of brain function, in situations where responsible medical opinion indicates its propriety, would be entirely consistent with Jewish law . . .

. . . Under appropriate circumstances, consistent with competent and current medical judgment the inclusion of brain function as a basis for the determination of death is entirely proper. The Rabbinical Assembly should therefore, endorse legislation which incorporates brain criteria in an appropriate manner."

Rabbi Siegel:

"From the point of view of Jewish law we can defend the thesis that if there is brain death and lack of spontaneous breathing (and heartbeat), then the individual should be considered dead even though his lungs may be ventilating by artificial means.

It is reasonable to assume that if the ancient rabbis had had artificial respirators or EEG's, they would have established different criteria of death than the ones they had."

Rabbi Siegel's position is underscored in another article:[54c]

The basic Talmudic definition is that death occurs when respiration ceases. The cessation of heartbeat was also taken into consideration. There are many today who believe that a better definition of death should be based on the cessation of brain activity as evidenced by the absence of EEG's (brain waves). When the brain waves stop, spontaneous breathing and heartbeat are impossible, and therefore the patient can be said to be dead even though his systems may be moving by means of machines. It was felt that when the rabbis defined death by referring to the circulation and breathing, they were reflecting the best scientific information available in their day, but now that we have means to measure the activity of the brain, the organ which is the central mechanism for the support of life, new criteria for death should be adopted.

A leading Conservative rabbi, Rudolph Adler, writing in *The Torch*[55] divides the subject into three parts, dealing separately with the laws as they may apply to the recipient, the donor, and the physician:

The Recipient: It goes without saying that the recipient must be vital enough to withstand this major operation. By removing a vital organ such as his heart, there is the danger of speeding his death. This would normally be prohibited by Jewish law. However, since by implanting a new and healthier heart in the recipient, his chances of living a longer life, if the operation proves successful would be increased, the normal prohibition may be set aside.

This exact question appears under different circumstances in a Responsa by Rabbi Jacob Reischer where a doctor asks if it is permitted to administer a medicine to a Jew which will either help him or kill him? Reischer permits it by quoting from the Talmud: "Where the chance for a longer life exists, we are not worried about the possibility that a shorter life is being sacrificed."

The Donor: According to Jewish law, we must not speed the death of any person nor withhold all means of saving life. Withholding medication or food in order to hasten death for a hopelessly suffering patient, or praying for his death and release from pain — these questions are discussed but are not decided in a clear-cut fashion. Can we make concessions in the case where the heart is needed and must be available thirty minutes after death?

Another concern is, at what state is a man dead? According to some physicians it depends on the brain, with others on the heart. How about modern machinery assisting people to live by taking over certain functions of life-giving organs? If a machine is turned on, the patient lives; if turned off, he dies. In that case, when is the donor alive and when not? Who will decide and do we have the right to turn off the machine? This leads us to the additional difficult problem of euthanasia, where Jewish law holds a very conservative view.

Next comes the problem of the desecration of the dead, as we are considering the removal of a vital organ from the donor. According to Jewish law the dead must be interred in their entirety but this law may be set aside in order to save another Jew. This discussion must lead to the entire problem of autopsy and Jewish law. A fierce controversy is still raging in this matter, yet most authorities would agree that if there is a known recipient, the donor may donate his heart. This may, however, depend also on the certainty of success of the transplant.

Because of the inviolable dignity attaching to the dead as well as the living according to Jewish law, the donor must give his consent. However, others hold that man's right over his body is limited during life as well as after death and even consent may not be valid in some cases.[56]

The Doctor: The prohibition of inflicting wounds on living persons in the process of taking out the ailing heart from the recipient, may be set aside in order to save his life. Removing the donor's heart and the ensuing desecration of the dead can also be overcome in order to save the life of a known patient. The major problem for the physician now as in the past remains: are these transplants sufficienty safe to justify the application of the Jewish law "for the purpose of saving life?"

Most authorities . . . will rely on the judgment of three competent medical specialists in that field, or majority opinion of same. How do we stand today with regards to the majority as to the safety of heart transplants? From all the available information it is proper to state that the greatest authorities on the subject are still completely divided and the majority would not recommend it as a safe procedure. It is recognized that the new heart transplant is a more delicate procedure than any other medical operation thus far performed.

In my opinion, Jewish law would permit heart transplants if the majority of experts would agree that there is a better than fifty-fifty chance of life; if not, the matter would be in the category of research which is not permitted. For in the latter case the Jewish laws of safeguarding the dying (Goses), not permitting one man to make a final decision in such a delicate matter could not be set aside.

## REFORM POSITIONS

In 1968 Rabbi Solomon Freehof submitted to the Central Conference of American Rabbis a responsum included in his latest volume[57] on the Jewish legal attitudes to transplants from the dead to the living.

Dr. Freehof stresses that "Jewish tradition and feeling . . . is absolutely opposed to hastening the death of a potential donor by even one second in order that the organ to be transplanted into another body be in good condition. Nothing must be done to hasten the death of the dying . . . the patient must be absolutely dead."

If the entire issue revolved around methods and materials used for healing, says Dr. Freehof, no further discussion would have been necessary. He marshalls sources which underscore this position. "The Talmud says that we may use any material for healing except that which is connected with idolatry, immorality and bloodshed"[58] Rather than commit any of these three cardinal sins, a person should undergo martyrdom, but aside from them, any medicine or method of healing would be permitted. Maimonides, himself a great physician, clarifies this issue:

> He who is sick and in danger of death, and the physician tells him that he can be cured by a certain object or material which is forbidden by the Torah, he must obey the physician and be cured.

There is a consideration quite apart from this, however, "that the body of the dead has a special sacredness in Jewish law. There is a general principle that the body of the dead may not be used for the benefit of the living (meth asur b'ha-a-na-ah, based on Sanhedrin

233

47b). If the two principles are taken together, the general permissiveness would then need to be restated as follows: We may use all materials except those involved in the three cardinal sins mentioned above and *except also*, the body of the dead."

Three issues are then raised: first, the question of the benefit to be derived from parts of the body of the dead; second, whether there is any difference as applied to organ transplants in using the body of a gentile or the body of a Jew. The third issue raised is that of the Halakhic requirement that the whole body undergo burial.

Dr. Freehof addresses himself to each of these questions and sums up his position:

> "The exceptional nature and rights of the dead body do not stand in the way of the use of parts of the body for healing of another body. The part taken is not taken into the living body as food. Hence it is not considered *derekh hana'ah*. The part becomes integrated into a living body and therefore the general principle first stated remains unimpugned, that "we may heal with any of the prohibited materials mentioned in Scripture." This is especially true, as Maimonides indicates, because the patients about to receive these implants are actually in danger of death, and for such patients any possible help is permitted by Jewish tradition."

NOTES

1. A recent item in the *Reader's Digest* notes: "In the midst of the much publicized series of heart transplants, a remarkable organ transplantation has been all but overlooked. Last fall in Ghent, a Belgian surgeon Fritz Derom transplanted a lung into Alois Vereecken, a 23 year-old steel worker whose own right lung had been destroyed by silicosis. In July, Vereecken was still alive and living happily at home, returning periodically to the hospital for checkups. No previous lung recipient had ever lived more than 28 days." The item quotes Dale Dauer in *Medical World News*.

1a. As of July 1, 1977, 346 heart transplants were performed on 338 recipients. 77 were alive on that date and the longest survivor has lived 8.7 years. Source: National Heart, Lung and Blood Institute. Courtesy: Stamford, Conn. Hospital. See also, David Dempsey, Transplants are Common: It's the Organs That Have Become Rare, New York Times Magazine, October 13, 1974, p. 56.

1b. See, "Cardiac Replacement; Medical, Ethical Psychological *and Economical Implications*, A Report by Ad Hoc Task Force On Cardiac Replacement," National Heart Institute, Washington, D.C., October 1969.

2. See, Paul Ramsey, "On Updating Death" in *The Religious Situation* 1969, Donald R. Cutler, Editor, Beacon Press, Boston, Mass. p. 253. See also, Vance

Packard, *The People Shapers*, Little Brown and Company, Boston-Toronto, 1977, p. 305.

3.*See*, Herbert Bronstein, "Ethical and Religious Issues in Heart Transplants," *Reconstructionist*, New York, May 31, 1968. *Also*, Immanuel Jakobovits, "A Modern Doctor's Dilemma," *Jewish Chronicle*, London, March 17, 1967. Also "Anatomical Gifts and Human Tissue Transplantation," *DePaul Law Review*, *Medico-Legal Symposium*, Chicago, Summer, 1969. For a radical view, *see* Joseph Fletcher, "Our Shameful Waste of Human Tissue: An Ethical Problem for the Living and Dead," *"The Religious Situation,"* 1969. For discussions on change of identity, see Azriel Rosenfeld, *Human Identity: Halakhic Issues*, Tradition, R.C.A. Vol. 16, No. 3,. Spring 1977. p. 58. Also by the same author, *The Heart, the Head and the Halakhah*, New York State Journal of Medicine, October 15, 1970.

4a. For a thorough analysis, see Fred Rosner, *"Heart and Other Organ Transplantations and Jewish Law,"* Jewish Life, U.O.J.C.A., Sept.-Oct., 1969, pp. 38-51. Also, in *Jewish Bioethics*, edited by Fred Rosner and J. David Bleich, Sanhedrin Press, New York, 1979.

4b. For interesting discussions of Sex Organ Transplants, See Azriel Rosenfeld, *Judaism and Gene Design*, Tradition, R.C.A., Vol. 13, No. 2, Fall, 1972, p. 75; J. David Bleich, *Contemporary Halakhic Problems*, Ktav-Yeshiva University Press, New York, p. 100. Solomon Freehof, *Reform Responsa for Our Time*, Hebrew Union College Press, Cincinnati, 1977, p. 196.

5. Shabbath 151b.

6. Mishnah, Yoma VIII, 6.

7. Exod. 22:1.

8. Exod. 31:16.

9. Lev. 18:5.

10. Yoma 85b.

11a. Sanhedrin 74a.

11b. See also, J. David Bleich, *Establishing Criteria of Death*, Tradition, R.C.A., Vol. 13, No. 3, Winter 1973, New York, p. 90. The same article appears in *Contemporary Halakhic Problems* by Rabbi Bleich, Ktav Publishing House, New York 1977, pp. 372-393. See also, J. David Bleich, *Time of Death Legislation*, Tradition, Vol. 16, No. 4. Summer 1977, p. 130. See also Daniel C. Goldfarb, *"The Definition of Death,"* Conservative Judaism, Vol. 30, No. 2. Winter, 1976, p. 10; also, Seymour Siegel, *"Updating Criteria of Death,"* ibid, p. 23. See also, William B. Silverman, *"The Ethics of Transplants,"* C.C.A.R. Journal, Vol. 21, No. 2. Spring, 1974, p. 56.

11c. Mishna, Yoma VIII, 7.

12. Gen. 7:22.

12a. Yoma 85a.

13a. Moses Sofer (1763-1839.) *See also*, Solomon, Freehof, *A Treasury of Responsa*, Jewish Publication Society, Philadelphia, 1963, p. 237 ff.

13b. See J. David Bleich, "Medical Experimentation Upon Several Organs," Tradition, Vol. 12, No. 1, Summer 1971, R.C.A., New York, p. 89.

14. Deut. 21:22-23.

15. The "his" is ambiguous and the Talmud later discusses to whom it refers.

16. Mishna, Sanhedrin VI, 5.

17. Sanhedrin 46b.

18. *Ibid.*

19. Later codes add arrival of relatives and those who will deliver funeral orations to the list of honors to the dead. Maimonides, Hilkhot Avel, IV:8 Yoreh Deah CCCLVIII 1.

20. Lev. 21:1-3. *See* Maimonides, Hilkhot Avel, Chapter 3.

21. Num. 20:1.

22. *Ibid.*

23. Deut. 21:4.

24. Sanhedrin 47b.

25. Baba Bathra 154a. *Also*, Yoreh De'ah CCCXLIX 7, quoted in Immanuel Jakobovits, *Jewish Medical Ethics*, p. 312, note 90.

26. II Chron. 32:33.

27. Rabbi H. Rabinowicz, A Guide to Life, *London Chronicle Publications*, London, 1964, p. 23.

28. *Dath Yisrael U'Medinath Yisrael*, 1951, quoted by H. Rabinowicz, ibid, p. 24. *Also*, by I. Jakobovits, *Jewish Medical Ethics*, p. 150.

29. Adler, Herman. *Anglo-Jewish Memories*, London, 1900, p. 137.

30. Rabbi Benzion Fierer, *Noam*, Vol. IV, Jerusalem, Israel, p. 200.

31. Deut. 21:21-23.

32. Sanhedrin 46b.

33. II Kings 4:35.

34. *See*, Fred Rosner, "Heart and Other Organ Transplantation," ibid., p. 42.

35. Immanuel Jakobovits, *Journal of a Rabbi*, Living Books, New York, 1961, p. 159.

36. *Hospital Compendium*, (Commission on Synagogue Relations) Federation of Jewish Philanthropies of New York, Inc. 1965, p. 12.

37. *Ibid.*, p. 26. *See also*, Fred Rosner, ibid., p. 42.

38. *Hadarom*, Rabbinical Council of America, New York, Nissan 5721-1961. The article, *"The Utilization of the Eyes of the Dead for Restoring Vision to the Blind,"* is digested in *Tradition*, Rabbinical Council of America, Vol. 4. Fall, 1961, by Immanuel Jakobovits. The Jewish Press, New York, January 1968, also quotes this responsum.

39. *Yearbook*, CCAR, Vol. LXIII, 1953, New York, p. 153.

40. *Ibid.*, CCAR, Vol. LXVI, 1956, New York, p. 106.

41. *Ibid.*, CCAR, Vol. LXXIV, 1964, p. 77.

42. *Proceedings*, Rabbinical Assembly, New York, Vol. XXV, p. 199.

43. The Jewish Press, Rabbi Sholom Klass, Ed., New York, Jan. 26, 1968.

44. Avodah Zarah 27b.

45. Immanuel Jakobovits, *Jewish Medical Ethics*, ibid., p. 263, note 69.

46. Immanuel Jakobovits, *Proceedings*, Orthodox Jewish Scientists, New York, 1966, p. 5.

47. Panim El Panim.

48. Fred Rosner, *ibid.*, note 34.

49. Rabbi Yizhak Weiss, Manchester, England, in *Hamaor*, Rabbinical Monthly Journal, Brooklyn, New York, Vol. 19, No. 5, August-September 1968,

"Whether it is Permissible to Transplant Heart from One Who is Dying, For the Sake of Healing."

Rabbi Haim Duber Golevesky, Brooklyn, New York, in *Hamaor*, Vol. 19, No. 6, October-November 1968, *Questions Regarding Heart Transplant.*

Hama'ayon, Jerusalem, Israel, Tebet-January 1969, Poalei Agudat Israel. Editorial comment on: *Medical Determination of Time of Death.*

Rabbi Yaakov Levi, Hama'ayon, September-October 1968, *When is it Permissible to Transplant and When is the Moment of Death?*

Rabbi Gabriel Kraus, Hama'ayon, Sept.-Oct. 1968, *Organ Transplant According to Halakhah.*

Rabbi Yehudah Gershuni, *Or Hamizrah*, Mizrahi-Hapoel Hamizrahi, New York, Vol. XVIII, No. 3, April 1969, *Organ Transplants According to Halakhah.*

Rabbi Yehudah Gershuni, *Or Hamizrah*, Vol. XVIII, No. 4, June, 1969. *Corneal Transplants and Other Organ Transplants According to Halakhah.*

50. *Hapardes*, Rabbi S. Elberg, editor, Brooklyn, New York, March-April 1969.

51. *See above*, note 47.

52. *See*, Nissan Gordon, "Heart Transplant in the Light of Jewish Law," New York, *Jewish Day-Journal*, May 20, 1969.

53. Fred Rosner, *ibid.*, p. 50.

54a. *Ibid.*, p. 51. See also J. David Bleich, *Contemporary Halakhic Problems*, ibid., p. 391: "Brain death and irreversible coma are not acceptable definitives of death insofar as Halakhah is concerned. The sole criterion of death accepted by Halakhah is total cessation of both cardiac and respiratory activity." Rabbi Bleich in *Tradition*, Vol. 16, No. 4, ibid., p. 133, states: "In oral communications Rabbi Feinstein has repeatedly stated that he, in no way, is prepared to accept any form of 'brain death' as compatible with the provisions of Halakhah . . ."

54b. *Conservative Judaism*, Stephen C. Lerner, Editor, Vol. 30, No. 2, Winter 1976, Rabbinical Assembly, New York, p. 22 ff.

54c. United Synagogue Review, *The Ethical Dilemmas of Modern Medicine: A Jewish Approach*, Fall, 1976, p. 4.

55. *The Torch*, National Federation of Jewish Men's Clubs, Philadelphia, Penna. *See*, "Cardiac Replacement," *ibid.*, p. 42. "The patient must be absolutely sure that his doctor does not become his executioner, and that no definition authorizes him to ever become one. His right to this certainty is absolute."

56. *See*, Immanuel Jakobovits, "A Modern Doctor's Dilemma" *Jewish Chronicle*, London, March 17, 1967, in which he takes issue with the doctrine of Justice Cardozo that "every human being of adult years and sound mind has a right to determine what shall be done with his own body," by saying that "Jewish law disputes this quite categorically."

57. Solomon Freehof, *Current Reform Responsa*, Hebrew Union College Press, New York, 1969, p. 118.

58 Pesachim 25a.

# PRE-MARITAL SEX

M ainstream Judaism has been consistently opposed to sexual relationships outside marriage, and even in the contemporary permissive society, religious leaders of the three denominations, however their approaches may differ, are in agreement over this.[1] Dissenting voices suggesting that, depending on the particular context, relationships with a certain amount of commitment and mutual affection might be allowed, are rare.[2]

Recent surveys show that men and women place less importance on chastity than they used to.[3] Although due to the rise in population growth and a greater frankness about sex, it may appear that more people are having pre-marital relations, statistics seem to show that the actual proportion has remained relatively constant.

Since Judaism is keenly aware of the sex drive, it has always been sensitive to the constant pressures upon young men and women. No religion is more candid in its attitude. Far from such a topic being considered improper, the Talmud devotes whole sections and tractates to it, without excluding any question from open discussion. Indeed, the deep insight of the rabbis of Talmud times is sometimes startlingly modern.

The Codes and responsa literature contain many problems relating to the sexual aspect of family life, and the needs and duties of marriage partners. To Judaism, procreation is only one part of marriage. Love and the giving and receiving of pleasure are equally important.

> The need to condition and prepare the wife for coitus is indicated in the talmudic suggestion that a man should seduce his wife.

238

Seduction is defined as endearing conversation and demonstrative love and desire . . . The male must satisfy the female's deep sexual yearning by giving her joy,i.e., an orgasm . . . The frequency of intercourse is considered an important aspect in marriage. Scholars are urged to engage in the sex act once a week, on the eve of the Sabbath; the very pious, once a week, on Wednesday, to prevent their wives from giving birth on the Sabbath and thus desecrating it; scholars who study at home, once a day, but they are cautioned not to "hang around" their wives like roosters . . . The wrong techniques of intercourse are pointed up in interdictions . . .[4]

Judaism has laid down that marriage should be the unique framework for the sexual relationship.[5] While the extreme Orthodox insist that even *negiah,* touching, is enough to stir the sexual urge and must be avoided, and other denominations use more rational arguments to persuade young people against pre-marital intercourse, Jewish standards are, in essence, the same. Spiritual leaders do realize, however, that the society in which they live lays great stress on "individual freedom and the fulfillment of personal desires."[6] Now that the idea that one should have no sexual experience before marriage is in disrepute, they are aware that "even a clergyman who is opposed to pre-marital sex on religious grounds cannot be dogmatic about his opinions in counselling. Students will simply not pay attention to a man who dramatically counsels abstinence unless that is what they wanted to hear in the first place."[7]

Judaism maintains that pre-marital continence is not only the correct mode of behavior but that it is in the best interests of the individual, the family and society.

A leading scholar, Louis M. Epstein, has analyzed the theme in depth:[8]

The Bible does not seem to consider non-commercial unpremeditated sexual contact between a man and an unmarried woman as harlotry.[9] In fact, the Bible has no prohibition against it, either for the man or for the woman. It takes up this subject only in connection with the rape or seduction of a virgin, and there it is treated not as a moral crime but as a civil case against the man for theft of virginity . . .[10]

During the Second Commonwealth, the age of exaggerated moral discipline, when even innocent sociability between the sexes was condemned, any unmarried contact between a man and a woman was, of course, cause for public outrage. But there is no legal verdict against the practice until the age of the early Tanaaim, when R. Eliezer taught that any unmarried contact between a man and a woman constituted harlotry.[11] The view of R. Eliezer did not prevail in the Halakhah, however, and his contemporaries as well as his successors drew a clear distinction between the prostitute who gives herself to many men either for gain or for gratification of passion, and the girl who succumbs to the temptation of intimacies with a lover. Unmarried cohabitation of the latter kind, in their view, did not constitute a violation of biblical command; the man, the girl, and her father, if he consented to it, suffer no penalty on the basis of the biblical authorities for immoral conduct. This peculiarly lenient view of the Talmud toward unmarried sex relations between lovers has never been challenged or modified by post-talmudic teachers on any legal grounds.[12] The impression was created by Maimonides that he considered such unmarried relations as biblically prohibited under the head of kedeshah,[13] and would therefore prescribe flagellation for violations. But in reality Maimonides condemns as harlotry permanent unmarried relations between a man and a woman, a "mistress" or a concubine. But he makes it clear that "there is no flagellation where cohabitation took place as a matter of accident . . . and where the girl had not premeditated it, for that has no permanency and is not usual."


However, the legal leniency toward non-professional harlotry should not mislead us into believing that the Jews tolerated unmarried relations between the sexes. The Jews have a super-halakhic standard of morality, the agaddic standard . . . That standard obtains its authority from public sensibilities and often proves more potent than the law. The various restrictions set up against the mingling of the sexes, the constant watch by the community over the conduct of young people, all were intended to prevent unmarried relations so that the bride might be a virgin and the groom pure at their marriage . . . Total elimination of premarital unchastity was, of course, never to be expected . . . but certainly the effort to stop such practices was not lacking, and the severity of communal enactments and their measure of enforcement had a telling effect. It is no exaggeration to say that down to the present time pre-nuptual sex relations among Jewish women has been a rare occurrence and when such a mishap occurred, the girl felt herself disgraced for life beyond redemption.

A number of rabbis and other authorities have in recent years made various statements which, taken together, will give us a comprehensive view on this subject. Rabbi Robert Gordis (Conservative) writes:

> Judaism maintains the principle that sexual relations are proper only within the marriage bond . . . Judaism is opposed to premarital relations. While it shows a realistic insight into the human impulses involved, it does not condone or sanction such relationships.[14]

According to Dr. Menahem M. Brayer (Orthodox):

> Pre-marital sex was never accepted in Judaism; instead the rabbis insisted on early, well-planned marriages . . . Pre-marital chastity is an old, still valid idea of the Jewish ideal of marriage. Through it a new and lasting relationship is to be built on the foundation of a tabula rasa — both sexually and emotionally, for a spiritual communion of body and soul and for the integrity of the family unit by two integrated personalities.[15]

According to Rabbi Richard L. Israel (Conservative):

> The traditionalist response to the problem of pre-marital intercourse is simple. Don't! It is unseemly for a Jewish boy to engage in pre-marital intercourse. Such acts are an indication of control over his *yetzer* (desire). For an unmarried Jewish girl to do so voluntarily is an act of *z'nut* (prostitution), perhaps not technically, but carrying just about the same social stigma.[16]

According to Monford Harris:

> The Jewish ideal is continence before marriage and fidelity within marriage.[17]

According to Trude Weis-Rosmarin:

> Jewish tradition demands *tzeniut* from women and men in their personal lives. The standard translation of *tzeniut* is "modesty." It

is not a semantically faithful rendition. *Tzeniut* is derived from a root which means "to restrain, to set limitations." Judaism demands "restraint." Judaism demands the setting of limits.[18]

## According to Rabbi Pinchas Stolper (Orthodox):

Sex relates to the most intimate bonds we can possibly establish with another person. It is a primary natural force which involves our total personalitites at the deepest levels of our being, an intensely private, personal matter . . . Together with other personality factors, it constitutes the cement which transforms two strangers into intimate, loving, life-long companions, committed to each other and to the building of a Jewish family. The laws of *tzeniut* (modesty, humility, and privacy) create an atmosphere of restraint, self-respect and self-discipline before marriage. They reserve the individual for the higher good of creating the relationship with the other, and insure that the physical impulse will be reserved for the chosen one, as an instrument of love, devotion and personal fulfillment. *Tzeniut* teaches us to control our appetites rather than be controlled by them . . .[19]

## According to Rabbi Roland Gittlesohn (Reform):

Chastity enhances happiness in marriage. To indulge in pre-marital intercourse is to isolate sexual union from all the other factors which go with it in love . . . The husband or wife who begin their experience with intercourse together are sharing the whole of life and love. They are building sturdy, integrated structure from the foundation up, rather than trying to piece together and repair various aspects of love which previously existed in isolation . . . Those who would insure themselves the greatest chance for happiness and success in marriage stand to lose by pre-marital adventures and to gain by waiting . . . Many experts who have devoted years to careful study of the factors which lead to a happy marriage have concluded that pre-marital chastity is one of them . . .

We cannot enjoy the purely physical, animal pleasures of pre-marital sexual indulgence and also achieve later the highest possible human level of sex-life and love. There is a price to be paid for every form of enjoyment or fun. In every important choice we gain something and lose something. Accurate knowledge of human nature and of mankind's experience through history leads to the conclusion that what we stand to gain through chastity is far greater than any temporary loss . . .[20]

According to Rabbi Eugene Borowitz (Reform):

. . . the general attitude toward pre-marital intercourse may be inferred from the indirect controls created in the first centuries C.E. to prevent any sexual relations but those of a married couple.

The rabbis went far beyond the biblical standards to sexuality They too esteemed virginity highly and sought to protect it by elaborating a stringent set of standards for female modesty . . . The effect of these laws is quite clear. They aimed not only at preventing adultery but any kind of sexual relations outside of marriage . . .

The traditional Jewish community was committed legally and morally to marriage as the only situation in which sexual intercourse should occur . . . Complete prohibition remains, apparently the position of our day.[21]

According to Rabbi Aaron Soloveichik (Orthodox):

. . . Pre-marital relation or any erotic experience between a man and a woman who are not married — even if it consists only of holding hands — is impure, because it emanates from lust. An erotic experience between husband and wife can be noble, lofty, and sacred because it emanates from love rather than lust. There is a fundamental and essential difference between lust and love. Lust is animalistic and parasitic. Love in humane and altruistic.

Pre-marital relation or extra-marital relation is parasitic for the simple reason that each partner is only interested in satisfying his or her impulse. In a marital relationship where husband and wife are sincerely united and attached to each other for better or worse, the erotic relationship is humane, altruistic and even angelic because the erotic act under such circumstances is only a physical manifestation of a total identification and union between husband and wife.[22]

While the Jewish position regarding pre-marital sex is clear, it must also be mentioned that any child born from such a relation is not illegitimate.

... The Halakhic norms of "pre-marital, extra-marital and adulterous" are not those of the Western Christian world. Jewish law does not know the concept of "illegitimacy" because intercourse establishes a legal union with a woman free to marry, although of course, there should be the *Ketubah* (marriage certificate) and the ceremony of *Kiddushin* (marriage). But even in the absence of the latter two, marriage is established and thus the child born of a legally and ceremoniously unconsummated union is legitimate. The Halakhic concept of "bastard" refers only to a child conceived in a "forbidden" union, especially with a married woman ...

To be sure, Jewish law, does not take a lenient view of the man who "gets the girl into trouble" and of the girl who lets herself be gotten into the situation of "unmarried mother." But the child — is the child of a Jewish mother — equal with all children of Jewish mothers.[23]

## NOTES

1. "Premarital Sexual Standards," *Siecus Study Guide* No. 5, New York, 1967, p. 8.

2. See Harriet A. Feiner, "Toward a Reconsideration of Sex Standards," *The Reconstructionist*, Jan. 2, 1970, pp. 17-20. The writer analyzes a discussion of the present subject at the Reconstructionist Convention and concludes that "though many specific traditional principles relating to sexual morality appear to need modification, the underlying philosophy of the tradition remains valid. Respect for the needs of the individual within the context of a living community, responsible behavior, and strong family ties remain guiding principles."

3. *New York Times*, May 20, 1970. See also, Richard L. Rubinstein, "The New Morality and the Jewish Family," *The Reconstructionist*, Nov. 17, 1967, p. 19.

4. Samuel I. Spector, "The Talmud and Sex," *The Jewish Spectator*, Feb. 1969, p. 19. See also *Code of Jewish Law* (Kitzur Shulhan Arukh), Solomon Ganzfried, translated by Hyman E. Goldin, Hebrew Publishing Co., New York, 1961, Vol. IV, pp. 13-17.

5. The Talmud, Sanhedrin 75b, offers this point of view in the following account: "R. Judah said in Rab's name. A man conceived a passion for a certain woman (Literally, set his eyes on a certain woman), and his heart was consumed by his burning desire (his life being endangered thereby). When the doctors were consulted, they said, 'His only cure is that she shall submit.' Thereupon the Sages said, 'Let him die rather than that she should yield.' 'Then (said the doctors) let her stand nude before him.' (They answered) 'Sooner let him die.' 'Then,' said the doctors, 'let him converse with her from behind a fence.' 'Let him die,' the Sages replied, 'rather than she should converse with him from behind a fence.' Now R. Jacob ben Idi and R. Samuel ben Nahmani dispute about this. One said that she was a mar-

ried woman, the other that she was unmarried. Now this is intelligible on the view that she was a married woman, but the latter, that she was unmarried, why such severity? R. Papa said, 'Because of the disgrace to her family.' R. Aha, the son of R. Ika said, 'That the daughters of Israel may not be immorally dissolute.' (i.e., in order that there be no looseness among the daughters of Israel.)"

6. Robert Gordis, *Sex and the Family in the Jewish Tradition*, Burning Bush Press, New York, 1967, p. 10.

7. Richard Rubinstein, "New Morality and College Religious Counseling," *Rabbinical Counseling*, Earl A. Grollman, editor, Bloch Publishing Co., New York, 1966, p. 29.

8. Louis M. Epstein, "Sex Laws and Customs in Judaism," American Academy of Jewish Research, 1948, pp. 167-170.

9. Deut. XXIII:18, "There shall be no harlot of the daughters of Israel."

10. Exod. XXII:15, Deut. XXII:13-21.

11. Yebemoth 61b. "R. Eleazar said: 'An unmarried man who had intercourse with an unmarried woman, with no matrimonial intent, renders her thereby a *zonah* (harlot).'"

See also, Robert Gordis, *Sex and the Family in the Jewish Tradition*, Burning Bush Press, New York, 1967, p. 54, note 56. Rabbi Gordis quotes the Talmud, note 57, (J. Pesahim 10:1) "He who eats matzah on the eve of Passover (i.e. before the advent of the Festival) is like a man who has relations with his betrothed in the house of his father-in-law (i.e. before marriage). He who is guilty of this offense (i.e. the eating of matzah) is punished by flagellation."

See also, Seymour Siegel, "A Jewish View of Sex," in *Jews and Divorce*, edited by Jacob Fried, Ktav Publishing House, New York, 1968, p. 175.

12. Robert Gordis, ibid., note 58. "According to the Codes, intimate relations by engaged couples are prohibited not biblically but only rabbinically."

13. Maimonides, Hilkhot Ishut, Introduction, Ch. I:4.

There are . . . four commandments, two enjoining duties, two prohibiting certain acts. Specifically, they are that: 1) One should marry a woman by means of a formal contract and the rabbinically enjoined rites, and 2) One should not have intercourse with a woman unless one has given her a marriage contract and performed the appropriate rites . . .

Before the time of the giving of the Torah, if a man met a woman in the street and they were both agreeable, he would give her her price, and they would have intercourse at the roadside, after which he went his way. This is what the Torah means when it speaks of the woman it calls a *kedeshah*.

However, once the Torah was given, the *kedeshah* was forbidden, as it is written: "No Israelite woman shall be a *kedeshah*" (Deut. 23:18). Therefore, anyone who has causal intercourse with a woman is to be punished at the order of the Jewish community court for the transgression of this commandment of the Torah, since he had intercourse with a *kedeshah*.

14. Robert Gordis, ibid., p. 41.

15. Menahem M. Brayer, "The Role of Jewish Law Pertaining to the Jewish Family, Jewish Marriage and Divorce," in *Jews and Divorce*, edited by Jacob Fried, Ktav Publishing House, New York, 1968, p. 3.

16. Richard L. Israel, "The New Morality and the Rabbis," *Conservative Judaism*, Vol. XXIV, No. 1, R.A., New York, Fall, 1969, p. 64.

17. Monford Harris, "Reflections on the Sexual Revolution," *Conservative Judaism*, Vol. XX, No. 3, Spring 1966, New York, p. 4.

18. Trude Weis-Rosmarin, "The Great Orgy," editorial, *The Jewish Spectator*, Oct. 1969, p. 30.

19. Pinchas Stolper, *The Road to Responsible Jewish Adulthood*, Union of Orthodox Jewish Congregations of America, New York, 1967, pp. 11-12, 35-37.

20. Roland Gittleson, *Consecrated Unto Me*, Union of American Hebrew Congregations, New York, 1965, selections from pp. 162-167, Rabbi Gittelsohn devotes three chapters to pre-marital sex. He gives the usual arguments for participation, "Everybody's doing it"; the relativity of ethics; the necessity that boys "sow their wild oats" before settling down to marriage; experienced men make better husbands and the complaint against the double standard. He then goes on to the reasons for chastity before marriage, sex might lead to pregnancy, danger of venereal disease, the uniqueness of sex in human as compared to animal life, and the likelihood that pre-marital chastity enhances happiness within marriage.
The quotation from Rabbi Gittelson is taken from the section dealing with the last argument.

21. Eugene Borowitz, *Choosing a Sex Ethic*, Schocken, published for the B'nai B'rith Hillel Foundations, Inc., New York, 1969, p. 49. Rabbi Borowitz's volume, the only one dealing exclusively with the issue of pre-marital relations, develops the thesis that biblically there is no prohibition, that until the time of Maimonides a difference existed in Jewish law between a *pilegesh*, concubine, who limits her relationship to one man and possesses semi-legal status, and a prostitute who gives her body for money. He notes that it was Maimonides who decreed that all intercourse outside of legal marriage be prohibited and while others disagreed with him and even attempted to restore the position of *pilegesh*, "moral development had made it indefensible." He also notes that Maimonides "did not succeed in his own day, although ultimately his position became the standard for Jewish law."
The author selected those statements from Rabbi Borowitz which underscore the present position on pre-marital intercourse. Here also is his treatment of the concubine issue:

"This (*pilegesh* relationship) closely resembles the modern ethics of mutual consent or of love, though in its semi-permanent nature, it seems far more like the latter than the former, which might well be quite temporary. So we must say that the Jewish tradition has in an earlier period given legal sanction to certain forms of non-marital, or better, semi-marital sexual relationships. That recognition or acceptance continued from biblical times through the Middle Ages, with a varying incidence of practice until Maimonides tried to put an end to it. He did not succeed in his own day, though ultimately his position became the standard of Jewish Law." (p. 46).

23. Trude Weis-Rosmarin, ibid., p. 5.

22. Rabbi Aaron Soloveichik, "Torah Tzniut Versus New Morality and Drugs," *Tradition*, Vol. 13, No. 2, Fall 1972, Rabbinical Council of America; New York, p. 54.

# SUICIDE

Every twenty minutes in the United States somebody commits suicide. The incidence of suicide is particularly high among college students, and teen-agers.[1a] The American Telephone Company has completed a universal code system which so covers the country that any individual dialing 911 will come into immediate contact with a local community emergency service center.

Massive studies of suicide, its causes and motivations are under way. In the past, a natural sense of repulsion against the act of self-destruction has seriously hampered complete analysis. Legal sanctions are gradually being lifted, though the moral stigma is more ingrained. Suicide is still considered a felony or misdemeanor in nine states, though these criminal statutes are rarely enforced. "It is not unusual these days to give a suicide a proper Roman Catholic funeral and a consecrated grave, on the grounds that 'his demented soul did not possess sufficient freedom of will for his heinous deed to constitute a mortal sin,' " writes a *Time* magazine editor. Nor for that matter, is the suicide always denied Jewish funeral rites though traditionally he is supposed to be consigned to a plot of ground outside the limits of the Jewish cemetery.

Until modern times there has been no word in Hebrew for suicide. In Hebrew the term *hitavduth*, or *m'aved atzmo ladaat* (he who consciously destroys himself) was coined. What does Judaism have to say about suicide? Are there any circumstances when it is permitted? How does suicide relate to martyrdom?

Judaism unequivocally condemns suicide as a violation of the life given by God. Only God has the right to determine when life should end. While Judaism deals harshly with the *proven* suicide it

247

is not as halakhically inflexible as people have been led to suppose in cases open to doubt. This is not to deny that "public rites were reduced to a minimum in the case of suicide or condemned criminals," as Salo Baron has written. Nor can the principle of the sanctity of life basic to religion be disregarded. Jewish law, however, has shown a great deal of understanding in particular cases, gaining support for this attitude from the passage, "Do not judge your neighbor until you are in his place."

Nor can it be denied that, while acts of self-destruction are widely condemned as, for example, by Bahya who notes that "suicide is a sentinel who has deserted his post," or Spinoza who believed that suicides are impotent of mind, there are exceptional occasions, such as during times of war, when acts of martyrdom and the heroism of those who refuse to acquiesce to evil even at the cost of their lives, are entirely appropriate. Religious literature is filled with examples of those who chose to die for "the sanctification of the name of God."

The official decisions arrived at within Judaism about the suicide question can of course be traced back to the Bible, Talmud, Codes, Commentaries, and Responsa.

**From the Bible:**

1. "Every creature that lives shall be yours to eat; as with the green grasses, I give you all these. You must not, however, eat flesh with its life-blood in it. *But for your own-life blood I will require a reckoning:* I will require if of every beast; of man, too, will I require a reckoning for human life, of every man for that of his fellow man.[1b]

This passage is regarded as the chief Biblical source prohibiting suicide.[2]

2. "You shall not murder."[3a]

This last means that, just as one should not kill another person, so he must not kill himself, a view which was accepted also by the Church Fathers, based on this verse. But the rabbis prefer to deduce the same prohibition from the previous quotation which admits of exceptions that could not be as easily inferred from the terse and absolute ring of, "You shall not murder!"[3b]

**From the Prophets — Events which Impinge on the Act of Suicide:**

1. The Philistines fought against Israel, and the men of Israel

fled and fell dead in Mount Gilboa. The Philistines followed hard upon Saul and his sons; and they killed Jonathan and Abinadab and Malchi-shua, the sons of Saul. The battle went badly against Saul, and the archers overtook him; and he was in great anguish by reason of the archers. Then Saul said to his armor-bearer, "Draw your sword and thrust it through me; lest these uncircumcised come and thrust me through and make a mock of me." But the armor-bearer refused, for he was afraid. Therefore, Saul took his own sword and fell on it . . .[4]

2. The lords of the Philistines gathered together to offer a great sacrifice to Dagon their god and to rejoice; for they said: "Our god has delivered Samson our enemy into our hand . . ." And it came to pass, when they were merry, that they said: "Call for Samson, that he may make us sport . . ." Now the house was full of men and women, and the lords of the Philistines were there; and there were about three thousand men and women on the roof who watched while Samson made sport . . . Samson called to the Lord and said: "Lord, God, remember me, I pray You, and strengthen me. I pray only this once, O God, that I may be this once avenged of the Philistines for my two eyes." And Samson took hold of the two middle pillars on which the house rested and leaned upon them, the one with his right hand, and the other with his left. Samson said: "Let me die with the Philistines!" He bent with all his might and the house fell on the lords and on all the people who were there . . . Then his brothers came and buried him . . .[5]

3. Ahitophel said to Absalom: "Let me now select twelve thousand men, and I will pursue after David tonight; and I will confront him while he is weary and weak-handed, and will frighten him . . . "And Absalom and all the men of Israel said: "The counsel of Hushai is better than the counsel of Ahitophel . . ." They came up out of the well and went and told King David: "Get up and pass quickly over the water, for Ahitophel has counseled against you . . . "And when Ahitophel saw that his counsel was not followed, he saddled his ass, and arose, and went home, set his house in order, strangled himself and died.[6]

4. Abimelech was prince over Israel three years. God sent an evil spirit between Abimelech and the men of Shechem . . . Abimelech rose up, and all the people who were with him at night and they lay in wait against Shechem . . . Abimelech came to the tower and fought against it and went close to the door of the tower

to burn it . . . A certain woman cast an upper millstone on Abimelech's head and broke his skull. He hastily called his young armor-bearer and said to him: "Draw your sword and kill me so that men may not say of me: 'A woman killed me . . .' " The young man thrust him through and he died . . .[7]

5. Zimri reigned seven days in Tizrah . . . The people who were encamped were heard to say: "Zimri has conspired and has also killed the King: "Wherefore all Israel made Omri the captain of the host, king over Israel that day in the camp . . . And Omri went up from Gibbethon and all Israel went with him and they besieged Tirzah. It came to pass that when Zimri saw that the city was taken, he went into the castle of the king's house, and burnt the king's house over him with fire, and died.[8]

6. When I say: "My bed shall comfort me,
My couch shall ease my complaint."
Then you frighten me with dreams
And terrify me through visions;
So that my soul chooses strangling
And death rather than these my bones.[9]

## From the Books of the Maccabees:

1. There was a certain Razis, one of the elders of Jerusalem . . . Due to his benevolence he was called Father of the Jews . . . Nicanor, wishing to show the animosity he felt toward the Jews, sent more than five hundred soldiers to put him under arrest . . . Preferring to die nobly rather than fall into the hands of a mob of sinners and to be outraged in a manner unworthy of his noble rank, he fell upon his sword.[10]

2. Eleazar, one of the foremost scribes, a man well advanced in years and one of the most noble of countenances, was compelled to open his mouth rather than live with pollution, and of his own free will went to the rack. Spitting out the food, he became an example of what men should do who are steadfast enough to forfeit life itself rather than eat what is not right for them to taste, in spite of a natural urge to live . . . "By departing this life courageously now, I shall show myself worthy of my old age, and to young men I shall have left a noble example of how to die happily and only on behalf of our revered and holy laws . . ." After saying this he immediately went to the rack.[11]

3. The account of Hannah and her seven sons.

**From the Books of Josephus:**

1. (Explaining the Masada event in which Eleazar ben Jair and his garrison refused to deal with and yield to the Romans. The Zealots agreed to commit suicide although Josephus tried to dissuade them).

What are we afraid of that we will not go up to the Romans? Is it death? If so, shall we inflict on ourselves for certain what we are afraid of, when we but suspect our enemies will inflict it on us? But someone will say that we fear slavery. Are we then altogether free at present? It may also be said that it is a manly act to kill oneself. No, certainly, but a most unmanly one, as I should esteem the pilot most cowardly, who, out of fear of a storm, should sink his ship of his own accord. Indeed, suicide is unknown to the common nature of all animals, and is impiety to God, our Creator. For no animal dies by its own contrivance, or by its own means. For the desire of life is as strong a law of nature with all . . . And do you not think that God is very angry when a man despises what He has bestowed on him? For it is from Him that we have received our being, and we ought to leave it to His disposal to take that being away from us. The bodies of all men are indeed mortal, and created out of corruptible matter; but the soul is ever immortal and is part of God and inhabits our bodies. Besides,if anyone destroys or misuses the deposit he has received from a mere man, he is esteemed a wicked and perfidious person; and if anyone cast out his own body, the deposit of God, can we imagine that He who is thereby affronted does not know of it? . . . So God hates suicide, and it is punished by our most wise Legislator. For our laws ordain that the bodies of such as kill themselves shall be exposed till sunset without burial, although it be lawful to bury even our enemies.[12] [13]

**From the Talmud:**

No clear-cut prohibition of suicide appears in the Talmud. Indeed, Talmudic literature indicates that while suicide was universally condemned, allowances were made in times of persecution in order to escape torture. A recent statement notes that, though suicide is normally wrong according to the Halakha, Rabbi Shlomo Goren, Chief Rabbi of Israel, had ruled that captured soldiers can kill themselves rather than reveal military secrets under torture.[14] In Roman times, during the Fall of Masada, the Crusades, the century of the Black Plague, and the Nazi Holocaust, such acts of self-destruction are recorded without a note of condemnation, but rather with implicit approval. It is interesting to note that the Rabbis viewed acts of suicide sympathetically, in cases of embarrassment or excessive grief, and were quick to declare that death had taken place through natural, or accidental causes and had not been self-inflicted.

The primary source in the Talmud regarding suicide is the following:[14a]

1. For a suicide, no rites whatsoever should be observed. Rabbi Ishmael said: "He may be lamented: 'Alas, misguided fool! Alas, misguided fool.'"

Whereupon Rabbi Akiva said to him: "Leave him to his oblivion, neither bless him, nor curse him!"

There may be no rending of clothes, no baring of shoulders, and no eulogizing for him. But people should line up for him and the mourner's prayer should be recited over him, out of respect for the living. The general rule is: The public should participate in whatsoever is done out of respect for the living; it should not participate in whatsoever is done out of respect for the dead.

2. Who is to be accounted a suicide?

Not one who climbs to the top of a tree or to the top of a roof and falls to his death. Rather it is one who says "Behold, I am going to climb to the top of the tree," or "to the top of the roof, and then throw myself down to my death," and thereupon others see him climb to the top of the tree or to the top of the roof and fall to his death. Such a one is presumed to be a suicide, and for such a person no rites whatsoever should be observed.

3. If a person is found strangled, hanging from a tree, or impaled upon a sword, he is presumed to have taken his own life unwittingly; to such a person no rites whatsoever may be denied.

4. It happened that the son of Gorgos ran away from school; his father threatened to box his ears. In terror of his father, the boy went off and cast himself into a cistern. The incident was brought before Rabbi Tarfon, who ruled: "No rites whatsoever are to be denied him."

5. Another incident is that of a child from Bene Berak who broke a flask. His father threatened to box his ears. In terror of his father, the child went off and cast himself into a cistern. The matter was brought before Rabbi Akiva, who ruled: "No rites whatsoever are to be denied him."

As a result of this, the Sages said: "A man should not threaten his child. He should spank him at once, or else hold his peace and say nothing."

6. For those executed by the court, no rites whatsoever should be observed. Their brothers and relatives should come and greet the witnesses and the judges, as if to say, "We bear you no ill will, for you have rendered a true judgment." They may not mourn, but may grieve, the latter signifying grieving in silence. The mourners' meal should not be prepared for them, as it is said, "Ye shall not eat over him whose blood has been shed" (Lev. 19:26). The court that imposed the death penalty would taste no food all that day.


The Talmud records a number of incidents/events which reveal the sensitivity of the rabbis to human tragedy:

1. Four hundred boys and girls are taken captive. The girls, learning that they were destined for immoral purposes, plunge into the sea. The boys learning what has occurred also take their lives in the same way.[15]

2. Hannah and her seven sons allow themselves to be martyred, one by one, rather than submit to idolatry.[16]

3. A maiden servant of Herod, learns that Herod has killed the entire household, and now seeks her. She takes her own life.[17]

4. Akiba recommends that one avoid placing the tephilin (phylacteries) in a public place, lest he be embarrassed should a harlot find them. A student, so embarrassed, had taken his life.[18]

5. The story of invited guests who give the host's child the gift of eggs prepared for them. The host, thinking that the child had taken them himself, thereby leaving nothing for the guests, is embarrassed. He strikes the child, who dies. In grief, the host and his wife, take their own lives.

6. Eleazar ben Dordia misbehaves with a harlot and when refused help as he seeks repentance, takes his own life; he prayed aloud till he died.[20]

7. Honi the Circle Drawer, asleep for seventy years, returns and finds that no one recognizes him. He prays for death, "either companionship or death." He dies.[21]

## From the Codes and Commentators:

1. For one who has committed suicide, no funeral rights are

performed, no mourning is observed, no lamentation is made; but the relatives stand in line (to be comforted), the Mourner's benediction is recited, and all that is intended as a matter of honor for the living is done.

Who is to be regarded as a suicide? Not he who was climbing to the top of the roof, "fell and died," but one who said: "Look! I am climbing to the top of the roof." If he was seen ascending it, agitated by anger and fear, and then fell and died, the presumption is that he committed suicide, but if he is found strangled or hanging from a tree, or slain, or fallen upon his sword, his status is that of any person who died. His obsequies are attended to, and none of the last rites are denied him.[22]

2. There is none more wicked than one who has committed suicide, as it is said, "And surely your blood of your lives will I require." For the sake of one individual was the world created, thus he who destroys one soul, is considered as though he had destroyed the whole world. Therefore, one should not attend to him, neither should one rend garments nor mourn for him who has destroyed himself, nor should a funeral oration be pronounced on his behalf. He should, however, be cleansed, dressed in shrouds and buried, for the rule is, whatever is done in honor of the living should be done for him.

Without proof to the contrary, a man is not pronounced to be wicked. If therefore a man was discovered hanged or choked, as far as possible the act of killing should be regarded as the deed of another person and not as his own deed.

> If a minor committed suicide, it is considered as if he had done the deed unwittingly. If an adult killed himself and it is evident that the act was prompted by madness or through fear of terrible torture, as was the case of Saul who feared the Philistines would act with him as they pleased, he should likewise be treated as an ordinary deceased person.[23]

The sources noted here laid the basis for later views on the question. There is no explicit biblical prohibition against suicide. As we have seen, however, from the Biblical statement, "but for your own life-blood I will require a reckoning," the Rabbis of the Talmud deduced:

" . . .who is the Tanna (sage) maintaining that a man may not in-jure himself? It could hardly be said that he was the Tanna of the teaching, "And surely your blood of your lives will I require," (upon which) Rabbi Eleazar remarked that it meant "I will require your blood if it is shed by your own hands" (for committing suicide) . . .[24]

Rashi notes on this source:

> . . . *your own blood*, although I have permitted you to take the life of cattle; yet your life I will require from him among you who sheds his own blood. Your life even though one strangles himself so that no blood flows from him, yet I will require it from him.

## An Historic Perspective

So, by inference, there can be found a biblical source prohibiting suicide.

Talmudic narratives begin to show the beginnings of a more understanding approach towards particular cases, and an attempt is made to avoid condemnation. The rabbis were hesitant to apply the sanction in cases of suicide in the face of threat, severe torture, or the demand for a betrayal of the faith; also, suicide committed under cir-cumstances of mental or physical pressure, as a reaction to acute grief or embarrassment or suicide committed on conscientious grounds, was treated by them with understanding. The suicide of Saul, described in the Bible, has given rise to the expression, "Anus K'Sha-ul," a case of pressure like that of Saul, and a lenient view is usually taken.

A recent comprehensive article on the Jewish attitude toward suicide by Ch. Reines in *Judaism*, states: ". . . practices such as the mutilation of the suicide's body and the confiscation of his goods are not consistent with the basic premises of Jewish law . . ."

R. Akiva (held) that the individual who committed suicide should be neither insulted nor honored. In keeping with this it was decided that there should be no public funeral, with the usual delivery of an eulogy, and that relatives and bystanders should not be required to tear their clothing as a sign of mourning. It was ad-ded, however, that, in keeping with custom, the bystanders should form a line to comfort the relatives after the burial, and that the blessing prescribed for this occasion be recited, the idea being that in cases of suicide, those rites which were provided for the honor of the deceased should be dispensed with, while those instituted for the sake of his relatives should be observed. From this it is obvious that the person who committed suicide was accorded customary burial, since this would make his relatives feel better.

Opinion was divided among the rabbis of the Middle Ages as to whether the relatives of a suicide should observe the prescribed mourning rites. Maimonides held that since these rites provide for the honor of the deceased, they should be dispensed with in cases of suicide. Nachmanides, however, held that since the relatives are to be comforted by the public, and since the prescribed blessing for mourners is to be recited in any case, it follows that the relatives are to observe the mourning rites. According to this view, the relatives have a duty to the deceased, regardless of the circumstances of his death . . .

Stringent requirements had to be met with before a death could legally be classified as a suicide. So, for instance, the deceased had to have announced his intention to commit suicide beforehand; there had to have been eye-witnesses to the act.

In recent centuries, harsher measures have been in force against suicide than are actually required by the spirit of Jewish law. This is probably due, in part, to the influence of the Christian envioronment. So, it became customary to bury the body of a suicide in a separate section of the cemetery. The rabbis, in these cases, show themselves far milder than popular practice. This is illustrated by the responsa of Rabbi Moses Sofer who strongly defended the view that relatives should be permitted to observe mourning rites for a person who had committed suicide. He argued that a suicide cannot be placed in the same category as unrepentant sinners, since this act was the only sin of which he was guilty and he did not have time for repentance . . . Rabbi Moses Sofer further stressed that the rabbi of the particular community concerned must take the feelings of the family into consideration, and not expose them to unnecessary shame. He also added that he saw no valid reason for not reciting the Kaddish under these circumstances.[25]

From this we can see that the rabbis showed a great deal of understanding both for the state of mind of the person who commits suicide and for the feelings of his family. It seems that they did everything they could to remove the stigma of suicide by allowing, *almost* equal mourning rites for the deceased.

This position is also adopted by the leaders of the various denominations within Judaism.


## THE ORTHODOX VIEW

The following statements have been made by Orthodox leaders:

1. A general view of Halakhah will convince us that a suicidal act cannot be accepted as a "sane act" under any circumstances. The laws are most liberal in recognizing the state of mind of the individual and, therefore, the word "suicide" would never be applied in the following cases:

a. temporary insanity

b. fear

c. pain

d. sanctifying the name of God (Kiddush Hashem).[26]

The same rabbi, in his capacity as the Executive Vice President of the Vaad Harabonim, the Council of Orthodox Rabbis of Massachusetts has said, "A general review of Halakhah will convince us that a suicidal act cannot be accepted as a 'sane act' under any conditions."[27]

2. The Rabbis consider only a premeditated and deliberate act of self-destruction to be suicide; but when there is an act of abberation or sudden impulse, or where there is a doubt, a more lenient view is generally taken and the deceased is given the benefit of the doubt. An instance is recorded in the Talmud. Threatened by his father with punishment, the young son of a citizen of Lydda ran away and killed himself. When the case was brought before Rabbi Tarphon (late 1st century) he decided that it was not suicide, saying that the boy was moved by fear of his father.

According to the majority of rabbinic authorities, in most cases of suicide, one may assume that the balance of mind was disturbed. It was considered inconceivable that a person of a sound mind would commit such an abominable act. Many rabbinic authorities, therefore, permit surviving members of the family of a suicide to observe mourning and to recite Kaddish in the synagogue for the soul of the deceased. In this way, they would be spared further humiliation and grief.[28]

## THE CONSERVATIVE VIEW

A leading Conservative Rabbi, the former Chairman of the Law Committee of the Rabbinical Assembly has stated:

> The Law Committee has generally regarded a suicide as an emotionally distressed and overwrought person, and therefore not responsible for his action. It would be almost impossible to ascertain a person's motives and lucidity at the time of such an act. We are inclined to say that he was not in his right mind at that time. He is, therefore, given burial and last rites in the same manner as any other deceased.[29] He may be buried in a Jewish cemetery since we now consider suicide to be the result of mental illness.[30]

## THE REFORM VIEW

The official Reform position is noted in the following:

> As for suicides, the Shulkhan Arukh and Yoreh Deah, say that none of the regular mourning ritual should be allowed. However, see the responsum in CCAR Yearbook. ". . . According to Jewish law one is considered a suicide only when there is absolute certainty that he premeditated and committed the act with a clear mind not troubled by some great fear or worry which might beset him for the moment and cause him temporarily to lose his mind. In the absence of such certain evidence, he is given the benefit of the doubt . . . Whenever possible we should try to spare the surviving relatives the disgrace which would come to them by having their relative declared a suicide."

> "In the spirit of the responsa (of Rabbi Moses Sofer, quoted above) it is the general custom among Liberal congregations to bury suicides in their family plots."[31]

A later, more detailed, and analytical responsum by the same scholar reaches a similar conclusion:

> "The long and complicated succession of discussions in the law on the matter of suicide amounts to this: An increasing reluctance to stigmatize a man as a suicide, and, therefore, an increasing willingness to grant more and more rights of burial and mourning. The only hesitation is with regard to eulogy. It would therefore seem to be in accord with the mood of tradition if we conducted

full services and omit the eulogy, provided this omission does not cause too much grief to the family. If the family is deeply desirous of some address to be given in the funeral service, then the address should be as little as possible in eulogy of the departed, and more in consolation of the survivors. For the general principle is frequently repeated in discussing this law: "That which is for the honor of the living shall be done."[32]

\* \* \*

To sum up, all the denominations of Judaism, have in general a very liberal perspective upon suicide. Certainly, the act is condemned as a violation of the dignity of man and the sacredness of life given by God. On the other hand, it is very difficult to make a death fit the legal requirements which would make it qualify as a suicide in halakhic terms. Every legal presumption goes against the likelihood of such a death being an act of suicide. Leniency in connection with mourning rites suggests that whatever is done for the survivors is the predominent consideration.

## Masada

The *Masada* suicides have been discussed by various authorities questioning whether "they were permitted or even commanded by Jewish Law" and how they should be regarded "as 960 martyrdoms, 960 cases of willful self-destruction, or something in between?"[33]

Professor Yigal Yadin, the famed archeologist, considers them as true martyrs.[34] Dr. Trude-Weis Rosmarin challenges this view. She suggests that the Zealots could only have been heroic if they died fighting. The idea that they committed suicide, which Yadin borrowed from Josephus, she considers to have come from a faulty source.

> ... self-annihilation is contrary to the basic Jewish conviction that "whosoever is joined to all the living has hope; for as a living dog he is better than a dead lion." (Ecclesiastes 9:4). This does not mean that Jews should cowardly avoid danger. One should, indeed, one must, risk his life for a worthwhile cause, *but*, then, a *risk* is never hopeless. Thus, when Samson, blinded and made sport of by the Philistines, grasped the two middle pillars which supported the building where his torturers were feasting so as to make it collapse, he cried: "Let me die with the Philistines." But

this was not deliberate suicide; it was taking a risk of almost certain death, but still with a chance of escape.[35]

In another issue of the quarterly, the writer brings up the case of the death of Saul:

> In the scale of Jewish values, life occupies the highest rung. Unlike the Romans and the Greeks, the Jews did not glorify those who died by their own sword on the battlefield. The Hebrew Bible has no praise for Saul and his armor-bearer who committed suicide rather than risk capture by the Philistines. Significantly, David's lament for Saul and Jonathan makes no mention of Saul's suicide so as to avoid death at the hands of the Philistines. Saul and Jonathan's bravery come in for due praise, but there is not a word of tribute to the heroism of Saul's death — the same type of valor which motivated the Zealots of Masada to die by their own hands."[36]

A study by Virginia Trimble[37] is supportive of Yadin's position:

> They must, at best, have been martyrs in the extended sense of Rabeinu Tam, since they killed themselves rather than suffer death. In addition, we must find a commandment in which they can be described as preferring to die rather than transgress . . . The commandment must have been one to refrain from serving any master but God, . . . Such a commandment can be derived from 'but if a servant shall say . . . I will not go free, then shall his master bring him unto God . . . and his master shall bore his ear throughout with an awl, and he shall serve him forever' (Exodus 21:-5). Rashi explained this by saying, 'The ear that heard at Sinai — they are my servants and not servants to servants.' Thus, evidently, a Jew has an *a priori* responsibility not to serve any master but God.

The author of the article concludes as follows:

> Willful self-destruction is forbidden and martyrdom required by Jewish law, while suicide under duress is forbidden but forgiven after the fact. The majority of authorities considering the deaths of the defenders of Masada have placed them in the third, forgivable category, along with the death of King Saul. We have

seen, however, that there is one line of thought within the mainstream of *Halakhah* . . . which would call the deaths permitted (though not compulsory) because of *m'nyat hillul hashem* (avoidance of the profanation of God's name).

## NOTES

1a. See, "College Suicide Study Discounts Impact of Drugs and Pressures," *New York Times*, March 23, 1970. See also, M. Krystol, "More Young People Commit Suicide," *Forward*, April 6, 1972, New York, p. 148ff. See also, Teen-Age Suicide *Newsweek*, Aug. 28, 1978.

1b. Gen. 9:3-5

2. "The Halakhic attitude toward suicide derives not, as one might expect, from the Sixth Commandment of the Decalogue — *thou shalt not murder* — but rather from the Noahide injunction — *and surely your blood of your lives will I require it* . . ." Masada, Suicide and Halakhah, *Conservative Judaism*, Virginia Trimble, Winter 1977, New York.

3a. Exod. 20:13.

3b. David Novak, "Law and Theology in Judaism," *Suicide in Jewish Perspective*, Ktav, New York, 1974 p. 82.

4. I Sam. 31:1-5. For a detailed study of the King Saul incident, see ibid, Virginia Trimble, note 1b, p. 50.

5. Judges 16: 23-31.

6. II Sam. 17:1-23.

7. Judges 9:22-54.

8. I Kings 16:15-18.

9. Job 7:13-15.

10. II Maccabees XIV:37-41.

11. II Maccabees VIII:18-31.

12. Josephus, Antiquities of the Jews, Vol. I, Ibid.

13. Ibid.

14. Time, New York, June 21, 1968.

14a. *Semahot*, Chap. 2 Judaica Series, Vol. XVII, Dov Zlotnick, translator, Yale University Press, New Haven, 1966, pp. 33-34.

15. Gittin 57b.

16. Gittin 57b.

17. Baba Bathra 3b.

18. Berakhoth 23a.

19. Hullin 94a.

20. Avodah Zara 17a.

21. Taanith 23a. See Ch. Reines, "The Jewish Attitude Toward Suicide, *Judaism*, American Jewish Congress, New York, Vol. 10, No. 2, Spring, 1961, p. 160. The author says: Honi, be it noted, did not actually take his own life. He achieved the same end with the help of prayer. But the legend implies that the feel-

ing of loneliness and the lack of esteem and sympathy of one's fellow men are likely to lead to despair.

22. Maimonides, Laws of Mourning, Code of Maimonides, Treatise IV:11, Vol. III, Yale University Press, New Haven, Conn., 1949.

23. Shulhan Aruch, Condensed Code of Jewish Law, Solomon Ganzfried, Translated by Hyman Goldin, Hebrew Publishing Company, New York, 1927, p. 108, This section is a shortened version of Yoreh Deah, Code of Jewish Law, 345:1.

24. Baba Kama 91b. See also, *Everyman's Talmud, Rev. Dr. A. Cohen, Dutton and Company, New York, 1905, p. 581. Also, Universal* Jewish Encyclopedia, Vol. 10, New York, p. 93. See also, David Novak, "The Law and Theology in Judaism," Ktav, New York, 1974, page 82.

25. Ch. Reines, "The Jewish Attitude Toward Suicide," ibid., p. 160 ff. The author has paraphrased selections from this article.

26. Samuel Korff, Mattapan, Mass., quoted by Earl Grollman, *Rabbinical Counseling*, Bloch Publishing Company, New York, 1966, p. 144.

27. Samuel Korff, quoted by Earl Grollman, *Suicide*, Beacon Press, Boston, 1971, page 22.

28. H. Rabinowicz, *A Guide to Life, Jewish Chronicle* Publications, London, 1964, p. 76-79.

29. Max Routtenberg in Ethics in Judaism, *Pattern of Ethics in America Today*, F. Ernest Johnson, editor, Harper and Bros., 1960, quoted by Earl Grollman, ibid., p. 144. Also in *Suicide*, Earl Grollman, Beacon Press, Boston, 1971, page 22.

30. Summary of Decisions of Committee on Jewish Law and Standards, Rabbinical Assembly, page 17.

31. Vol. 33, p. 63, Solomon Freehof, *Reform Jewish Practice*, Hebrew Union College Press, Cincinnati, 1944, p. 145.

32. Ibid.

33. For a study of these issues, see Virginia L. Trimble, "Masada, Suicide and Halakhah," *Conservative Judaism*, Vol. 31, No. 2, Rabbinical Assembly, Winter 1977, pp. 45-55.

34. Yigal Yadin, *Masada: Herod's Fortress and the Zealots Last Stand*, New York, Random House, 1966.

35. Trude Weis-Rosmarin, Editor, The Jewish Spectator, New York, October 1967.

36. Ibid., Nov. 1966.

37. Ibid., Virginia Trimble, p. 54-55.

# GLOSSARY OF WORDS AND TERMS

AGGADAH (Plural, Aggadot)

That part of Talmudic and of later Rabbinic literature which does not deal with legal matters; rather with homiletic, figurative, ethically instructive, and legendary themes. It may also be taken as historical background.

AMORA (Plural, Amoraim. Speaker, expositor, expounder.)

Title given to Jewish scholars who flourished in the third, fourth and fifth centuries. C.E., whose debates, discussions and evaluations are embodied in the Gemara, the second part of the Talmud, the first division being the Mishna, presided over by the sages called Tannaaim.

BARAITA

An extraneous Mishna, containing a Tannaitic tradition (from the 1st and 2nd centuries) not incorporated in the Mishna as collected by Rabbi Judah the Prince, ca. 200, but cited in the Gemara and Midrash.

BIBLE

The Hebrew Bible consists of three main groups: a) Pentateuch, called also Five Books of Moses, b) Prophets, subdivided into First Prophets (Joshua through Kings) and Second Prophets (Isaiah through Malachi) and, c) Sacred Writings (Psalms through Chronicles).

CODES

Literary, systematic structuring of Jewish law and practice, following the Gaonic period, ca. 1100, by leading authorities into codes and compendia, designed to provide easier reference and investigation. Many codes, containing expositions, explanations, and adjustments, by popular fiat, became the bases of religious living and possessing the power of law.

GEMARA (Literally, learning, tradition.)

That part of the Talmud, (the second) which is made up of the legal and homiletic discussions and disputations of the Amoraim or positors, on the contents of the Mishna. The Gemara was codified about 500 C.E., three centuries after the Mishna was officially closed.

GAON (Literally, excellency, illustrious; plural, Gaonim)

The title held by the religious heads of the Babylonian academies in post-Talmudic times, from the seventh to about the twelfth century.

HALAKHAH (Literally, procedure, rule, way. Plural, Halakhot)
An accepted decision in rabbinic law which may be based either on argument from Scripture or Mishna, or on tradition. The term is used also to define those parts of the rabbinic literature which deal with legal problems and issues as distinct from Aggadah, which embraces material of an homiletic and edifying character and miscellaneous non-legal topics. Halakhah is also used to mean Law, Jewish Law, in reality — Way of Jewish Life.

MIDRASH (Literally, investigation, exposition)
Various collections of homiletical expositions and commentaries of Scripture in which the sages engaged.

MISHNA (Literally, teaching)
The collection of traditions, discussions and legal decisions of the sages of the first two centuries, called the Tannaim, based on the Bible, and edited and arranged into six orders by Rabbi Judah the Prince, about 200 C.E. The Mishna provides the text to which the Gemara is the commentary, the two constituting the Talmud. It is the first part of what is also called the Oral Law or Teaching, that is, the teaching which, in time, followed the Written Law or Teaching, originally transmitted orally from teacher to student, and only later, reduced to writing.

ORAL LAW . . . (see Mishna, Talmud)

RABBIS (Literally, teachers, masters)
The title of one duly ordained and hence authorized to offer decisions on Jewish law and practice. In the context of this book, the term "the rabbis" or "the sages" generally refers to the scholars and rabbis of the Talmudic era, to 500 C.E. Rabbi was the title of Tannaim while Rav (Rab) was the title of the Amoriam.

RESPONSA (Literally, a response, a letter. Singular: responsum)
The literature describing the rabbinic correspondence during the last 1000 years by which answers questions posed for guidance and decisions to legal and religious issues were provided for the Jewish people. The medium by which new problems arising in each generation are expounded by rabbis and teachers whose knowledge and mastery of Jewish law and piety were recognized and their authority and decision accepted. It remains today the method by which the rabbis adjust Jewish law to new matters and problems.

SCRIBE (Hebrew, Sofer, Plural, Soferim)
The title of post-biblical scholars dating back to Ezra the Scribe, about 400 B.C.E. A term loosely used to apply to rabbis of the subsequent period who preserved the Oral Law or Teaching.

SHULKAN ARUKH. (Literally, Prepared Table. Code of Jewish Law)

The official name of the Code of Jewish Law, edited by Rabbi Joseph Karo, 1654, and the most recognized and authoritative code and source. Since decisions and comments reflected primarily the school of Spanish Jewish thought, a gloss, added by Rabbi Moses Isserles (the RaMa), presenting Polish-German Jewish thought and practice, became part of the total Shulhan Arukh. The gloss is called, *Mapat HaShulhan, The Table Cloth*. The term "Prepared Table" suggests that the code is set out for the Jew to live by.

SANHEDRIN

The council of state and supreme tribunal of the Jewish people during the century or more preceding the fall of the Second Temple, 70 C.E. It consisted of seventy one members, and was presided over by the High Priest. A minor court (for judicial purposes only) consisted of twenty three members and was called the Small Sanhedrin.

TORAH (Literally, teaching, learning, instruction)

The most significant term in Judaism. It has many meanings and embraces wide areas. It can mean simply the Pentateuch, the Written Law, or the entire Bible, or the entire Written *and* Unwritten Law, as it can mean the whole body of Jewish religious and rabbinic literature throughout the centuries. It may also mean the concept of total Judaism in every aspect.

TALMUD (Literally, learning. The Oral Law or Teaching)

The name of the combined Mishna and Gemara: the first reduced to writing in about 250 C.E. and the second, codified about 500 C.E. It is the Oral Torah or Law/Teaching as the Bible is the Written Torah/Law or Teaching.

TOSEFTA (Additional)

A collection of legal decisions of the Tannaim, not included in the Mishna and codified by Rabbi Hiyya, disciple of Rabbi Judah the Prince. Third century C.E.

TANNA (Literally, teacher. Plural, Tannaim)

The name of the sage of the Mishnaic period (to 200 C.E.) who studied, discussed, and debated the text of the Mishnah.

UNWRITTEN LAW

See Oral Law, Mishna, Gemara. Originally unwritten after the Bible period, transmitted orally, and later reduced to writing. Called also the Oral Torah. (Torah She-b'alpeh).

WRITTEN LAW

The Bible, recorded by Moses at God's behest or by inspiration, is known as the Written Torah, (Torah She-bikhtav).

# RECOMMENDED SOURCES FOR
# FURTHER STUDY

## Orthodox

In addition to HaPardes, Noam, HaMaor, rabbinic monthly journals, and *Jewish Life, Judaism*, published by the Rabbinical Council of America, provides regular Halakhic sections and articles on new issues.

Books of recent vintage which have postured the Orthodox position are:

J. David Bleich, *Contemporary Halakhic Problems*, Library of Jewish Law and Ethics IV, Ktav Publishing House Yeshiva University Press, New York, 1977.

Immanuel Jakobovitz, *Jewish Law Faces Modern Problems*, Yeshiva University, New York 1965.
*Jewish Medical Ethics*, Bloch Publishing Co., New York, 1967.
*Journal of a Rabbi*, Bloch Publishing Co., New York, 1966. Published also, N.H. Allen, London, 1967.

Louis Jacobs, *What Does Judaism Say About* . . . New York Times Books, New York, 1973.

Fred Rosner, *Modern Medicine in Jewish Law*, Yeshiva University, Ktav, New York, 1972.
*Medicine in the Bible and Talmud: Selections from Classical Jewish Sources*, Library of Jewish Law and Ethics V, Ktav, New York, 1976.

Moses D. Tendler, *Medical Ethics*, Committee on Religious Affairs,

Federation of Jewish Philanthropies of New York, New York, 1975

Abraham Scheinberg, *What is the Halakhah?*, Shulsinger Bros., New York, 1974.

Irving J. Rosenbaum, *The Holocaust and Halakhah*, Ktav, New York, 1976.

Fred Rosner and J. David Bleich, editors, *Jewish Bioethics*, Sanhedrin Press, New York, 1979.

### Conservative

*Conservative Judaism*, the official quarterly of the Rabbinical Assembly, the *Proceedings* of the Rabbinical Assembly often recording the position of the Committee on Law and Standards, and the *United Synagogue Review*, provide basic sources for the views of Conservative Judaism. In addition, the following volumes, though not always official, reflect views of Conservative Judaism:

Louis M. Epstein, *Sex Laws and Customs in Judaism*, Ktav, (American Academy of Jewish Research, 1948) New York, 1967.

David M. Feldman, *Birth Control in Jewish Law*, New York University Press and University of London Press Ltd., 1968.

Robert Gordis, *Love and Sex: A Modern Jewish Perspective*, Women's League for Conservative Judaism, New York, 1978.

Isaac Klein, *Responsa in Halakhic Studies*, Ktav, New York, 1975.
     *A Guide to Jewish Religious Practice*, Jewish Theological Seminary of America, New York, 1978.

David Novak, *Law and Theology in Judaism*, Ktav, New York, 1975.

Seymour Siegel, *Conservative Judaism and Jewish Law*, Rabbinical Assembly, New York, 1977.

### Reform

The *Yearbook*, which includes decisions of the Committee on Responsa, and the quarterly *CCAR Journal*, (now called Journal of Reform Judaism), both published by the Central Conference of American Rabbis, provide current positions of Reform Judaism

The following books are basic to the understanding of Reform's postures on various issues:

Solomon B. Freehof, *Reform Jewish Practice*, Hebrew Union College, Cincinnati, Ohio, 1944.

*The Responsa Literature*, Jewish Publication Society of America, Philadelphia, 1955.

*Reform Responsa*, Hebrew Union College, Cincinnati, 1960.

*Recent Reform Responsa*, Hebrew Union College, Cincinnati, 1963.

*Current Reform Responsa*, Hebrew Union College, Cincinnati, 1969.

*Modern Reform Responsa*, Hebrew Union College, Cincinnati, 1971.

*Reform Responsa for Our Time*, Hebrew Union College, Cincinnati, 1977.

Jacob Z. Lauterbach, *Studies in Jewish Law, Custom and Folklore*, Introduction by Bernard J. Bamberger, Ktav, New York, 1970.

# INDEX

Abaye, 65, 216
Abba Saul, 91
Abortion, 35-62
Abrahams, Rabbi Israel, 224
Adler, Rabbi Hermann, 95, 213
Adler, Rabbi Rudolph, 231
Adoption, 63-73
Aggadah, 42, 76, 81, 127, 223, 240
Agudath Israel of America, 103
*Aharonim*, 19, 21
Akiba, Rabbi, 16, 92, 252, 253, 255
American Civil Liberties Union, 192
*Amo-ra-im*, 17
Arieli, Rabbi Yitzhak, 98
Aristotle, 43, 171
Artificial Insemination, 74-86
Ashi, Rabbi, 17
*Ashkenaz*, 18
Autopsy, 87-107, 211, 217, 223, 224, 232
Avneri, Uri, 158

Bachrach, Rabbi Yair Hayyim, 44, 45, 49
Bahya, 248
Bar Nahamani, Rabbi, 65
Baron, Salo, 248
Bebai, Rabbi, 113
Begin, Menahem, 51
Ben Azzai, 143, 144
Ben Sirah, 76, 81
Ben Zoma, 75
Bet Din, 30, 68
Bet Hillel, 16, 110
Bet Shammai, 16, 110
Bet Shemuel, 77
Birth Control, 109-137
Bleich, Rabbi J. David, 163, 183
Bokser, Rabbi Ben Zion, 132
*Book of Beliefs and Opinions, The*, 156
Borowitz, Rabbi Eugene, 243
*Brave New World*, 85
Brayer, Dr. Menahem M., 165, 241
Brown, Governor Jerry, 182

Carney, Rabbi Shalom, 51
Casper, Rabbi Bernard, 224
Catholic Israel, 28-31
Catholicism, 38-40, 42, 43, 47, 74, 75, 78, 85, 109, 139-140, 172, 247

Celibacy, 138-150
Central Conference of American Rabbis (CCAR), 26, 49, 56, 59, 69, 80-82, 106, 126, 128, 129, 178, 182, 221, 233, 258
*Chabad*-Lubavitch Movement, 69
Chronicles, 64
Cohen, Rabbi Jack J., 33
Cohn, Rabbi Hillel, 183, 184
Columbus Conference, 23, 25
Conservative Judaism 11, 12, 26-32, 37, 43, 47, 48, 52-56, 58, 70-72, 82-84, 103, 104, 130-134, 138, 156, 179-181, 205-208, 222, 223, 229-233, 241, 258
Cryobiology, 151-157, 179

Danzig, Rabbi Abraham, 21
Deuteronomy, 163, 168, 195
*Dina d'Malchuta Dina*, 68
Drake, Donald C., 185
Draper Commision, 109
Drugs, 158-170

Ecclesiastes, 259
Edwards, Dr. Robert G., 84
Eger, Rabbi Akiva, 115
Eleazar, Rabbi, 199, 255
Eleazar ben Zadok, Rabbi, 30, 64
Eliezer, Rabbi, 142, 198, 240
Emden, Rabbi Jacob, 45, 49, 93, 218
Epstein, Louis M., 239
Essenes, 138
Esther, 65
Ettlinger, Rabbi Jacob, 94, 95
Euthanasia, 156, 171-191, 211, 229, 232
*Even Ha-Ezer*, 19
Exodus, 260
Ezra the Scribe, 15

Federation of Jewish Philanthropies, 102, 159
Feinstein, Rabbi Moshe, 51, 52, 84, 99, 102, 103, 116, 118, 120, 164, 167, 185, 227-229
Feldman, Rabbi David, 46, 47, 48, 83, 120, 207
Fibley, E.E., 171
Fletcher, Joseph, 171
Fond, Dr. Morris S., 47

**Temple Israel**

Minneapolis, Minnesota

IN HONOR OF THE BAT MITZVAH OF
SARAH HARRIS
FROM
ROBERT GREENBERG